The Making of
Modern
Ireland

An alternative history

This edition first published in the UK in 2009

© Buttercup Books Ltd., distributed by Green Umbrella Publishing Ltd

The right of Geoff Robinson to be identified as Author of this book has been asserted by him in accordance with the Copyright, Designs and Patents Act 1988.

Printed and bound by MPG Books

ISBN: 978-1-907311-05-5

The Making of
Modern
Ireland

An alternative history

Seathrun Mac Roibin
Geoff Robinson

Contents

Author's Preface

Though born and educated in England, I am now an Irish National; having lived in Ireland for fifty years it was a decision I decided to formalise, in 1972. I did this in protest at the Derry Massacre of 26, civilian, protestors in January, of that year, an event which could never have happened had it not been for the employment, in the North of young inexperienced troops, wholly unprepared to deal with a situation other than conventional warfare, where their enemies are recognisable, who could easily have been unnerved by any apparent IRA activity, in the background of the Civil Rights march.

Once an unswerving believer in the rectitude of the Irish cause, hardly surprising as many of my close friends were involved in the 1916 Rising or the War of Independence while others had come to England to escape the internecine strife which followed the signing of the 1921 Treaty. Consequently, I already had a number of contacts when I decided to take up residence in Ireland in the late 1950s. Among them was Commandant Vincent Horgan, through whom I met Mr Thomas Crosbie, the owner of the Cork Examiner, a close associate of Michael Collins, who was killed in an ambush at Beal na Bliath. It was only when I met Vincent's brother Ned, who had fought on the opposite side, during the Civil war, that I discovered that but for this tragic accident, this conflict could have been ended within four months. During the next twenty years, I encountered many people, covering a wide spectrum of Irish political life, from my friend, Maureen O'Shee whose father had been an Irish Parliamentary Party MP, at Westminster, to Dan Breen, who is attributed with firing the first shots in the War of Independence, apart from others, including the Editor of the clandestine "Irish Republican News", or "Bulletin", as it was known, not to mention those who had taken part in the Easter Rising, including a civilian witness who has every reason to have a vivid recollection of it.

By the time I met my future wife, Bernadette Tiernan, a national teacher, I had become more Irish than the Irish, as the saying goes, and had developed an intense interest in the Irish political scene, but it was then that I discovered that such was the lack of a critical examination of the events surrounding the Rising, or its aftermath, in the curriculum of Irish schools that children are brought up in ignorance of the fact that, but for it, all Ireland today could have had a fully devolved administration yet, would have been protected from both the sectarian abuses, in the North, and the flagrant misuse of power, in the South, by being part of a Home Rule Government which would have had a fully devolved administration.

This prompted me to compare the official account of Irish history with that contained in the *Short History of the English People* by the Rev John Richard Green, published by Macmillan, in 1881, from which it was clear that that the former depended for its veracity not only on carefully selected facts, but equally significant omissions.

Few realise that but for the defeat by the French, during the 100 Years War and the subsequent emergence of the House of Tudor, following the Wars of the Roses, both Britain and Ireland might still be subject to the Angevin Empire, whose Plantagenet rulers, of the House of Anjou, were to control an area from the Banks of the Shannon to the centre of France, following the invasion of Ireland, by Henry 11, in 1169. Nor are we told that similar repressive provisions applied to England as those contained in the Statute of Kilkenny; so much for the assertion that England occupied Ireland for 800 years.

What passes for the official record of a nation is, at best subjective, otherwise it depends on the political outlook of the chronicler which is perforce fashioned by an admixture of truths, half truths and statistics taken out of context to which, in the case of Ireland, is added the mythology of a past age to form the propaganda of the Fenians, which provided the motive for the ill thought out, mistimed and unpopular Rising of 1916. There is, however, evidence both documentary and circumstantial of Unionist involvement in precipitating it, in order to prevent the implementation of the Home Rule Bill, due to be enacted following the conclusion of World War 1. This insurrection would by now have been long forgotten were it not for the over-reaction of the British authorities and the despatch of the Black and Tans, hardened, unemployed War veterans, to Ireland in 1919, to restore order, but whose resort to reprisals against the civilian population, in response to attacks by the IRA, was responsible for the War of Independence. The subsequent 1921 Peace Treaty was rejected by the militants, leading to the Civil War which raged until 1926, when de Valera founded his, constitutional, republican Party, Fianna Fail, which renounced violence, as a means of settling political disputes.

A statesman of international renown, de Valera evolved from militant nationalism, over the years, to become a social conservative and foremost opponent of Fascism, as evidenced by his statements to the General Assembly of the League of Nations and subsequent secret war against this evil. Since then the State has been ill served by politicians who have, with one or two notable exceptions, been self-serving. Particularly within the last thirty years as evidenced by the testimony given to the various Tribunals of Enquiry, while others conceal their political ineptitude by a spurious appeal to a nationalism.

It is the purpose of this book to present a chronicle of Ireland, shorn of the mythology which so often passes for history by presenting the facts as they are, rather than others would have us believe them to be, and, in so doing fill in the omissions on which so much of the recorded account of Ireland depends for its veracity, thereby freeing her people from the tyranny of brainwashing to which they have been subjected by those who would use the noble, but as yet unrealised, social aspirations of past patriots to cover their own ignoble ends.

CHAPTER 1

Ireland and the Angevin Empire

Before tracing the evolution of the various political and social movements that have formed in Ireland since the dawn of republicanism it is necessary to fill in the background, as without it much that follows would be incomprehensible. It is essential to delve into history to dispel some of the widespread inaccuracies and misconceptions that are commonly taken as gospel truth.

It is not generally appreciated that the real story of the occupation of Ireland by Britain began not in the twelfth century but in the sixteenth. This is because Normandy had ceased to exist as a separate entity following its assimilation into the Angevin Empire on the marriage of William the Conqueror's grandson, Henry II (or Henri II), to the Countess of Anjou. In so doing, and following his invasion of Ireland in 1169, he became sovereign of a dominion that extended from the banks of the Shannon to the centre of France.

Unlike the conquest of Britain by William, the invasion of Ireland by his grandson Henry II was undertaken by predominantly Norman troops, in view of his suspicion of the discredited Earl of Pembroke, who was known as Strongbow. He had fled to Ireland and offered his services as a mercenary to Dermot, High King of Leinster, who had also been banished from his domain and had unsuccessfully sought the aid of Henry to retrieve his lost possessions. After a short military campaign Strongbow successfully helped Dermot regain his position and married his daughter Eva. On Dermot's death, Strongbow became High King of Leinster, giving rise to the fear that he might attempt to make common cause with any British troops already in Ireland, and prompting the High Kings of Ireland to mount a rebellion against him. This dispute was finally resolved, but only when Strongbow agreed to relinquish his new found kingdom, thereby presenting Henry with a valuable foothold in Ireland.

From that time forward Ireland and Britain were to become subject states of the Angevin Empire, whose Plantagenet rulers remained in power until 1399, when France occupied the Empire. They continued to hold power in Britain, maintaining the hope of using that country as a springboard to regain their lost dominion. Nevertheless it was only following the end of the Wars of the Roses, in 1485, that the Plantagenets, so called because of the *planta genista* a badge which they wore in their helmets, reinvented themselves to form the Tudor dynasty and, at the same time resurrected England, which until its Danish rulers had laid the foundation for its political unity, in the 11th Century, did not exist as a nation.

The actual conquest of Ireland by England was, however, not undertaken until the arrival on the throne of the tyrant and self-styled King of Ireland, Henry VIII, although it is true that both King John and King Richard II invaded the country to restore order between the Normans who had remained there and the Irish tribes. This is the cause of the confusion regarding the date when Ireland first became subject to England, which has been further confounded by the unwillingness of British commentators to admit that England was long subject to a foreign power.

The Norman invasion of Ireland is in part a misnomer; inasmuch as Norman troops were used they were under the control of the Angevins. However, unlike the decision of William Duke of Normandy to occupy England for purely strategic purposes, the Plantagenet sovereign Henry II to invade Ireland had been prompted directly by the eclipse of the Golden Age, which had been inaugurated by St Patrick, during which the country had become the main centre of Christian culture and learning in Europe.

This idyllic situation led to the beginning of Ireland's decline, with the coming of the Danes. For just as the Celts had been inspired by the Christianity of Patrick, so too did they admire the efficiency of their Danish conquerors. They were indeed marauders like their own forebears, and in truth the nature of the Celt was more given to marauding than to learning.

Consequently the Danes, while they succeeded in establishing the cities of Dublin and Waterford, which made up the original pale, were unable to penetrate into the heart of the country. Their defeat at the battle of Clontarf was followed by a period of war between the remaining Danish settlements and the Celtic tribes surrounding them. Inevitably these tribes, led by their High Kings, began fighting among themselves for the spoils of war, leading to anarchy, hatred and division that grew deeper with each passing generation.

By the twelfth century the Christianity that had been such a vital force in the eighth century had degenerated into mere superstition; mythology took the place of true learning. The resultant moral decadence left the Church powerless and the slave trade, which had been suppressed, was flourishing once again. But as a number of his subjects had been abducted and sold into slavery, Henry II had a ready excuse to persuade Pope Hadrian IV to give his blessing to a crusade to Ireland. The Normans, who had originally invaded the country, were permitted to remain to maintain garrisons in Drogheda, Wexford, Waterford and Cork and were to play an important part in the development of Ireland but their greatest and perhaps only visible contribution is the legacy of many fine churches and cathedrals that exist throughout the country. A more accurate indication of the history of those years is to be seen in the remains of forts they built along the banks of the Shannon, to protect them against the incursions of the High Kings of Ulster and Connacht, whom they never succeeded in subduing.

The murder of Thomas Becket and the outbreak of war between the Empire and France forced Henry to return to Angers, leaving Norman planters in charge of Ireland. Had the High Kings united at this stage, not only would the remaining invaders have been driven into the sea but a new spirit of national identity might have been born. However this was not to be for the division between the tribes was now too deep rooted.

This was to see the beginning of a period of forays by the barons outside the enlarged pale. But following the intervention of Richard II a stalemate developed, after which the conflict between the Irish clans and the Normans became ever more bitter, culminating in the Battle of Athenry when some 11,000 Normans were killed and almost the entire clan of the O'Connors was wiped out.

Completely frustrated, it was not long before feuds broke out between the Normans and their Angevin rulers. Richard's successor John divided the country into counties but neither this nor the Statute of Kilkenny had any effect. Both measures were aimed at preventing the integration of the Irish tribes with the remaining British and the Norman barons, who had become more Irish than the Irish themselves, but such was the dissention among the barons that with the passing of the years they joined the tribes, even becoming High Kings.

The outbreak of the Hundred Years War (1336-1431) and the Wars of the Roses (1450-1471), between two descendants of Edward III, who had assumed the titles of Duke of Lancaster and Duke of York, was to stop the clock in Ireland for centuries. Thus it was not foreign rule but the complete breakdown of law and order, without a central government, native or otherwise, that was to see Ireland bereft of all her former glory by the time of the restoration of stability to the English monarchy with the accession of Henry VII, the first Tudor monarch.

At this stage Ireland was no further advanced, politically, than it had been when the Normans had first invaded the country. There was no central government and what initial progress had been made was counterbalanced by the incessant internal strife. This had taken its toll on the church, whose bishops had become involved in the fighting, while whole dioceses, left without priests, were now in a state of decay. Yet despite this chaos Christian tradition had been kept alive in the monasteries and religious institutions that housed the schools. Unlike his successors, Henry VII endeavoured to bring peace to Ireland but his conciliatory gestures were spurned by both by the native Irish and the Normans, whose integration with the Irish was now complete.

Another fact that is completely overlooked is the position of England. The Angevin suppression of that country was so complete that for decades French became the official language and every effort was made to stifle the revival of English literature, until the collapse of the Empire in 1399 following its invasion by France. Traces of this are still to be seen today in contemporary documents that were written in old French, such as the motto of the Knights of the Garter – Honi soit qui mal y pense.

Ireland was to be occupied by England for 400 years following the ascent to the throne of Henry VIII, the self styled King of Ireland, who set in motion a train of events that resulted in a legacy of bitterness and hatred between the two countries that was to last almost to this day. For in order to achieve his aim of bringing Ireland under English domination he began the process of colonising the country with settlers, with the ostensible purpose of ending the power of the warring tribes.

His endeavours to suppress the Celtic customs and traditions, however, together with the introduction of the 'new religion', had the exact opposite effect to what he had anticipated. Not only did he succeed in bringing about a rebirth of the old religion in opposition to Protestantism, but his actions also resulted in the re-emergence of Ireland as a nation. The people had discovered a new sense of identity and for the first time were united – against the Crown.

Henry's equally ruthless successor, Elizabeth I, continued the process of establishing English rule in Ireland by gaining control of the southern part of the country and initiating a reign of terror. But it was many years before she managed to wrest control of Ulster, first from Shane and then from Hugh O'Neill, and only completed the process with the introduction of settlers from Scotland. This is referred to as the Plantation of Ulster, yet could just as accurately be described as the homecoming of the people of Ulster, for these planters were for the most part descendants of the Celts who had originally invaded Scotland. From this time forward, however, no English monarch could rule Ireland other than by force of arms or by fostering divisions – a policy that was to lead to disaster within 40 years of Elizabeth's death.

It came in 1641, during the reign of Charles I, when a secret conspiracy in Ulster led to the near extermination of the Protestant settlers, no less than 50,000 of whom were butchered throughout the length and breadth of the land. This lead to a terrible revenge, exacted by the regicide Oliver Cromwell, who became Lord Protector and the first republican leader in the contemporary Western world, whose actions were to result in his becoming the symbol of British oppression to the Irish.

The wars fought in Ireland from the period of Henry VIII's reign until the invasion of William of Orange were religious rather than political. Following the degeneration of the Celtic Golden Age into mere savagery by the time of the Tudors, Norman influence had brought about a revival and the actions of Henry VIII and his successors, which began with the suppression of the monasteries, had resulted in Catholicism becoming the mainspring of Irish nationalism. This gave rise to the sectarian divide and explains how religion and politics became inextricably intertwined.

Contemporary Irish history begins with the Williamite conquest that culminated in the Battle of Limerick in 1691. A period that has never been examined by Irish Catholic nationalists until comparatively recently, it is of such importance to the mythology of Ulster Protestant Unionists that it is necessary to examine the events leading up to it in some detail. They are directly responsible for the fears, whether real or imaginary, that Ulster Protestants continue to carry with them.

King James II had attempted to re-establish the Catholic religion, by the forcible suppression of his Protestant subjects, not only in his own country but also in Ireland, and the wholesale executions in England on the orders of the infamous Judge Jeffreys, had led to fears of the revival of the 'Popish Plot', a product of the imagination of the equally notorious Titus Oates. This was to lead to similar treatment of Catholics on the accession of William of Orange to the throne of Britain. The situation would have been better if James, who was William's brother in law, had had the courage or wisdom to introduce a measure granting freedom of religion to all his subjects. However he had neither of these qualities and his whole reign was characterised by weakness and savage cruelty.

James was no respecter of persons and, himself childless, proceeded to invent a son, the existence of whom would sound the death knell to William's progressive plans as well as his position as heir apparent to the throne. William had so far been content to oppose James by constitutional means, but when the Queen fell pregnant it became vital for him to rid England of its tyrant.

Realising the extent of the opposition to him, which had built up over the years, James set about preparing himself a haven in Ireland. To this end Richard Talbot, an Irish Catholic leader, had been elevated to the English peerage as Earl of Tyrconnell and appointed Lord Deputy of Ireland. All Protestants were dismissed from the army, to be replaced by Catholics and at the same time all posts in the judiciary and local government were taken out of Protestant hands.

This caused fears of another massacre to grow among the settlers and many fled across the sea while those who remained behind concentrated in Derry and Enniskillen. Meanwhile James's policies at home made him ever more isolated and in a state of abject fear. Following his failure to replace the English army with Catholics drafted from Ireland, he fled to France where he mustered what troops were still loyal to him and landed in Kinsale. From there he immediately began to march north in an endeavour to crush all Protestant resistance.

No less than half of Tyrconnell's army was sent against Derry, where only the walls of the city and a few old guns protected the panic-stricken residents. It was here that the phrase 'No surrender', which was to become a byword among Unionists during the latter part of the twentieth century, was first coined. The courage and bravery of the defenders of Derry cannot be underrated and is comparable only with the defence of Limerick by Sarsfield against Williamite forces.

The siege of Derry lasted 105 days, during which many perished from starvation and disease rather than capitulate, and it was only brought to an end by the arrival of an English ship, when no more than two days' supply of food remained. Taken off their guard the besiegers fell back, only to be routed at the siege of Newtown Butler by the men of Enniskillen.

During all this time William had been powerless to intervene, his hands being tied due to the political unrest resulting from a territorial dispute between Britain and France. He was also in a quandary, as he was now perceived as the saviour of the Protestants, so his plans to end religious divisions were put in jeopardy. In addition, despite James being away from England in France, he had no claim to the throne. This disability was removed when the Whigs and Tories finally united to pass a Bill of Rights that removed the hereditary title or 'divine right' of Kings, thereby making it possible for Parliament to depose the monarch or alter the order of succession, should it think fit.

William was thus the first King to be elected by Parliament and, despite the threat of a Jacobite rebellion, decided that his first priority must be to secure his position in Ireland. His defeat of James, whose cowardice became legendary, at the Battle of the Boyne in July 1690, proved to be the final turning point in the English conquest of Ireland. It is for this reason that this battle and the siege of Derry are commemorated annually by Northern Unionists. The occupation was completed with the Treaty of Limerick, which was signed on Sarsfield's surrender, but it was never ratified by the English Parliament to the dismay of both William and Sarsfield. With all hope of the freedom of religion that this would have guaranteed now extinguished, Sarsfield and his army now sought refuge in France, leaving the Irish in the grip of a pitiless legal tyranny that had resulted from Tyrconnell's collaboration with James I.

At this time Catholic landlords outnumbered Protestants by five to one but they were dispossessed of their land and by the eighteenth century very few of them survived. Nearly all of them were forced to profess Protestantism and those who refused were reduced to a state of penury. On the other hand, for practical reasons it was impossible to eradicate the Catholic religion and, to that extent, Ireland was spared the full extent of the persecution that was taking place in England.

In 1782 the agitation of Grattan and Flood succeeded in persuading Lord Rockingham that many of the disabilities under which Catholics had been suffering since 1691, and the consequent unrest, could be ended if England were to end the judicial and legislative authority that it exercised over the Irish Parliament. As a result Ireland was to become independent, for all intents and purposes, the only remaining link being the allegiance of both countries to the same sovereign.

This independence, however, turned out to be nothing more than the uncontrolled and uncontrollable rule of a few families, members of a corrupt aristocracy, at whose mercy Ireland was now left. Indeed so corrupt was the rule of these 'Parliamentary Undertakers', as this small group of noblemen were known, that at the time of the Act of Union no fewer than 60 seats in the Irish Parliament were controlled by three families – the Downshires the Beresfords and the Ponsonbys. Ireland, under the Grattan administration, far from having advanced had gained the reputation of being the worst governed country in Europe.

Prior to this period there had lately been a slight easing of the repression, and the subordination of the Irish Parliament to the English Privy Council had resulted in a brake being put on the worst excesses of the plundering aristocracy and landlord classes. A few Catholic families had profited under the Grattan administration, but they had no power in this overwhelmingly Protestant administration and the state of misery suffered by the majority of the people, in particular the peasantry, was worse than before. In these circumstances it would seem that revolution was the only means of freeing the country.

CHAPTER 2

The 1798 Rising

The father of Irish Republicanism was Theobald Wolfe Tone, a Presbyterian solicitor practicing in Dublin. Unfortunately those who would claim him as their founding father today have perverted his teachings out of all proportion. Viewed in the light of history, it is evident that his separatism was the product of circumstances that are no longer relevant but were pertinent in his day, if his main aim of uniting Catholic, Protestant and Dissenter in a common cause was to be achieved.

This was due to the continued existence, during the eighteenth century, of the British penal laws, which had made the practice of the Roman Catholic faith in England an offence punishable by death. In Ireland, where these laws were more difficult to enforce, adherence to this religion entailed the loss of all rights, civil or otherwise.

These laws, originally enacted for fear of the political power of Rome, applied equally though they were less harshly enforced to Dissenters, who were regarded with equal suspicion by the Establishment, a situation that had pertained ever since the restoration of Charles II on the overthrow of Cromwell's Puritan republic. In passing it should be noticed that in this context 'Establishment' is used, as it was originally understood – to denote the rule of the Established Church. This is quite different from its modern connotation, which refers to the social order.

In Ireland there is a common misconception, as a result of this change of usage, that Tone was a member of the Establishment. In reality he was one of its victims, who looked to the emancipation of all religions to solve the communal strife in Ireland and in this he had the support of the Earl of Rosse, among others.

Drawing his inspiration from the American War of Independence and the new ideas of liberty, equality and fraternity that had emerged from the French Revolution, he envisaged a New Ireland, where Catholics, Protestants and Dissenters would enjoy equality of esteem and freedom to practice their religion. But in order to initiate this new order it was essential to break the link with England, for it was the source of all Ireland's ills, which stemmed directly from the legal constraints imposed by the British Government.

In 1791 Tone, together with others who were attracted by his ideas, founded the Society of the United Irishmen in Belfast. This city was a natural choice inasmuch as the greater part of the Protestant populace was situated in Ulster, as a consequence of the Elizabethan and Cromwellian plantations. Common cause was made with the

Roman Catholics and it was not long before the organisation had rapidly expanding cells in every part of Ireland.

The following year, however, Prime Minister William Pitt, who like Tone had been impressed with the ideals of the French Revolution and had little time for the Irish Parliament due to that body's rejection of his plans for free trade, used the imminent threat of war with France to gain the acceptance of measures providing for the admission of Catholics to the franchise and to civil and military offices within Ireland.

But Tone's plans for a rising were now well advanced and two events combined to make the coming revolution inevitable – the prevarication of the Irish Parliament in considering, much less putting into effect, Pitt's proposals, despite the pleas of Grattan and Lord Fitzwilliam, and the atrocities being committed by the Orange yeomanry in suppressing minor riots that had been taking place.

Tone went first to America and then to France to elicit support, while Belfast witnessed a colourful parade of the United Irishmen that surpassed anything that had been seen in that City. Ostensibly held to celebrate the French Revolution it served, as its originators intended, not only to stir the hearts of Catholics and Dissenters alike, but also to forge links with revolutionary France. Indeed the French Tricolour was carried at the head of the procession.

This flag was adapted, with its colours changed to green, white and orange, to signify the unity of Catholics, Dissenters and members of the Established Church, became the emblem of the United Irishmen, before evolving into the symbol of the Irish Republic.

With the success of Tone's visit to France ensured, a national uprising was planned to take place on 12 March 1798, However by 1793 the ideals that had inspired the French Revolution were replaced by the naked terror of the Commune. This state of affairs continued until the time of Napoleon, whose successful conduct of the war against England enabled him to overthrow the Directory and become the First Consul of the Empire.

As late as 1792 Britain had endeavoured to avert this conflict by refusing to take part in the coalition against France and had agreed to remain neutral, on receiving an undertaking that France would cease violating the independence of neighbouring states. The invasion of Holland in clear violation of this agreement brought about the rupture of diplomatic relations between the two countries and, in February 1793, France declared war on England.

This gave added impetus to the plans for the Rising and, seeing the danger, in 1795 the authorities made a vain attempt to wean Catholics away from the growing movement by founding Maynooth College. The object was to discourage students from emigrating to France where they were likely to come into contact with revolutionary politics.

The British were not alone in their apprehension of such a development. There was disquiet throughout Europe as the Revolution had degenerated into a squalid struggle for power between a number of anti-clerical factions who had prostituted its aims to suit their own ends. By the time Napoleon came to power, France had become notorious as the home of atheism and anticlericalism.

Indeed there can be little doubt that Tone, who was an idealist, had some misgivings at this stage, but they were soon dissipated as a result of the short-lived Terror, which had been whipped up in England by Edmund Burke. He feared a republican plot following the publication of Thomas Paine's *Rights of Man* and saw an opportunity to put an end to Pitt's reformism.

Pitt was driven by Burke's agitation to introduce draconian measures, against his better judgement, in order to assuage public opinion. The Habeus Corpus Act was temporarily suspended and with the widening of the Statute of Treasons public meetings were prohibited. In addition the press was subject to censorship, resulting in numerous prosecutions, but of even greater significance was that in Ireland the sermons of many dissenting clergymen were indicted as seditious.

Despite these measures Pitt was to find himself alone in wanting to make peace with revolutionary France, and was denounced by Burke in his *Letters on the Proposals for a Peace with the Regicide Directory,* when he endeavoured to open negotiations with the French in 1796. Irish historians, however, ignore the genuine zeal for reform that was characteristic of Pitt. Rather they tend to blacken his name by concentrating on the repressive measures he was forced to take due to the agitation of Burke, whom they extol, and the Act of Union in its final form, which they wrongly attribute to him.

In this they are totally inconsistent for excellent orator though he no doubt was, Burke although sympathetic to Catholic emancipation, unlike Pitt, was a dedicated monarchist but was otherwise opposed to any progressive reform in Ireland or in England. Furthermore the original aims of Pitt's Act of Union were distorted out of all recognition by his successor.

These same chroniclers would have us believe that, at the time of the Rising, informers betrayed the plans of the United Irishmen. This is not only unlikely but it was also unnecessary, as the British had already been alerted by Hoche's unsuccessful attempt at a landing in 1796. Consequently the ranks of Tone's supporters would have been infiltrated and such a penetration would have ensured that his plan of campaign would have been well known to the authorities in advance of the date set for the Rising.

Tone would have accompanied Hoche on this abortive expedition, which had set out with a squadron of 43 ships and 15,000 men, for Bantry Bay on the coast of West Cork. As luck would have it they encountered adverse weather conditions when only 500 yards from the shore, and after waiting for six frustrating days they were forced to return to France. Meanwhile Napoleon, abandoning the United Irishmen, had decided to switch his attention to Egypt. It was not long before most of the leaders of the United Irishmen were apprehended and had it not been for the treatment meted out by the yeomanry to their prisoners it is highly probable that the Rising would have been stillborn.

In the event the enraged populace of Wexford decided to go ahead as planned, but following the arrest of the leaders the rest of the country was completely disorganised. The premature revolt, which took place on 26 May 1798, was accompanied only by smaller outbreaks in Antrim, Down and Leinster, all of which were easily contained.

Meanwhile the long-awaited help from France arrived and landings took place in Lough Swilley in Ulster and Killalla in County Mayo, but the forces were not only pitifully inadequate but arrived far too late to have any effect. It can only be concluded that Napoleon wanted to have a clear indication as to how the insurrection was faring before committing himself, as it is clear from the strength of the forces involved, amounting to no more than 300 and 1,000 in the respective locations, that this was a mere token force to precede a full-scale invasion should the Rising prove successful.

The invaders were easily overcome and when Tone, who later took his own life, was captured, the Rising was over to all intent and purposes bar the brave resistance put up by the United Irishmen in Wexford. These men, though hopelessly outnumbered and outclassed in weaponry, succeeded in advancing throughout the county to Oulart, Gorey and Bunclody, but were defeated at New Ross. Attempts to extend the insurrection into neighbouring Wicklow met with a further setback at Arklow.

The outcome was now inevitable and it was only a matter of time before the remaining insurgents were encircled following the battle of Vinegar Hill on 21 June, barely a month after the beginning of the Rising at Boolavogue. Nevertheless the spirit of the United Irishmen lived on and was to have a considerable impact on future events. In the immediate aftermath of the Rising most of the rebels were rounded up, many being executed, while others were transported to Australia and New Zealand where their descendants are to be found today, many in important positions in the Crown Service. Others were not so fortunate. Some 30,000 Irishmen were killed in the battles and by the end of the century no less than a 250,000 Ulster Protestants had been forced to flee across the Atlantic due to the continuing unrest.

During the immediate aftermath of the Rising, Pitt who had considerable sympathy with the reasons that had provoked it, determined to introduce sweeping reforms in Ireland but could see no hope of progress until "this farce of independence", as he described the Grattan Parliament, was abolished. Though nominally committed to the measure, not only had it delayed his plans for Catholic Emancipation and driven many of the uncommitted into the ranks of the United Irishmen, but it was doing nothing substantial to protect the Catholics and Dissenters from the bigoted fury of the Protestant yeomanry who supported the Established Church.

CHAPTER 3

Ireland is Wracked by Political Ferment and the Famine

It was Pitt's sympathy with the inequities that had provoked the Rising and his anger at the procrastination of the Grattan Parliament that had made it inevitable, that determined him to set out on a course of action that, had it been successful, would have achieved more than Tone could have hoped to gain by the Rising. Pitt planned the Act of Union, which as originally envisaged by him could have been one of the most comprehensive packages of social legislation affecting Ireland in the nineteenth Century; Pitt, who had no little contempt for the ruling classes, was ahead of his time in that he despised hereditary titles.

His policy was based on the concession of full religious liberty to all and the abolition of the religious Tests that had limited the exercise of the franchise. It meant that nobody, however humble, be they Catholic or Dissenter, would be debarred from holding any office in the nation and in due course it would become possible to establish a parliament representative of all the Irish people.

Grattan on the other hand, whose paramount concern was protecting the power of the Irish landowners and tradesmen, whose interests were mutual, had also championed Catholic Emancipation for no other reason than to quell the growing agitation among the peasants. Consequently he came to adopt an anti-British stance, but on account of this his significance has been magnified out of all proportion and he has been portrayed as a patriot and champion of the people. Yet otherwise he was opposed to any progressive reforms.

Earlier, when Pitt had endeavoured to end a situation whereby English landowners effectively barred the import of agricultural produce from Ireland, Grattan had supported the Irish landlords, who were suspicious of any measure of free trade. The Irish Parliament rejected the proposals out of hand. This well-intentioned reform was, however, misused in the future by unscrupulous 'gombeen men', the pejorative term for small-time 'wheeler-dealers', who lined their pockets during the famine years by exporting much needed grain to Britain. In the ordinary course of events such free trade would have increased the prosperity of the farming community who, up till then, had been denied an export market.

In the circumstances the Irish Parliament was asked to introduce legislation that would effectively put an end to its existence. The first vote saw the Assembly almost equally divided on the issue, for many felt that the proposed Act of Union would afford them the opportunity of holding the balance of power between the Whigs and the Tories, which they could use to block any future reformist measures directed at Ireland.

Although it was alien to his nature, Pitt realised that the assent of the Irish Parliament would have to be bought with hard cash and the creation of a number of peerages. Eventually it was to cost the better part of £1 million (£800 million in today's money) to persuade its members to agree to its dissolution. It was bribery, but he had no option if the Union was to be brought about, together with an end to the abuses to which the people had been subjected.

With the passing of the Act of Union free trade was gradually introduced and these abuses were indeed ameliorated. Nevertheless Pitt had to tread carefully for fear of alarming the English Protestant Parliament. Consequently when he suggested that Catholic and Dissenting clergymen be paid the same stipend as members of the Established Church, he took care to reassure Parliament that the proposed measure would ensure the loyalty of Catholics.

Among other provisions, he had made arrangements for the hated tithes to be commuted, but his scheme was so progressive that he could not win the assent of his Cabinet and his intentions were leaked to the King. This resulted in a furious encounter between Pitt and George III that concluded with the Prime Minister's resignation.

Pitt was replaced by Addington, a Protestant every bit as bigoted as the King himself. He made it his business to see that the Act was used to introduce repressive measures, which negated the planned reforms. The original Union, as envisaged by Pitt, was thus altered out of all recognition, giving credence to the myth that the Act was a trick perpetrated by Pitt.

Meanwhile the Rising of 1798 was to become a milestone in Irish history for Republicans in much the same way as the Battle of the Boyne was to symbolise the conquest of Ireland for Unionists. Unfortunately, however, the accounts of this period by both sides, though they contain some undoubted facts, consist in the main of propaganda conveyed in the form of ballads. Most of them are highly coloured, but while some contain an element of truth others are completely unreliable and are the product of the balladeer's imagination.

Thus a new mythology was born out of the ashes of the Rising. It was to wreak havoc in future generations, for these ballads were to survive until comparatively recently in the form of rebel songs, which in the absence of a properly documented narrative were once taught in schools in conjunction with selected facts. At the same time no consideration is given to the fact that the United Irishmen, as originally constituted, ceased to exist as a political entity after the Rising. Nor is the part that many of its leaders were to play in the growth of the Orange Order generally known.

Subjected to this subtle yet unintentional indoctrination, it is hardly surprising that so many young minds in the south grew up with an inbuilt anti-British bias. Conversely Unionist thinking is conditioned by the Orange Order, which came into being in 1795 to unite the various Orange Societies that had appeared, during the past decade, to protect landlords who were members of the Established Church from the ferocity of the attacks made on them by their Catholic tenants, who had been goaded into action following 100 years of unremitting repression.

Prior to the removal of Pitt from office and the passing of the Act, the Order had strongly resisted the Union. However not only was it opposed to the Papacy but the link between Catholics in Ireland and revolutionaries on the Continent was not lost on its members. They feared that emancipation would be the prelude to a fate similar to that suffered by members of the French aristocracy, and later the bourgeoisie, at the hands of the Commune. But like their counterparts in France they had failed to appreciate that the possibility of such an eventuality being brought about was the result of conditions of their own making.

The initial opposition by the Orange Order to the Union gives the lie to the belief, fostered by Nationalist chroniclers that Pitt had no other motive but to bring Ireland under the domination of England. In order to sustain this myth they quote history out of context, completely oblivious to Pitt's attempts to form a Cabinet made up of leading progressives on his return to office following Addington's retirement.

In this he was again thwarted by George III, who refused to ratify his chosen administration. However he was not alone in trying to bring about Catholic Emancipation. Later the Granville Ministry, whose enlightened policy had seen the abolition of the slave trade, endeavoured to introduce this measure, but the King sacked him on his refusal to give an undertaking that he would not bring the matter before parliament. It was not until 1829 that the British Government was committed to this measure, and this time it was forced on an unwilling Tory administration that feared that the outcome of Daniel O'Connell's successful agitation in Ireland would be a civil war.

It was left to Daniel O'Connell to make the first move in what was to prove to a long, drawn-out struggle against British rule. Educated in France, he had watched unfolding events there with interest, but the atrocities committed in the name of the Revolution had filled him with revulsion. This was to have a profound effect on his future actions, which were dominated by his abhorrence of violence.

With the passing of the Catholic Relief Act he had travelled to London to be one of the first Catholics there to be admitted to the bar, and it was his genius as a lawyer that was largely responsible for his success as a politician. He therefore determined to make a careful study of the brief he had set himself in order to determine why previous movements had failed.

The defeat of the United Irishmen had signalled the end of the fragile alliance between Catholics and Dissenters that had made the Rising possible. However in Ireland there is a completely false perception that this society was a mainly Catholic entity that had the support of Tone and some Protestants. Rather the reverse is true, for this body consisted of a hard core of disaffected, middle-class Presbyterian radicals, who though committed to Catholic Emancipation by no means shared Tone's zeal for it. Indeed many of them regarded the necessity of recruiting Catholics to their ranks with a mixture of apprehension and distaste.

Nevertheless O'Connell concluded that the society could have achieved its aims if it had restricted its activities to mounting demonstrations rather than resorting to violence. Initially there had been considerable sympathy among the Dissenters for the plight of the Catholics, due to the degradation to which those professing that faith had been reduced. But they soon had reason to fear the violence of the downtrodden Irish Catholics, whose ferocity they compared to that of the *sans culottes* who had seized power from the bourgeoisie in France. After one particularly horrific agrarian outrage one of the founders of the United Irishmen, the poet William Drennan, voiced their feelings when he questioned the wisdom of "committing arms and rights to such savages as these Catholics". However, he was persuaded to support O'Connell's peaceful agitation.

During the years immediately preceding the passage of the Act of Union, Pitt had succeeded in gaining support for Catholic Emancipation. But once he was relieved from office the reforms that were introduced were diluted to such an extent that they amounted, at best, to reliefs rather than any genuine revision of the existing legislation.

Nonetheless the penal laws had, to all intents and purposes, ceased to exist. This was not from any good will on the part of the government, but it is clear that the King had finally heeded Pitt's advice in order to obviate the possibility of any further attempt at revolution in Ireland. He had, however, set his face firmly against Catholic Emancipation, but the Catholic Relief Act, passed in 1793, meant that the Irish were no longer barred from being elected in the English Parliament and the legal profession was now open to them.

Surprisingly, in view of the pivotal part they had played in the Rising, the Dissenters were the main beneficiaries of the Catholic Relief Act because all the disabilities to which they had been subjected prior to the Union had been removed. Freed from their former constraints, their fear of the underprivileged Catholics drove those who remained in Ireland to join the Orange Order, where they were to become pillars of the Unionist ruling class.

Robert Emmet, one of the few to remain loyal to their ideals, staged a brave but futile revolt in Kildare and Wicklow in 1803. It collapsed after he led an attack on Dublin Castle and he fled, probably as much in fear of this rabble as of the authorities. But he was to prove himself to be a far greater orator than he was a military tactician and his oft-quoted 'Speech from the Dock', in which he gave a brilliant exposé of the aspirations of the Society of United Irishmen, was to earn him a place in posterity. Nevertheless Nationalist mythology omits to mention the defection of many of the United Irishmen to the Unionist camp.

It also confuses Pitt's plans for a Union, which would have brought emancipation to the entire Irish people, with the Act as introduced by Addington. Not only does it blame Pitt for its future misuse but paints an entirely false picture of the events of the time, which has been perpetuated ever since. However it is doubtful whether the myth that Pitt's plans for a Union were simply a device to bring Ireland under the complete domination of England could ever have been sustained, but for the methods he was forced to employ to rid Ireland of the discredited Grattan Parliament.

O'Connell realised that Catholic Emancipation would not be gained simply by political action, however skilful its advocates, but only by carefully planned and massive demonstrations. Consequently the 1820s saw the growth of a mass movement, initiated and sustained by him. In 1823 he formed the Catholic Association with the aid of the clergy and set out to tour Ireland, making rousing speeches that gave the country new hope and encouragement.

Though himself a landlord, he used the Association's funds to fight cases against the landowners on behalf of their tenants and pay for the printing of newssheets and pamphlets to use at his meetings. Failing to appreciate that O'Connell would neither have supported nor advocated an insurrection; the government reacted by banning the Association. O'Connell, however, used his legal skill to ensure that the organisation kept well within the law and resuscitated it under the title of the New Catholic Association.

The general election of 1826 afforded the organisation an opportunity to flex its muscles and O'Connell the chance to prove the extent of his following. Prior to this it had been accepted that tenants would simply vote for the candidate of their landlord's choice, but O'Connell chose four test constituencies, Monaghan, Roscommon, Louth and Waterford, each representing one of the four Provinces, and urged tenants to vote for the candidates who supported Emancipation. In every case these candidates were overwhelmingly successful and for the first time landlords found themselves confronted with a challenge and the possibility of losing their influence.

Their fear of the emergence of a new spirit of defiance was heightened when, in the Clare by-election of 1848, O'Connell himself secured the nomination against the powerful and popular Vesey Fitzgerald. His resounding victory at the polls with a margin of two to one brought him renown, not only at home but also internationally, and it now became clear to the British Government that it could no longer delay implementing a measure granting full emancipation to Catholics, as any attempt to prevent such a man from taking his seat in Parliament would do immeasurable damage to England's image abroad.

In addition to this consideration, renewed fears of a rebellion in Ireland persuaded many MPs, who were becoming increasingly apprehensive, that such a revolt might spread to England. There it would have the backing not only of their co-religionists but also of growing radical elements, who were already beginning to voice their support for Catholic Emancipation. The upshot was the introduction of a bill that was passed without delay in 1829, resulting in O'Connell being hailed as 'the liberator' by Irish and English Catholics alike.

However the value of this reform to tenant farmers in Ireland was eroded by a further amending Act that restricted the exercise of the franchise to those whose holdings were valued at £10 or more (around £10,000 today), whereas formerly it had been set at £2. Thus only the more wealthy Catholics were able to become members of the English Parliament.

O'Connell was anything but satisfied with this turn of events and set about pressing for further reforms. As a result the 1830s saw the introduction of new social legislation, particularly regarding education and the administration of the legal and police systems. Workhouses were also established during this period to cater for the increasing population of the destitute and those living in abject poverty, which the Irish viewed as the result of the repression that had followed the introduction of Addington's Act of Union.

This prompted O'Connell to form the National Repeal Association with the object of establishing a new Irish administration, free of the corruption that had characterised the Grattan Parliament. He called for the Act of Union to be rescinded and based his tactics on those he had used so successfully in the campaign for Catholic Emancipation. As the tenants, joined by others opposed to the Union flocked to join him, so his following increased

The country soon became the scene of massive demonstrations once more, but no support came from England or the Protestants of North-East Ulster, who had fared comparatively well under the Union. They were firmly against the new movement and the situation was further exacerbated by fear of O'Connell and the triumphalist attitude of the Catholic Church.

The Orangemen had watched his progress with ill-concealed dismay. Not only had he succeeded in wresting Catholic Emancipation from no lesser man than the Duke of Wellington, but also now he was out to break the Union. Ever since its inception the Orange Order had played on the fears of past massacres to instil nothing short of dread of Catholics into its members.

His mass meetings generated considerable anxiety among the Protestant community. They now looked to the connection with England, which many of them had so vehemently opposed in the past, as the only means of guaranteeing their privileged position. Undaunted by this setback O'Connell continued to build up his following.

Meanwhile a number of young writers, including Thomas Davis, Charles Gavan Duffy and Thomas Dillon, formed a group calling themselves the Young Irelanders and founded a newspaper – *The Nation* – aimed at reversing the sectarian trend and uniting Irishmen of all denominations. The Young Irelanders travelled the length and breadth of the country, enlivening fairs and other local events with readings from their paper, which consisted in the main of ballads composed at the time of the 1798 Rising.

Simultaneously O'Connell's agitation was gathering momentum and was to reach its zenith on 11 August, when approximately 250,000 people turned out to hear him address them at the Hill of Tara in County Meath, the ancient seat of the High Kings of Ireland. The significance of his choice of venue for this meeting was not lost on the Protestant landlords, whose fear of the angry peasantry had now reached fever pitch.

It would seem that it now only needed a spark to set off an insurrection and this led O'Connell to cancel a planned demonstration, which would have been even more impressive, to have been held in Clontarf in October. Like the authorities, who had also banned the meeting, he feared the possibility of a confrontation between his supporters and the troops sent to Dublin Bay to enforce the ban, as he was against the use of physical force to achieve his objectives, he agreed not to proceed with this meeting.

The British then made one of those unbelievable errors that have characterised much of their dealings with Ireland. Not only did they fail to appreciate O'Connell's nature but they also seriously underestimated his influence and power. Instead of realising that they were dealing with a man of peace, whose strength and popular support was such that he was capable of controlling a crowd of any size even at a time when a headlong clash seemed inevitable, they mistook his action for weakness and had him arrested.

In so doing they lent credence to the militants, led by John Mitchell, William Smith O'Brien and Thomas Meagher. Consequently when he was released 12 months later he found his people riven with dissention and came into conflict with the Young

Irelanders, who had now joined the Fenian camp. He no longer had the stamina to organise the revival of the movement, which he had led so effectively, and died in Genoa in 1857.

After his death he was vilified not only by the Young Irelanders but by also those who were influenced by their writings to commit evil deeds in the name of the land they professed to love. But when these are long forgotten the name of O'Connell, who except for Parnell was unquestionably the greatest leader to emerge in nineteenth century Ireland, will continue to be revered.

Indeed had it not been for the methods adopted by the physical force movement, which was a legacy of the Rising of 1798 and the subsequent revolts instigated by future leaders that culminated in the Fenian Movement, the Union would have died a natural death. Further, the reasons that had prompted the separatism of Tone had long ceased to exist.

Today a very different situation pertains and it is understandable why, in the light of the situation that continued to exist for the better part of the twentieth century, Britain was slow to relinquish its foothold in Northern Ireland, for The Republic of Ireland was declared not by Eamonn de Valera but by the Inter-Party Government which, on coming to power in 1948 repealed his External Relations Act (1936). Since then the Irish State has refused to cooperate in any arrangements for collective security, despite its membership of the European Union, while maintaining pitifully inadequate defence forces as distinct from a highly efficient peacekeeping unit.

With the cessation of the conflict ignited by the Provisional IRA in Northern Ireland, there can be little doubt that Britain would be only too willing to extricate itself from that Province. But its hands are tied in the light of continued activities by both loyalist and dissident republican paramilitaries, and there can be little doubt that American foreign policy will be the deciding factor in any future decision.

The 1840s were to witness the greatest natural disaster ever to befall Ireland. Coming as it did during the period when O'Connell's agitation had left a legacy of unrest in the country, this catastrophe was to have far-reaching implications particularly among Irish Americans, many of whose forebears were victims of the last great famine in Europe.

Between 1800 and 1841 a population explosion had taken place in Ireland and the population had increased dramatically from 5,000,000 to 8,175,000, a very large proportion of whom derived their living from the land. Of these no less than a third of the entire community depended on smallholdings of between one and five acres. For their subsistence they relied on a good quality crop of potatoes that could be stored over a long period.

Portents of the impending doom came with the failure of a number of crops in mainland Europe, between 1818 and 1842, accompanied by similar outbreaks of blight in continental Europe and Canada in 1825. But it was not until September 1845 that the disease reached Ireland, where it first made itself manifest in the form of a foul-smelling fungus that rotted all around it. Although the initial outbreak confined itself to the southeast of the country, it soon spread to neighbouring counties.

A completely unknown phenomenon, the cause of this disease was unknown, as was the cure. Those living in the affected areas were to find starvation staring them in the face as prices began to soar beyond their reach. Sir Robert Peel, the British Prime Minister, thought that the famine would be short-lived and sent to America for a consignment of maize, with the exchequer making £100,000 (£75 million today) available for the purpose.

On its arrival it was sold at low prices by the Famine Relief organisations that had been set up to deal with the emergency. But the people, unused to eating cereals, found them hard to cook and harder still to digest. In addition, as so often happens today when dealing with humanitarian crises, much of this food fell into the hands of the unscrupulous gombeen men and other merchants, who saw the chance of making an exorbitant profit out of the distress of the people whose scant earnings, from the public works established to provide employment, were soon exhausted, but the full force of the famine was yet to be felt.

In 1846, despite the import of good seed potatoes, the potato blight returned with even greater severity and swept through the entire country, obliterating all before it. Then came the worst winter in living memory, with storms, lashing winds and icy gales. It seemed that the whole of nature was pitted against the helpless peasantry, who were now dying in huge numbers, while those who could still muster sufficient strength struggled to find anything in the field, even roots and berries, that would kill the pangs of hunger and keep body and soul together.

It is difficult for us today, when it is possible to make contact with any part of the world in a matter of seconds, and when supplies can be airlifted to disaster areas within hours, to appreciate the enormity of the problem facing the government. Not only was communication slow and ponderous but transport by sea was hazardous in bad weather. There were therefore inevitable delays but they were the result of the winter of 1846 and subsequent years rather than the result of any procrastination on the part of the authorities. However perceived tardiness on their part was to assume political significance, for the hard-pressed Irish people were bearing the brunt of what was probably the worst catastrophe to have been experienced in these islands since the Black Death swept England in 1348.

Aided by numerous voluntary agencies and organisations, including the Society of Friends and the British Famine Relief Organisation, the government set about the well-nigh impossible task of alleviating the situation. Free soup kitchens came into being and by August 1847 some three million souls depended on them for survival. There is also no doubt that the Catholic Church, or at any rate individual clergymen, forbade their parishioners to use them for fear that attempts would be made to convert the people away from Catholicism.

The workhouses that had originally been built as a last resort for the homeless were hurriedly extended to cater for 100,000 people. They soon become overcrowded and by 1849 the better part of one million people were herded into them to escape the bitter winter. This brought about the dreaded famine disease, which was to cost more lives than the famine itself.

Added to this was the action of some, but by no means all, landlords who showed no pity in evicting their tenants. This was done either in genuine fear of the disease by some but others, like their Scottish counterparts seized the opportunity to rid themselves of crofters, in order to obtain more land for grazing. Such treatment condemned the people to almost certain death, for they were barred from entering urban areas by the townspeople who, in their own close living conditions, feared contamination by the fever.

A ray of hope existed for some – those who could afford the passage to America. But for others the dream of seeking a new life in the land of limitless opportunities was turned into a nightmare by Liverpool ship-owners who seized the opportunity to make vast profits out of these unfortunates. The scene aboard the ill-equipped vessels provided for the voyage across the Atlantic, into which all who could afford it were packed like cattle, beggars description. For many, weakened as they were by hunger or wracked by disease, it was a journey to a watery grave.

In these circumstances it is hardly surprising that the Young Irelanders should have attempted their ill-fated revolt in 1848. Occurring as it did, so soon after the agitation of O'Connell and when the Rising of 1798 was still fresh in the minds of the people, though it was easily put down, it was to assume enormous political significance. The famine itself was to have far-reaching repercussions and the actions of the less scrupulous landlords, ship owners and gombeen men were to produce yet another myth.

Such was the prevailing mood that any failure on the part of those responsible for distributing famine relief was magnified out of all proportion and the government was blamed for the actions of those over whom they had no control. Legislation to curb profits and prices was unheard of and the authorities were as powerless to prevent the activities of dishonest Irish traders as they were to control the Liverpool merchants who owned the 'coffin ships', or the actions of those who were exporting much needed grain from the country not to mention those of the Irish bailiffs, whose duty it was to attend to the affairs of absentee landlords, including the fixing and collecting of rents.

There can be little doubt that many bailiffs took advantage of their employer's absence to see how much money they could extract from poverty stricken tenants. Indeed many such bailiffs and stewards vied with one another in the pitiless exploitation of the misery of the tenant farmers and were responsible for actions that were subsequently attributed to the landlords.

In order to appreciate the difficulties facing the government and the constraints placed on the authorities in their endeavours to alleviate the worst excesses of those who exploited the famine victims, it is necessary to examine the social background in England during this period. The prevailing attitude was one of *laissez-faire*, an economic doctrine enunciated by the Manchester School, which brought untold misery to the working masses as the industrial revolution gathered momentum.

The rapid expansion of trade that accompanied this resulted in a *nouveau riche* capitalist class, which together with the merchants possessed formidable political muscle. Though there were honourable exceptions these people were, if anything, even more pitiless than the most heartless Irish landlord. They condemned their workers, living in smoke blackened hovels, to a condition not far removed from slavery and women toiled for long hours in the mills. Even children were not spared, being forced to crawl up and clean the soot-laden chimneys. Many exposed to the horrific conditions of the sweatshops chose to die of starvation rather than enter them.

Parts of England had also been affected by the famine, so taking into account the complete lack of social conscience that characterised the bourgeoisie that grew up with the industrial revolution throughout much of Europe; it is surprising how much aid was made available to Ireland. But in the wake of the bitterness that followed the famine only the bad was remembered; the people had little, if any, knowledge of conditions outside the country, which prompted Karl Marx to write his *Communist Manifesto* in 1848. Subsequently Fenian propagandists gave rise to the belief that the Famine was an act of genocide against the Irish people, which has since become part of the mythology that so often passes for Irish history.

Another myth, to which mention has already been made, regards the 'soupers' who it is said delivered soup to starving people in the hope of being able to convert them from Catholicism. Those in charge of this relief operation were the Society of Friends, or Quakers as they were called, and their activities in Dublin disprove this malicious slander. In 1865 it became possible to wind up their Famine Relief Operation and they used the balance of the funds available to found the Royal Hospital, Donnybrook, or Hospital for the Incurables as it was then known.

This was possibly the only non-denominational institution of its kind in the country. Archbishop Cullen, the Catholic Archbishop of Dublin, who was to become one of its

Governors, not only praised the hospital for admitting so many Catholic victims of the famine but also for ensuring that arrangements were made to for them to attend Sunday Mass at nearby Donnybrook Church.

The evils produced by the famine, rather than the famine itself, were to provide the basis for poisonous propaganda and the subsequent social unrest that was to stem from it. Other events that took place during this period were either wholly or partially airbrushed from Irish history. Indeed this was otherwise a period of great material progress in Ireland, which was not unaffected by the spirit of invention and adventure that prevailed abroad.

One noteworthy achievement was the erection of what was then the world's largest and most powerful telescope, in the grounds of the estate of the Earl of Rosse in Birr, County Offaly. Another development that nearly revolutionised rail transport – the vacuum-powered railway – was designed to enable trains from Dublin to Kingstown (now Dun Laoghaire), to climb the steep gradient over Bray Head in Dalkey, near Dublin. The first of its kind in the world, it was so successful that for a while it seemed that it might replace steam-driven locomotives; it was faster, not to mention being pollution free, but fell into disuse with the rapid development of the steam engine. In this connection it is well worth recording that during the latter half of the nineteenth century Ireland became famous for many feats of engineering connected with railways, leading to the development of a number of industries in the small towns served by them.

Many of these railways subsequently fell into disuse due to Fenian agitation in the area, and more recently due to political failure to appreciate the necessity to decentralise industry from Dublin and the major cities to the regions rather than the other way round, as well as the imperative to replace the internal combustion engine as a means of locomotion. Few of the railways that were developed almost immediately after the Famine have survived to this day, following the decision taken during the 1950s to dismantle all but the main lines.

Paradoxically, in view of the criticism levelled at it by Irish historians, it was the Act of Union that made it impossible for England to ignore Ireland's plight. Had Ireland been independent it could have been treated like any other foreign nation. Just as the Irish townspeople barred the country folk from their cities to save them from the famine disease, all links between the two countries would have been severed and English ports would have been closed to ships crossing the Irish Sea, on the pretext that they might spread the contamination to England.

However the famine itself, and the events that preceded it, were to make the establishment of Home Rule in one form or another inevitable in the long term. But of even more importance for Ireland's future development was the birth in 1846 of two men who were to play a crucial role in the country's future.

Michael Davitt and Charles Stewart Parnell came from widely disparate backgrounds. The former was born into a small farmer's family in Straide, County Mayo, and had experienced all the horrors of the famine. As a young boy he had been present when his parents were evicted. The latter was the son of a wealthy Protestant landowner with an estate at Avondale, County Wicklow, and had enjoyed all the advantages of an English education and a comfortable home environment.

Davitt and his family had been forced to emigrate and, arriving in Lancashire, soon became inured to the sufferings and hardship that were the lot of an English working-class household. When only eleven years of age he worked in the cotton mills and it was there that he met with a serious accident to his right arm, which had to be amputated at the shoulder.

He was fortunate to obtain less arduous work in the pay of a local postmaster. Prior to this he had been accustomed to working a 12-hour day, but now he had time on his hands that he put to good use by studying, developing a love of learning that was illustrated in his future literary activities. It was during this period that he began to read and absorb the revolutionary doctrines of the Young Irelanders. Later he joined the Fenian Movement founded by James Stephens and Jeremiah O'Donovan Rossa. Known also as the Irish Republican Brotherhood, or IRB, this secret society had come into being following the abortive revolt of 1848 and had branches in England and America, as well as in Ireland.

The Fenians were planning for an early armed insurrection but preparations were thwarted by the outbreak of the American civil war in 1861, making much needed money and supplies from that country no longer available. Even so there was considerable divergence of opinion between those who wanted to ensure an uprising "sooner or never", and others who felt that they should wait for a more opportune time. Eventually it was agreed that a revolt should be planned to take place on 7 March 1867.

Such was the delay, however, that it dealt a deathblow to the campaign, as their activities had become known to the authorities through the publication by the IRB of a newspaper entitled *The Irish People*. It had been intended to prepare the Irish people for an insurrection while defending the Fenians from the hostility of the Catholic Church. Hence Dublin Castle had become alerted as to their intentions and the spies planted within the organisation were able to report their every move.

When the revolt took place it was a fiasco. No more than 12 people were killed but many hundreds of prisoners were taken and received long jail sentences. The only incident of any note took place in Manchester, when an attempt was made to rescue two Fenians from a prison van. In the ensuing fracas a police constable was killed;

subsequently three Irishmen were convicted and executed. There may or may not have been a miscarriage of justice, in that it is possible that the wrong people were arrested. To Irish minds there was no doubt that this was the case and the myth of the Manchester Martyrs was born.

Davitt himself was arrested in 1870, having been convicted of gun-running, and received a 15-year prison sentence but served less than half. On his release he went first to America, where he made contact with John Devoy, a leading Fenian activist who had himself served a term in jail, and together they made plans for the future.

On his return to Ireland, Davitt found his people dejected and in a state of apprehension. American exports of grain were now reaching Ireland in such vast quantities that supply exceeded demand, and prices had fallen to such an extent that the income of tenant farmers who had switched to grain production was now below subsistence level. These people now faced even greater difficulties than before, as the landlords were adamant in their refusal to reduce rents to meet the new situation. They fell into arrears and the country witnessed evictions on a large scale. Nature was also playing a grim hand and the terrible weather of the next few winters gave grounds to suspect the approach of a new famine. In response the government and the Famine Relief Associations poured some £2 million into Connacht alone.

In the circumstances, when in October 1879 Davitt founded the Land League, he had little difficulty in organising the smallholders, who were already fiercely determined to end their exploitation by the bailiffs. These men naturally purported to act on behalf of the landlords, many of whom were now absentees – for obvious reasons. Meanwhile in 1875 Parnell had been elected to Parliament to represent the Meath constituency, and together the two men were to represent a formidable alliance. But just as their backgrounds differed widely, so did their methods.

Parnell placed his reliance on constitutional politics while Davitt, whose father had been the leader of one of the agrarian secret societies in County Mayo, had become the leader of the Irish Republican Brotherhood. This organisation was pledged to continue the revolutionary tradition of the United Irishmen and the Young Irelanders, with a view to breaking all connection with England and the establishment of an independent Irish Republic. This would be achieved through militant action, and he saw his Land League as a means whereby he could achieve his dual aim of freeing the tenants from exploitation by their landlords, and preparing the country for a future uprising. Nevertheless, being a pragmatist he fully appreciated the value of Parnell's agitation for Home Rule in Parliament, where he had made a name for himself as a shrewd and able debater, which was to ensure his leadership of the Irish Parliamentary Party on the death of Isaac Butt.

However whereas the Parliamentary Party was well established among nationalists of all classes, inasmuch as unlike the Grattan Parliament it proposed a Home Rule assembly that would give an equal voice to both landlords and tenants, Davitt's movement was as yet in its infancy. However he was impressed with Parnell's progressive ideas and it occurred to him that if Parnell could be persuaded to lend his support to alleviating the lot of the tenants, he could unwittingly become an invaluable ally in building up the revolutionary movement.

At first sight the prospect of Parnell, the Irish Protestant landlord, becoming the leader of the Irish Catholic peasantry might seem something of an anachronism. Yet this apparent paradox is explicable in the light of information that Davitt had received from the IRB in New York, from which it would appear that Parnell was very much influenced by his American-born mother and her father, Commodore Charles O'Connor. The family had emigrated from Belfast during a period when anti-British feeling there was at its height and he had fought against the British in 1812.

For his part, Parnell was concerned at the growing disorder that was becoming apparent, following meetings of the Land League, and feared that this might be counterproductive in securing the aims of the tenants. But as he was wholly unaware of Davitt's connection with the IRB he saw no inconsistency in a strategic alliance and so when Davitt approached Parnell he agreed to become President of the Land League.

He counselled that strict discipline would be needed to obviate the violence that had characterised previous agrarian movements and pointed out that the use of force could have but one consequence – the proscription of the organisation. Davitt was also aware that premature action by the tenants could well jeopardise his planning to secure his main aim, so the upshot of their meeting was an agreement that Parnell should address a vast meeting of the League in Westport, County Mayo. He saw this as an opportunity to bring about the unity of the tenants in their struggle to obtain security of tenure, while pledging members to non-violent action and winning their support for his endeavours to secure Home rule by constitutional means.

Any misgivings that Davitt might have had were dispelled by the success of the large protest meetings that were organised wherever an eviction was to take place and at which every obstacle short of actual physical force was placed in the way of the authorities and the landlords concerned. Land-grabbers, be they landlords or tenants who purchased the land of those who had been evicted, were shunned and were to meet with a wall of silence wherever they went. Such was the case of the infamous Captain Boycott, which is where the term to refuse to have dealings with a person or group entered popular usage, who was to find it impossible, as were others like him, to obtain the necessary supplies or men to work their lands. The League defended anyone arrested for Land League activities and, within a comparatively short time, the courts found themselves overburdened and unable to secure convictions.

With Parnell behind it, the agitation soon spread to the entire country and it seemed inevitable that such a well-organised and disciplined campaign was to bear fruit. The first breakthrough came in 1881 when Gladstone, the Liberal Prime Minister, succeeded against strong opposition from the landowners in getting the first Land Act passed. This in itself was no mean achievement, for when similar legislation had been suggested to Palmerston on a previous occasion he had dismissed it contemptuously with the words, "This is a house of landlords."

This Act was a substantial advance, for not only did it guarantee security to all who paid the rent, as laid down by the Special Courts set up to put an end to the arbitrary fixing of rents by landlords or their bailiffs, but it also contained provisions to enable tenants to sell the interest in their land to other smallholders. Nevertheless the measure fell far short of the demands of the Land League, as it did not protect those who had already fallen into arrears with their rent, and neither did it provide for those who wished to sell their land rather than a mere interest in it. The campaign therefore continued unabated and the League counselled the withholding of even those rents fixed by the Land Courts. The authorities, at their wits' end to know how to stem the growing unrest, finally decided to arrest Parnell and the other leaders of the agitation.

How foolish this error was soon became apparent by the trail of destruction left by the angry peasants. Left to their own devices and without the restraining hand of Parnell, they were now completely out of control and many serious crimes were committed against the innocent as well as the guilty.

Gladstone, realising the magnitude of the miscalculation of his advisers, immediately sought peace with the leaders of the Land League. An agreement, known as the Treaty of Kilmainham, was drawn up whereby they were released and the government gave an undertaking that it would rescind all the remaining oppressive laws operating against the tenants, while funds were to be made available to pay the rents of all those who had fallen into arrears. Finally, the Rents Courts were empowered to reduce existing payments by up to 20 percent. The treaty was followed by Asbourne's Land Act, which provided long-term loans for those who wished to buy out their holdings. However lasting damage had been done to the cause of those who envisaged obtaining their objectives by peaceful means.

Parnell was incensed by crimes committed with little respect for persons or property in the name of the Land League while he was interned during the tenant riots. Being also outraged by the murder in 1882 of the newly appointed. Lord Lieutenant of Ireland by a section of the IRB calling themselves the Invincibles, he agreed to cooperate with the government by lending the whole weight of his authority to its bid to quell the disturbances and restore order. It was at this point that he and Davitt became estranged, for Parnell made it clear that he could have no further truck with the Fenians unless he could rely on their cooperation in his efforts to bring peace to the country.

Thus two separate traditions were to grow up side by side, in opposition to one other. One, with its controlling body the IRB led by Davitt., was pledged to revolution as a means of delivering Ireland from British rule; the other, under the National League founded by Parnell, opted for a constitutional approach to obtaining Home Rule by Act of Parliament.

During the period when Parnell was President of the Land League, much had been achieved by collective non-violent action. Now, in spite of the split, his National League was to meet with even greater success. In the ensuing general election no fewer than 85 of his candidates were elected and the following year Gladstone introduced the first Home Rule Bill. This measure was bitterly opposed by the Ulster Protestant landlords, who not only feared a decline in the trade that had built up in the province since the onset of the industrial revolution, but were even more daunted by the prospect of being ruled by a Catholic dominated assembly. Nevertheless, despite an increasingly acrimonious and trenchant debate and riots among the Unionists in Belfast, not to mention the activities of the Fenians who were equally opposed to any such measure, the Bill was defeated by a mere 30 votes.

Despite this defeat, following the 1886 general election Gladstone remained firmly committed to Home Rule. On his return to Office in 1892 he reintroduced the Bill, which was passed by the House of Commons but vetoed by the House of Lords. This setback spurred Parnell to even greater efforts and he set about rousing support for the measure in England. His stature in that country was greatly enhanced when, in 1889, letters were published in the London *Times* purporting to link him with the Phoenix Park murders. But when these documents were exposed as a crude attempt at character assassination his reputation was restored, along with the growing sympathy for his cause.

Within a year, however, his plans were to receive a disastrous setback. He had one secret that he thought was unknown to all – his love affair with Kitty O'Shea, the Englishwoman with an aristocratic background – but this matter was brought to light when her husband sued for divorce. This attracted considerable publicity and, as is the case with so many politicians whose private lives fall below the exemplary, he was forced to pay the price.

Many of Gladstone's supporters demanded that he break all links with Parnell and the Irish Catholic hierarchy echoed these calls. Parnell protested in vain that his private life was his own affair and, while many Irish MPs continued to support him, a split developed within the party. Seeing the danger to the Home Rule Bill, a majority eventually favoured his stepping down.

Meanwhile Parnell, equally anxious to save the Bill, found himself forced to write to the Irish Parliamentary Party suggesting that he relinquish the leadership, but it was at this stage that he made a fatal error. Relying on the support he had built up in Ireland, he set out on an unremitting tour of the country in a bid to restore his good name. Ironically, however, the only aid he received was from Davitt and the Fenians, with whom he had renewed his association.

This was to result in the loss of many of his erstwhile supporters, while others abandoned the attempt to achieve a separate identity within a British framework and joined forces with the revolutionaries. By now physically and mentally exhausted by his strenuous campaign, Parnell became ill and died at the age of 45, embittered by his downfall and failure to maintain his support.

Davitt, now free to give his whole attention to revolutionary politics, contacted James Stephens, one of the most militant leaders of the IRB, whose uncompromising stance had won him the following of the younger nationalists. This led inevitably to the growth in the power of the Fenians, who were the main beneficiaries of Parnell's demise, while 1898 saw the death of Gladstone himself.

Great though his contribution to Irish politics had been, Parnell, like so many who came after him, had made the fatal error of putting his own interests before those of his country and the movement he had built up. Had he listened to the pleas of Gladstone, the outcome for the Home Rule Bill would have been beyond doubt and the course of Irish history would have taken a different direction.

Instead the opponents of Home Rule, whether nationalist or unionist, were able to take full advantage of the hiatus provided by his downfall and the mistakes made by the British during the subsequent period of Tory rule. The failure to obtain support for the measure by constitutional means played into the hands of the physical force element and many lost all confidence in the possibility of obtaining independence other than by revolution.

Parnell's death saw the invention of yet another myth. Irish historians would have us believe that his downfall had been engineered by the British Government, which had persuaded Kitty O'Shea to seduce him. This is a contention that depends entirely on circumstantial evidence. Had there been any truth in this suggestion it is clear that the extremists in Ireland, of whatever hue, would have had an equal motive in ensuring his political demise, for the Fenians were just as vehement in their opposition to Home Rule as were the Protestants of northeast Ulster. This was not be the first time – nor would it be the last – that opposing extremists united to secure a common objective; evidence of such collusion was to emerge later.

With Parnell out of the way, the IRB succeeded in capitalising on the prevailing sense of disillusion to gain credence for their propaganda, which on closer examination appears to be a heady mixture of carefully selected facts taken out of context and Celtic mythology. This is exemplified by the story of the famine, as presented by these propagandists and accepted as fact by Irish chroniclers. It is perfectly true that between the years 1845 and 1851some 800,000 perished, a further 1,259,000 were forced to emigrate and 49,000 were evicted from their homes, yet no consideration is given to the difficulties of those trying to ship relief supplies across the Irish Sea during the bitter winters. Only the activities of unscrupulous individuals, over whom the government had no control, are highlighted. Neither is there any mention of the fact that many of the absentee landlords were themselves victims of the famine, in that they were forced to emigrate to escape from the disease that it had unleashed

England has been blamed for the large-scale emigration that then took place, which is difficult to see how it could have been avoided in the face of a disaster of this magnitude. This trend, far from abating, has been actively encouraged by successive Irish governments since the foundation of the state, until Ireland's decision to join the European Community made possible a degree of prosperity during the 1990s.

Just as the mythology of nationalism was sustained by presenting the Fenian propaganda of the nineteenth century as history, so that of Unionism relies for its credibility on tales of past massacres from which, as they see it, they were delivered by William of Orange in 1690. In so doing they overlook the fact that William's main aim of bringing his war with James II to an end in Ireland was to prevent further sectarian violence. In this instance, however, he appeared to be the protector of the Protestants, which is why Orangemen have associated themselves with the House of Orange, from which they took their title. Thus began a myth that they have perpetuated to this day, although their loyalty to the British crown is by no means unconditional.

England, though once again dominated by a Tory government adamantly opposed to Home Rule, nevertheless, passed a number of imaginative measures, aimed at quelling the agitation in Ireland, and redressing the grievances of the Irish tenants. Among these was the Wyndham Land Act, by which the state made funds available for smallholders to purchase land from their landowners. The money was distributed to the tenants by means of loans that were repayable through land annuities.

When the Liberals were returned to power following the 1910 general election, Prime Minister Asquith enacted legislation to limit the power of the House of Lords and reintroduced the Home Rule Bill, which by January 1913 had passed all stages in the Commons. Further delaying tactics were employed by the Lords to block its passage, but they would have had no option but to assent to it had it not been for the outbreak of war on 4 August 1914, when all legislation had to be was put on hold until the end of hostilities.

CHAPTER 4

Prelude to a Revolution

The Irish Renaissance was the culmination of a number of movements that developed during the latter part of the nineteenth century. Following the political assassination of Parnell, a number of thoughtful people who agreed with the Fenian analysis banded together with the aim of reviving the ancient Irish customs and culture that existed prior to the Norman invasion.

During this period a number of organisations came into being, all of which were to play an important role in the shaping of future events. Among them was the Gaelic Athletic Association, founded by Michael Cusack in 1884 and whose primary aims were to foster and develop Gaelic games and to reawaken an interest in the Irish language, music and customs. To this end, participation in foreign games was banned and the membership restricted to exclude the police and British servicemen.

This Association has proved to be remarkably successful over the years and today boasts a greater following than any other sporting organisation in Ireland. But however noble its original aspirations, it became bitterly introverted and sectarian in outlook until comparatively recently. Indeed for more than a century its direction was to remain as much political as sporting. Until recently the ban on foreign games was strictly enforced and within living memory it was customary to introduce the games by the playing of the triumphalist Roman Catholic hymn 'Faith of our Fathers'. For a time it seemed that it would become no less ultra-nationalistic than when it first saw the light of day but, now that it has opened its doors to all codes, it is a great asset to the sporting life not only of the entire country but to community life in general.

Alongside this development Eoin Mac Neill and Douglas Hyde established the Gaelic League. By contrast this was, as its founders intended, strictly non-political and non-sectarian, its purpose being to accommodate all who had an interest in the Irish language, irrespective of political opinion or religious persuasion, including Unionists. But unknown to the founders, the prime movers were forging a weapon that would bring about the destruction of the League as originally constituted.

By far the most momentous event was the emergence of the Irish Literary Movement, which had its beginnings in 1892 when as a result of the reawakening of interest in Irish history and culture; a number of writers and poets formed the Irish Literary Society in London. Simultaneously the National Literary Society came into being in Dublin when a number of literati, notably Standish O'Grady, Lady Gregory and

W B Yeats, came to the fore with stories, poems and plays involving such legendary characters as Oisin, Deidre and Cuchulainn. This was to have a critical bearing not only on what was happening in Ireland but also on future events in the development of European nationalism in the wake of the 1914-1918 war.

Douglas Hyde, who was later to become the first President of Ireland, gave the inaugural lecture to the Society, which he entitled *The necessity for de-Anglicising Ireland*. He spoke at length on the decline of the Irish language and the need to preserve and foster Irish literature, but above all on the necessity for the people to develop a culture distinct from that of the British.

The Fenians, who had been watching the growth of the new movements with interest, now seized the opportunity to use the enthusiasm generated to build up the cult of Celtic nationalism. By this means they added a new myth to their propaganda, that of a pure Celtic race and civilisation that was superior in every way to that of the British – or for that matter any other European culture. In later years a similar theory was used to whip up support for Fascism, in Italy and National Socialism in Germany, which made use of German mythology to build up the cult of a pure Aryan race to justify the extermination of the Jews.

Such a development could not have been foreseen, much less intended, by those who brought about the Irish renaissance. Nevertheless it was the result of the interaction of developments that took place in the long history of repression, not to mention institutional injustice, to which Ireland had been subjected since her colonisation by Henry VIII, and which Germany was to suffer with the imposition of the iniquitous Treaty of Versailles.

An important by-product of this cult of Celtic nationalism was the propagation of a misconception, commonly held by the Irish people today, that they are the descendants of a unique Celtic race that has its own distinct culture. This ignores the origins of Celtic Ireland and the characteristics of the Celts whose nature was twofold. On the one hand there were men of great culture who invented the Brehon laws, while on the other there were adventurers whose origin is to be found in an area of southeast Europe bounded by the Adriatic. From these lands marauding tribes invaded much of Europe, including Ireland, where they endeavoured to annihilate the native inhabitants, the Firbolgs, but never quite succeeded. The survivors' descendents are still to be found in parts of the West of Ireland, where they produced a breed of 'mountainy men' as a result of contact with soldiers who came over to Ireland with Cromwell's armies.

On their conquest of Ireland, the tribes began to fight each other for the spoils of war and this resulted in the emergence of the High Kings of Ulster, Connacht, Leinster and Munster. Following the arrival of Patrick in Ireland, peace was restored and the Golden Age was established. But by the twelfth century, when the Norman soldiers invaded, chaos had returned. However by the twentieth century Ireland could be said to be one of the most of cosmopolitan countries in Europe.

More than a few Irish can trace their ancestry back not only to the Normans and Anglo-Saxons but to the survivors of the Spanish Armada or to those who, like the Huguenots, had fled to Ireland from the Continent to escape persecution. While the Celts undoubtedly form the majority in Ireland, the Celtic race as such is to be found mainly in Ulster to where having invaded Scotland, many were to return during the Plantation of Ulster during the reign of Elizabeth I. Hence Ireland and Scotland, particularly the Western Isles, share a common heritage that is possibly unique in these islands.

The new racist cult was invaluable to the Fenians, who set about the systematic infiltration of the ranks of all the new movements. The Gaelic League soon became an organ of militant Irish Republicanism rather the cultural organisation its authors had set out to create. As a result the Unionists left the League, as did Douglas Hyde himself in 1915.

There were others who had become disenchanted due to the delays in obtaining Home Rule following the death of Parnell, among whom was Arthur Griffith, founder of the newspaper *The United Irishmen*. This he used to advocate a middle-of-the-road policy, between that advocated by the Irish Parliamentary Party on the one hand and the Fenians on the other. He advocated the withdrawal from Westminster of all Irish MPs, with the aim of setting up of an Irish national Parliament in Dublin. In 1905 he then founded a new political party, Sinn Fein, with the object of undermining the British administration by peaceful means.

He counselled non-cooperation with England, insisting on changes in the legal and political administration that would result in Ireland having its own Law Courts and civil service. His doctrine was one of Irish self-sufficiency and he advised his readers to buy Irish-made goods rather than those imported from Britain or elsewhere. Nevertheless he envisaged the continuation of the link with the British Crown. In so doing it could be said that he was, to some extent, responsible for the concept of Commonwealth as opposed to Empire.

However his failure to be returned at the 1908 general election, due to his abstentionist stance, was to drive himself and his followers into the camp of the militants under the control of the IRB, now led by such men as the Leitrim-born Sean Mac Dermott and Tom Clarke, who had already served fifteen years in British jails. At a later date these men usurped the name Sinn Fein as an umbrella to cover all those who supported their revolutionary activities.

They too published a newspaper, *Irish Freedom*, in which they advocated the use of force to overthrow British institutions, appealing to Tone's dictum of 1798 to break the connection with England. Though still with few members the IRB, having subverted all the national movements that had come into being as a result of the Irish renaissance now made plans for a rising. But in parallel with this development a militant workers' movement had come into being in 1896, which though it shared similar aims to the Fenians had a very dissimilar agenda in that they sought a revolution as a means of delivering the country, not only from British Rule but from the capitalist system of wealth production and its replacement by an international workers' socialist republic.

By the beginning of the twentieth century, following successive Land Acts, many smallholders had come to own their land and this was to foreshadow the development of cooperatives by Sir Horace Plunkett, which enabled them to band together to make the best use of their land and secure a reasonable return for their produce. By 1910 many living in the rural areas of Ireland enjoyed a reasonable standard of living.

By contrast in the urban areas, particularly in the City of Dublin where the working masses lived and worked under appalling conditions, the situation was very different. Over a third of the population of the metropolis was herded into overcrowded and unsavoury tenements where whole families, condemned to poverty, were housed in a single room and the ever-present disease was further aggravated by hunger. Work was not easily come by and those fortunate enough to obtain it were paid a pittance, amounting to little more than slave wages.

A report published some two years later, reported that the death rate in Dublin was the highest in the world, surpassing even cities in Tsarist Russia and plague-ridden Calcutta. Against this background, James Connolly conceived the idea of one big trade union, whose membership would not depend solely on the proficiency of individual members but on their rights as members of the working class, to which smaller unions would be affiliated, giving them the industrial muscle to fight for decent wages and conditions of employment.

This saw the establishment of the Irish Transport and General Workers Union in 1909, which by the following year had 3,000 members. In 1911 it set up its headquarters in the Northumberland Hotel, on the corner of Eden Quay, Dublin. Now derelict this building had a long history and had been the venue for meetings of the Young Irelanders as well as the Dublin branch of the Land League. Renamed Liberty Hall, it was to provide the focal point for the activities of the Union, whose first move was to unite the formerly loose federation of unions making up the Irish Congress of Trade Unions. This had as yet no political platform, so the domination of Redmond's Irish Parliamentary Party at annual meetings of the Congress had defeated efforts to create a distinct republican and socialist party.

Connolly, who had been secretary of an international organisation that called on the industrial workers of the world to unite, also saw the opportunity of using growing national revolutionary fervour to his advantage. Just as the Fenians had taken control of the national movement, so he planned to use their proposed Rising to establish the first Workers' Socialist Republic in Europe. He clashed with the IRB when his intentions became known to them, although they were to realise that his cooperation, so long as they remained in control, was essential if their venture was to be successful.

Connolly's tactic of linking a revolutionary concept of trade unionism with nationalism attracted many, including a number of advanced thinkers, and its use of direct action against the employers was to usher in an unprecedented era of turbulence. By 1912 the Union had become a potent force, spreading its influence from the dockworkers and porters to shipping, the construction industry, engineering, the coal industry, and those employed on the railways and in the marshalling yards. In short, it spread to every industrial enterprise employing manual labour.

Thus began a prolonged period of industrial unrest, as Dublin, Belfast and Cork were hit by strikes, to which the employers replied with lockouts. Wexford was to have a foretaste of things to come when a local union, which subsequently merged with the ITGWU, challenged the right of employers to prevent them combining in a union. The employers replied by locking out 500 workers in three foundries, and during a grim struggle that lasted for some months, were adamant in their refusal to negotiate, replying to union attempts at conciliation by axing other workers in the town, for no other reason than that they were members of the union. Police, who had been brought in to protect blackleg labour drafted in to fill jobs, batoned striking demonstrators.

In June of that year the Irish Employers' Federation came into being, a prominent founder of which was William Martin Murphy, whose vast interests ranged from the Independent group of newspapers to Dublin United Tramways. The Federation included every principal employer in Dublin, who pledged themselves to enforce a ban on their workers joining the ITGWU. The battle lines for the coming conflict were drawn.

For some months during the summer of 1913 there had been agitation among workers employed by the Dublin United Tramways, following a decision taken by William Martin Murphy to dismiss any worker who was a member of the Union. This was the spark needed to ignite the 1913 strike, which broke out on August 26, the first day of the Horse Show. There followed the arrest of a number of the leading members of the Union, including Jim Larkin, on charges of sedition. On appearing before a magistrate they were released on bail, and a meeting scheduled to take place on Sunday 31 August was proscribed.

During the week leading up to the date of the banned meeting tension grew as strikers attacked those trams that were still running. They were set on by police wielding batons and hundreds were injured in the running battles that ensued. By the eve of the meeting, which was scheduled to take place in O'Connell Street, the violence had reached its peak and there was intense speculation as to what might happen the following morning. The day began quietly enough for some people to be under the impression that the Union had postponed the meeting, but by midday an enormous crowd had assembled. Some people expected trouble and others were merely curious spectators, many of whom were ordinary citizens returning from Mass or other church services.

It was at this stage that Larkin suddenly appeared at a hotel window overlooking the crowd assembled below. This was the signal for hundreds of police, concealed in the narrow streets surrounding the hotel, to move in with batons drawn. They attacked all before them, be they demonstrators or innocent passers-by. Many hundreds of men, women and children, caught up in the baton charge, were so seriously injured that by the end of the morning O'Connell Street resembled a battlefield, strewn with bodies, many of which were covered in blood. This was the first of a number of demonstrations to take place over the following decades, and became the first to receive the acronym 'Bloody Sunday'.

The following morning employers imposed a lockout and so began a titanic struggle. The question at issue did not concern wages or even the long hours and conditions the workers suffered. The sole point was their right to combine to secure a bargaining position. Precipitated by the intransigence of the founder of the Employers' Federation, who had persuaded its members to join him in forcing his workers to sign a document undertaking that they would not join the Union, and if they had already done so would have their membership repudiated, this action was to bring hundreds of hitherto uninvolved workers out in sympathy. At the height of the dispute 20,000 wage earners were involved, affecting the better part of a further 100,000 men, women and children. Ranged against them were 400 employers, pledged to resist the demands of their workers and stand together in compelling them to sign this document.

These events received considerable publicity abroad and comment at home, for in the circumstances the resistance of the workers was nothing short of heroic. On the other hand the obduracy of the employers raised the indignation of some of the most advanced thinkers in the country, as evidenced by the open letter addressed to the 'Masters of Dublin', which 'AE' (George Russell), the collaborator and friend of W B Yeats, sent to the *Irish Times* in October.

Having referred to the Dark Ages, he wrote: "It remained for the twentieth century and the capital city of Ireland to see an oligarchy of 400 masters deciding openly on starving one hundred thousand people and refusing to consider any solution except that fixed by their pride." He concluded by reminding the employers that "Your insolence and ignorance of the rights conceded to workers, universally, in the modern world, is incredible and is as great as is your inhumanity."

As the conflict became ever fiercer, more and more workers became involved while the police protected blacklegs and used force to disperse demonstrators. Raids on working-class tenements became commonplace. It was then that a decision was taken to form the Irish Citizen Army to protect the workers. Founded by James Connolly and organised by Captain J H White, it was to play an important part in future events. Meanwhile the workers' struggle had attracted considerable support among members of the Literary Movement, as evidenced not only by the writings of 'AE' but also by those of playwright Sean O'Casey, who was already a member of the workers' movement, as well as those of the poet Padraig Pearse.

The outcome of the struggle, which lasted six months, was a deadlock. While the costly lockout was over without either side having made real any concession, the price paid by the workers was horrendous. They had held out against insuperable odds, but when the children in the unsavoury slums of the north inner city began to die of hunger and cold, they could take it no longer.

The dispute could have been settled months earlier had the employers not underestimated the determination of the workers. It was not until they found themselves facing heavy losses due to the stoppage that they were prepared to consider easing their demands. As it was, the situation that unfolded in 1913 gave an added impetus to those who were planning a Rising.

The Great Lockout had overshadowed a growing political crisis that had been developing ever since the passage of the third Home Rule Bill in 1912. This had seen the proclamation of Sir Edward Carson's Solemn League and Covenant, pledging the people of Ulster to oppose its implementation, together with the formation of the Ulster Volunteer Force to resist its application to the Province – if necessary by force of arms.

To counteract this threat the Irish Volunteer Force was formed in Dublin on 23 November, under a provisional committee headed by Eoin Mac Neill. Although initially the Irish Parliamentary Party, which then had the overwhelming support of the Irish people, had remained aloof from this development, their supporters made up the majority of the Volunteers. This organisation also contained members with no political affiliation, as well as members of Sinn Fein and, significantly, those who were responsible for setting up the Volunteers in the first place. These were members of the secret IRB, although to begin with they kept a low profile. Meanwhile, the growing strength of their units throughout the country prompted John Redmond, the leader of the Irish Parliamentary Party, to demand that representatives of his party be appointed to the Provisional Committee.

At this time a political crisis had developed in Britain, with a deepening rift between the Liberals and Conservatives, who in May proposed an amendment to the Home Rule Bill aimed at excluding the nine counties of Ulster from the jurisdiction of any future Irish Government. As the Bill had already been passed by the Commons and could no longer be delayed by the Lords due to the recently enacted Parliament Act, discussion was deferred, in July, with the approach of World War One.

This amendment was in fact never discussed due to future events that occurred in Ireland, which were to render the implementation of Home Rule impossible. But it was to form the basis of the 1921 negotiations, which were to see the division of the country, when the Irish Free State ceded six of the nine counties of Ulster but retained Donegal, Cavan and Monaghan.

CHAPTER 5

The 1916 Rising

A knowledge of the events immediately preceding the 1916 Rising, and its consequences as well as the underlying motives of those who participated in it, is essential if this crucial period in Irish history is to be assessed in its true perspective. But the Irish people have been kept in total ignorance of these facts and few know anything of the Rising other than that it took place.

The IRB had been encouraged by the example of the Ulster Volunteers and the Citizen Army to form their own military wing, the Irish Volunteers. This body, while many of its members sympathised with the workers' struggle for recognition, took its cue from Sir Edward Carson whose Ulster Volunteer Force was the first paramilitary force in Ireland. It contained a considerable number of disaffected Protestants, whose immediate aim was to prevent the implementation of the Home Rule Bill even if it meant the use of force and rebellion against England.

In this they had the support of the IRB and the militant wing of the Irish Volunteers, but this movement was from the outset divided into two groups due to the influx of recruits who outnumbered the original members. Knowing nothing of the intentions of the IRB, they perceived the Volunteers as a means of advancing the cause of Home Rule by forming a force to defend Ireland in the event of attack. Nevertheless they were to prove an unwitting aid to the militants, who by joining with them in drilling were provided with a means of training in the use of weapons – an opportunity that they had previously been denied.

An irreconcilable rift also existed in the Citizen Army. Sean O'Casey, who saw the workers' struggle as paramount, brought it to a head. To him the Volunteers were an elitist force and he clashed on more than one occasion with Countess Markiewicz, who had played a prominent role in the suffragette movement and was now one of the Sinn Fein leaders, as well as with the leaders of the Gaelic League, from which he eventually resigned. He also objected to the lack of worker representation in Sinn Fein, which he regarded as an essentially right wing organisation, despite the support of Padraig Pearse for the worker's struggle.

Connolly, on the other hand, was a pragmatist, who could see the potential of an alliance with the Irish Volunteers, whom he hoped would create a viable force with which to instigate a revolution. Thus he counselled cooperation between the two groups lest they defeat their own object. O'Casey, however, insisted that no useful purpose could be served by an alliance between the Citizen Army and a movement that he regarded as the product of middle-class intellectuals.

Though half blind and self-taught, O'Casey had become a playwright of note. Born in a tenement, he had experienced all the deprivations of the average worker of the day. By contrast, the Fenians were led by a group of extreme nationalist poets and writers, whose actual lack of experience of real life made them prone to utopian and impractical ideas. Nevertheless Connolly saw the advantage of an, albeit temporary, alliance with them and the subsequent marriage of the two factions was to give birth to the Irish Republican Army.

The year 1914 was to prove fateful not only for the world in general but also for Ireland in particular. The outbreak of World War One on 4 August saw a further delay in implementing the Home Rule Bill as all pending legislation, other than that relating to the war, had to be put on hold until the cessation of hostilities. This was to afford Carson a valuable breathing space to plan the death of the measure.

His Ulster Volunteer Force now consisted of 100,000 men pledged to resist the imposition of Home Rule on Ulster by force of arms. He also had the backing of the 470,000 signatories of his Solemn League and Covenant, which he had drawn up in September 1912. He was also assured of further support when British officers, stationed at the Curragh Camp outside Dublin, staged a mutiny and declared that they would refuse to obey orders, should they be given, to march on Ulster.

His agents had already penetrated the IRB, whose plans were well known to him. This had presented him with little difficulty, for when the Fenians had infiltrated the cultural movements they had unwittingly laid themselves open to a risk, for their association with literary men was to produce new leaders. However as O'Casey had feared, unlike their predecessors they were impractical visionaries who were naïve enough to believe that they had an ally in Carson.

This was strikingly illustrated in the description given by David Hogan, a contemporary republican chronicler, of the first meetings in Galway and Cork to launch the Irish Volunteers, which took place in the late Autumn of 1913. Eoin Mac Neill called on these gatherings to express their support for Carson and the UVF, whose opposition to Home Rule he regarded as an expression of the demand of the Irish people to govern themselves, even if they did not agree with the reason for the stance taken by the Unionists.

Just as Carson's lead had helped to fashion the Volunteers, he now set about showing them how to prepare for an insurrection while providing a means to defend Ulster in the event of a Rising in the South. Money for arms was collected and, on the 24 April 1914, a consignment of 35,000 rifles and a million rounds of ammunition were landed at Larne, County Antrim, from Germany. There was no resistance from the authorities in Northern Ireland, who turned a blind eye to the operation.

This was followed by the Howth gunrunning, masterminded by Erskine Childers, for the Irish Volunteers. They also received a supply of arms from Germany on 26 July 1914, less than a fortnight before the outbreak of the war. Childers and his wife had received a sizeable ketch as a wedding present, and he used this vessel to ferry 15,000 rifles from Hamburg to Howth. A further landing was made at Kilcoole in County Wicklow.

Surprisingly he was not apprehended and the arms were landed safely, with mere token resistance by the police and army, who were by no means sympathetic to the republicans. Yet later that day three people were killed when the police opened fire on a crowd of protestors in Bachelors Walk, Dublin. It is possible, of course that a decision had been taken at the highest level in Dublin Castle not to react further for the sake of public order.

Strangely the credentials of Erskine Childers as an Irish revolutionary have never been questioned. Though he was of Irish birth, most of his life was spent in the service of England, where he had equally strong connections. A conservative by nature, he had been educated at Haileybury College and Cambridge University. He first came to prominence during the Boer War, in which he served as a British officer, and his expressed anger at the actions of John Mac Bride, who had raised an Irish-American brigade to fight for the Boers, is on record.

Following the war he rose rapidly through the ranks of the English civil service to reach the most coveted post of all, that of Clerk of the House of Commons. Only weeks after he had planned and executed the Howth gunrunning he was back in the British forces, this time in the Navy, where he rose to the rank of Lieutenant Commander. Not only did he receive the DSO but he also did not see Irish soil again until 1919.

His acceptance by the Irish and the British at the same time, though at first sight inexplicable, presents no mystery. Either he was one of those rare enigmas, thrown up by history from time to time, or he had been persuaded by Carson and the Unionist faction in Ireland, together with the English conservatives, to play the part of a double agent. There is in fact abundant circumstantial evidence to indicate that the latter was the case.

This is reinforced by his imperialist background and subsequent actions that do not run true, either to his known character, or to his newfound identity as an Irish republican. This was later vividly illustrated during the delicate negotiations that preceded the Treaty of 1921. De Valera had appointed him as Secretary to the Irish Delegation at the Peace Conference yet, despite his known reputation as a stickler for detail, he failed to report back to Dublin when the delegates were divided on the terms of the Treaty.

This omission resulted in the Delegates' acceptance of terms that had not been submitted to the Provisional Government – an error that was to precipitate the Civil War, which might well have destroyed the infant Free State. Childers then joined the Irregulars and, prior to his capture and execution by Free State forces, de Valera trusted him implicitly, so much so that he placed him in charge of both his administration and propaganda.

The fact that his son, Erskine Hamilton Childers, remained on to become President of Ireland effectively killed any speculation as to his father's possible involvement in Carson's intelligence network. But it is not sufficiently appreciated that those who are engaged in such activities do not disclose the fact to anyone, let alone their nearest and dearest. It is thus likely that the late President would not have been aware of the role played by his father.

The situation in Ireland in 1914, with the approach of the Great War, had become highly complex, revolving as it did round the question of Home Rule. Several factions now existed, including the Ulster Volunteer Force; the Irish Volunteers divided between those who supported John Redmond and his Irish Parliamentary Party and the Republicans, who were demanding a unitary State, divorced from Britain. The latter group was divided into the more extreme nationalists and the Citizen Army, which looked to a rising as a means of establishing the first international socialist workers' republic in Europe. With the exception of the Volunteers who were loyal to Redmond, all four movements, though their motives were disparate and even contradictory, shared a common aim in the destruction of the Home Rule legislation, while the UVF hoped that the militants would stage an insurrection that would put an end to the Bill.

Redmond, who earlier in the year had become aware of the existence of the IRB, had misjudged the strength of the militants. Though he had realised that there might be some infiltration into the ranks of Volunteers, he had nonetheless felt safe in the knowledge that the majority of the Volunteers favoured Home Rule. Now, however, he feared civil war between his own supporters and the UVF, if not with the other factions that made up the coalition against Home Rule. He therefore determined that he should become the leader of the Volunteers and suggested to the leaders of the IRB that cooperation with Britain, in the event of the outbreak of war with Germany, would be the best way of securing their aims.

The militants, who realised that his presence would act as an effective cloak for their activities, welcomed his move. Consequently he had little difficulty in securing acceptance for his proposition. However the IRB and the militants, who held that Ireland had no quarrel with Germany, saw the war as an ideal opportunity to put Tone's dictum that "England's difficulty was Ireland's opportunity" into practice, and set about forming a secret Military Council to make plans for a rebellion.

However there was some dissention among them that was voiced by Eoin Mac Neill who, while he fully supported their aims, did not consider the moment for an insurrection to be opportune. He strongly argued that to take up arms when Britain was at war would be counterproductive. This led to a split and an Inner Council, consisting of Padraig Pearse, Sean Mac Dermott and Tom Clarke, was set up. Henceforth Mac Neill was kept in ignorance of their plans for a Rising.

Pearse then became the undisputed leader of the IRB. Born in Dublin in 1870 he had, as a young man, been strongly influenced by the Irish Renaissance and the new interest in the Irish language, culture and folklore. Following his education by the Irish Christian Brothers, a lay order of teachers, he joined the Gaelic League, which appointed him editor of an Irish language publication it financed. Though a lawyer by profession, he abandoned his chosen profession to take a cottage in Rosmuc, a village in the Connemara Gaeltacht, in order to develop his knowledge of Celtic mythology. This was to become an obsession.

In retrospect, there can be little doubt but that his otherwise brilliant mind had been turned by his contact with pagan mysticism. His pronouncements indicated an unnatural interest in human sacrifice and he welcomed the outbreak of the Great War, which he concluded was a necessary bloodletting that would purge the world from the evils afflicting it. Similarly he insisted that only a blood sacrifice would free the Irish nation from English domination.

On his return to Dublin, determined to indoctrinate the young with the new ideas, he founded St Enda's school in Rathfarnham, which was then a hamlet three miles from the centre of the city. There he taught the children in Irish and encouraged them to model their lives on the legendary hero Cuchulainn.

Pearse first came to the attention of the public at the funeral of Jeremiah O'Donovan Rossa, when he gave the first indication that anything unusual was afoot. One of the early Fenian leaders, Rossa had spent many years in English jails or in exile, but on his death his body was returned from England for burial and Pearse delivered a graveside oration to the large crowd that had gathered to pay their respects.

Addressing them, he said: "Life springs from death, and from the graves of patriot men and women spring living nations. The defenders of the realm have worked well, in secret and in the open. They think they have pacified Ireland but – the fools, the fools – they have left us our Fenian dead and while Ireland holds these graves, Ireland unfree shall never be at peace." His remarks, though stirring, went unnoticed by Dublin Castle as the Redmondites and the Ulster Volunteers were vying with one another to prove their loyalty to the English war effort. The latter hoped to boost their case against Home Rule, while Redmond's promise that the Volunteers would defend

Ireland enabled the release of much needed troops garrisoned there. Eventually 200,000 Irishmen joined the British army.

By the beginning of 1916 the plans for a rising were well advanced and in January the Military Council decided to take Connolly into their confidence. Prior to this, such was their fear that he might go it alone in order to establish his socialist workers' republic, that plans had been considered to abduct him should the need arise. It was then agreed that Easter Sunday of that year should be fixed as the date for the Rising and Sir Roger Casement was sent to Germany to seek aid, his intention being to secure at least a sufficiency of small arms, a quantity of machine guns and, if possible, some artillery. He also hoped to persuade the Germans to land a small expeditionary force.

However for some reason that is not entirely clear, the IRB did not entirely trust Casement. They therefore sent Robert Monteith to Germany to replace him. Casement discovered not only that his dangerous journey had been undertaken in vain, but also that Monteith had agreed to accept a consignment of 20,000 obsolete rifles and had made plans to ship them to Ireland. Casement was now in an unenviable position. It was impossible to get word back from Germany, so the only option open to him was to return immediately, whatever the danger from friend or foe, and warn the leaders of this debacle. He was a practical man to whom it was obvious that in the absence of up-to-date weapons and a back-up force, the proposed rising would be a fiasco.

As luck would have it the vessel chartered for the gunrunning, the *Aud*, was seized off Tralee Bay and Casement, who had been put ashore by a submarine, was captured almost as soon as he landed. This was unfortunate for a number of reasons, not the least being that had he succeeded in eluding his captors he could have been instrumental in putting a stop to the Rising. However Eoin Mac Neill, though no longer a member of the Inner Council of the IRB, had been made aware of their plans and, as he was still Commander-in-Chief of the Volunteers, sent out an order cancelling the drilling on Easter Sunday morning, which was to have been the signal for the beginning of the Rising. A copy of this order was published in the *Sunday Independent* .

This was the second occasion on which Mac Neill had intervened to countermand the Rising, for when the plan had first been discovered by him some days earlier, he had issued instructions to the effect that "all orders issued by Commandant Pearse are hereby cancelled". However on that occasion, having been informed of the imminent arrival of aid from Germany, he had been persuaded to change his mind. But as it now had become clear that no such aid would be forthcoming, he had had no option but to act but for a time it seemed that saner counsels would prevail.

Meanwhile Sean O'Casey had endeavoured to prevail on Connolly not to become involved in the insurrection, which he doubted would advance the workers' cause, but his pleas had proved unsuccessful and he had therefore withdrawn from the movement. The feeling of many others was summed up by William O'Brien of the All for Ireland League, who demanded to know: "What did the men who attacked England in the midst of a war think they were going to gain for Ireland?"

Pearse however, oblivious to all warnings, was determined that the Easter Rising should go ahead. On Easter Monday morning he marched into the centre of Dublin at the head of a column made up units of the Citizen Army and the Volunteers, to seize control of the General Post Office. The ill-fated Rising had begun.

No attempt had been made by the authorities to prevent the Volunteers from drilling openly, no doubt due to Redmond's assurances of their loyalty, which appeared to be born out by the fact that the majority of them had joined the forces. However for some unaccountable reason the formation of the Military Council by the IRB had not come to their notice, despite the rift that had developed in the movement. It is, however, inconceivable that they should have failed to take some precautions, in the light of the Larne and Howth gun runnings, but the pressure of the war was such that they were forced to rely on the few units that still remained in Ireland to keep order. These consisted, in the main, of men who were on leave from the front.

Nevertheless the government was aware that it could count on the average man in the street, for the populace as a whole despised the remaining Volunteers, rather than regarding them as potential liberators. This was particularly so when they viewed them parading in the safety of their own land while so many of their compatriots were engaged in the bitter struggle now taking place in Flanders.

It was a Bank Holiday and the city was well nigh deserted when a motley collection of men aged between 15 and 60 headed by Padraig Pearse, representing the combined forces of the Volunteers and the Citizen Army, made its appearance in O'Connell Street. Few if any of the passers by could have suspected their intentions, much less realised that this was an advance party and that they were witnessing the beginning of an insurrection.

Pearse must have realised that he was leading his men to their deaths but that was of no consequence to him, for he believed that such a sacrifice was a prerequisite to the success of the Rising. There was an air of grim determination among the marchers as they made their way towards their chosen objective; an imposing building that could be taken without a shot being fired. The GPO was seized by the insurgents and was to remain their headquarters for the remainder of the week. His base secured, Pearce began to read his proclamation from the steps outside the building.

A grandiloquent document, it is noteworthy only for its promises of reform in the social field, many of which have remained unfulfilled to this day. Pearse, its undoubted author, referred to a number of past revolts, which other than the 1798 rebellion and the Young Irelanders rising in 1848 were of no particular significance and scarcely amounted to more than mere riots. He then proceeded to announce the establishment of an Irish Republic and the Tricolour was hoisted above the GPO. His proclamation, addressed to the 'people of Ireland' and headed 'The Provisional Government of the Irish Republic' read as follows:

"Irishmen and Irishwomen. In the name of God and the dead generations from which she receives her old tradition of nationhood, Ireland, through us, summons her people to her flag and strikes for her freedom. Having organised and trained her manhood through her secret revolutionary organisation, the Irish Republican Brotherhood and the Irish Citizen Army; having patiently perfected her discipline; having resolutely waited for the right moment to reveal itself, she now seizes that moment and supported by her exiled children, in America and by gallant allies, in Europe, but relying, in the first instance, on her own strength, she strikes in full confidence of victory.

"We declare the right of the people of Ireland to the ownership of Ireland and to the unfettered control of Irish destinies as sovereign and indefeasible. The long usurpation of that right, by a foreign people and government, has not extinguished this right nor can it ever be extinguished except by the destruction of the Irish people. In every generation the Irish people have asserted their right to national freedom, six times during the past three hundred years they have asserted it in arms. Standing on this fundamental right and again asserting it in arms, in the face of the world, we hereby proclaim the Irish Republic as a sovereign independent State and we pledge our lives and the lives of our comrades in arms to the cause of its freedom, of its welfare and its exaltation among the nations.

"The Irish Republic is entitled to and hereby claims the allegiance of every Irishman and Irishwomen. The Republic guarantees civil and religious liberty, equal rights and equal opportunities to all its citizens and declares its resolve to pursue the happiness of the whole nation and all its parts, cherishing all the children of the nation equally and oblivious of the differences, carefully fostered by an alien government, which has divided the majority from the minority in the past.

"Until our arms have brought about the opportune moment for the establishment of a permanent national government, representative of the whole people of Ireland and elected by the suffrage of all her men and women, the provisional government hereby constituted will administer the affairs of the Republic in trust for the people.

"We place the cause of the Republic under the protection of the Most High God, whose blessing we invoke upon our arms and we pray that no one who serves that cause will dishonour it by cowardice, inhumanity or rapine.

"In this supreme hour the Irish nation must by its valour and discipline and by the readiness of its children to sacrifice themselves for the common good, prove itself worthy of the august destiny to which it is called."

This document was signed by Thomas Clarke, Sean Mac Donagh, Eamonn Ceant and Joseph Plunkett.

Obviously the work of a middle class intellectual, such a document could not be expected to appeal to the working masses, who were more concerned with bread and butter issues, and for whom in many cases the Great War had provided much needed employment. Consequently the public reaction to it was predictable. Indeed, apart from one paragraph that promised equal rights and equal opportunities to all the children of the nation, nothing could have more calculated to infuriate all sections of the community. For long those members of the Volunteers who had chosen to remain in Ireland had been treated with outright derision and contempt, but these feelings were now replaced by anger and hatred, for many had lost sons, husbands and loved ones fighting what Pearse had referred to as "our gallant allies in Europe".

The people were not fools and were well aware that the only ally the insurgents had was Germany, and they looked not to "the dead generations" but to their own men folk locked in deadly combat in Flanders while these gentry had, apparently, been playacting as soldiers. Now it seemed that these mountebanks were nothing more than traitors, who had stabbed their own people in the back. Naturally this is precisely how their actions were regarded across the water, where they were to destroy all hope of the Home Rule Bill being enacted, thereby playing into the hands of Carson and the Northern Unionists.

Public opinion in England, which had come to accept the necessity for Home Rule, was so outraged that no government could resist the pressure to abandon the necessary legislation, while in Ireland Pearse seems to have gone out of his way to alienate the better part of the population. His mention of the part played by the IRB, a secret society condemned by the Catholic Church, brought angry denunciations from the hierarchy and the Archbishop of Dublin.

Indeed there is little more in this document worthy of mention except, perhaps, to refer to the penultimate paragraph which, although this was certainly not Pearse's intention, expresses sentiments similar to those that have been used to justify the establishment of more than a few modern military dictatorships. The proclamation also contains a number of aspirations that, however worthy, have yet to be fulfilled. If he wanted a blood sacrifice he was certainly going the right way about it.

The very wording of this document was sufficient to destroy whatever support he and his followers might have had in the country as a whole. Consequently the insurrection was confined for the most part to Dublin, and Irish historians put the number of those who actually took part at no more than 3,000. Indeed, for reasons that will appear later, it is doubtful that even half that number was involved.

It was at this stage that the British made their first and, in the light of future events, possibly their most crucial error. The failure of their intelligence services to discover the existence of the Military Council or the plans for the Rising in time to prevent it taking place, no doubt rankled with High Command, which could ill afford to keep tied down in Ireland troops that were badly needed in France,. They were totally unprepared for the insurrection when it happened, and wholly unaware of its probable extent. They were therefore misled by Pearse's Proclamation, which gave the impression of a countrywide rising backed by Germany.

In the event they over-reacted and the rebellion, which could have been contained by a handful of troops in a matter of hours had they been forewarned, assumed a significance out of all proportion to its size. Artillery was brought up from the Curragh and, during the next five days, the centre of the city was subjected to a ceaseless bombardment by the British on the one hand and attacks on civilian property by the IRA on the other.

The rebels were proving themselves to be no cowards and their resistance, though foolhardy in the extreme, was nothing short of heroic. Though hopelessly outnumbered and outgunned, they succeeded in establishing a number of bases at strategic points leading to the city centre, the most noteworthy being those at Jacob's factory, Boland's Mills, the Four Courts and the South Dublin Union. In addition they had strongholds, one of which, Riley's pub, was converted into a fort. There was also a house in Mount Street Bridge from which de Valera, with a handful of Volunteers, endeavoured to halt the march of a British army contingent en route to the City from the docks at Dun Laoghaire. This group continued fighting until they were forced to surrender, having run out of ammunition.

By the Wednesday not only was the garrison at the GPO on the point of collapse, but much of the building itself had been destroyed by the shelling and most of the surrounding buildings were either gutted or in flames. Despite this Pearse and his men held out for nearly three more days, until the Saturday afternoon, when he ordered the evacuation of what remained of his headquarters. By now many civilian lives had been lost, having been caught up in the crossfire, and even Pearse must have realised the futility of prolonging the agony.

The Rising had cost 1,000 lives, while almost an equal number, the vast majority of whom had had no part in it, lay wounded. Some £8 million worth of property had been razed to the ground. The overwhelming reaction of the people was to curse the insurgents for having brought this calamity to their country and devastation to their capital city.

Not only had the insurrection been mistimed but also the bungling that had characterised it was such as to infuriate Michael Collins who, though in the GPO, was not yet in the confidence of the leaders. It was this that determined him, in the future, to establish a first class intelligence service. Meanwhile he had seen rapid promotion in the ranks of the IRA.

So lacking in cohesion had been the organisation of the Rising that it would have been a non-event had the British not been taken completely off their guard. Indeed the first intimation they had of what was afoot was when 20 Volunteers attempted to capture Dublin Castle. A sentry fired a shot into the air and, when the guard turned out, the rebels fled after shooting an unarmed constable who tried to block their path.

Nevertheless a new mythology was born out of the Rising. It succeeded in concealing the fact that while those manning the strong points resisted bravely, they had little regard for the plight of the civilian population, which was subjected to great intimidation. We are told that after the shooting of the policeman at Dublin Castle, firm instructions were given, and strictly obeyed, that no civilian should be molested. We are also given to believe that a gunboat that was brought up the Liffey to bombard the city brought about the destruction of Dublin.

It is interesting to compare this version of events with that of an eye-witness, the late Lily Meagher, who went on to become a singer at the Metropolitan Opera in New York. Then in her twenties, she lived at the White Horse Inn, Eden Quay (later Daley's Hotel), overlooking the river. According to her account the insurgents had been systematically setting fire to the property of those who would not cooperate with them. She herself was burnt out of her home on the refusal of her father to let the inn be used as a strong point. Together with her sister she was rescued by British troops who escorted them to safety under a hail of machine-gun fire.

She stated that there was indeed a gunboat tied up at the quay but it remained at its berth and was at no time engaged in the battle. She further said that units of the Volunteers, aided by looters from the nearby slums, had set a large area of O'Connell Street ablaze and when the army attempted to intervene they were met with heavy gunfire from the GPO. On returning the following day with heavy artillery they shelled not only the insurgents' headquarters but also levelled many of the already gutted buildings, which had become unsafe. Meagher's experience is not untypical and quite a few paid with their lives for refusing to quit their homes at the Volunteers' behest. Indeed many were under the impression that the Germans had invaded.

When Pearse had undertaken the 1916 adventure he must have been well aware of its eventual outcome. Britain was at war with Germany and not only had he rebelled while thousands were dying at the front, but he had deliberately invoked the enemy as an ally, thereby sealing his fate and that of his comrades. He regarded the shelling of Dublin as a bonus that would in the long term ensure the realisation of his dreams. Himself a fanatic, he was relying on the predictable response of the British to bring about a blood sacrifice that would lead a people already tired of waiting for Home Rule to fight for their independence. But he had not counted on the reaction of the public, which ran contrary to his expectations.

In view of Redmond's assurances, the existence of the Volunteers had been tolerated because conscription did not apply to Ireland, and in any event he had pledged that they would defend the country if attacked. To that extent they had been regarded as an auxiliary force to the British army, particularly as many of them were now serving abroad on the Western Front. But now some of those who had remained behind had mutinied and there was only one penalty for traitors – death.

The year 1916 had proved to be an unmitigated disaster for the Irish people, not only at home but also abroad. Thousands of their compatriots were yet to die in the looming Battle of the Somme and the consequences of the Rising were to bedevil relations between Britain and Ireland for decades.

CHAPTER 6

Sinn Fein rises from the Ashes

In the immediate aftermath of the Rising, the country was in a state of confusion due to the spread of wild speculation and, in the absence of any concrete news, the impression gained credence in the country that something of enormous import had taken place in Dublin, but that the authorities were playing it down. Meanwhile most of those who had surrendered with Pearse received long terms of imprisonment, but between 3 and 12 May he and 15 leaders of the insurrection were executed following summary courts martial.

The Irish people had little sympathy with Pearse; indeed the majority felt that he and his comrades richly deserved all that they got. But as execution followed execution they were staggered, and many were incensed at the manner in which Connolly's sentence had been carried out. They knew little or nothing of Pearse but they could identify with Connolly, with whom many had been active in the labour movement. During the fighting he had been injured, yet he was forced to face a firing squad sitting in a wheelchair.

This year also saw the most horrific of all the battles of World War One – the Battle of the Somme – in which the Irish contingents in particular were involved. This advance saw the massacre of Allied forces and in all 419,614 British troops, many of whom were Irish, lay dead on the battlefield. Many thousands more who survived were maimed for life. Thus horror was heaped upon horror and it was not long before many who had been opposed to the Rising began to question Ireland's participation in the war.

A number of new political parties, or groups, came into being. Prominent among them was the Nation League, formed to oppose Lloyd George's latest proposal to solve the Irish question. This was to be a compromise whereby, now that the possibility of introducing Home Rule had become a non-runner, an amending Act would be brought in that would provide for the partition of Ireland. Lloyd George now regarded Ireland, with exception of the Northern counties of Ulster, as a liability rather than an asset.

In coming to this conclusion he had been influenced by the political situation at home. The people, wholly unaware of the motives behind the Larne and Howth gun-runnings and the part played by Carson in helping to precipitate the Rising in order to destroy the Home Rule Bill, had fallen for the loyalty displayed by the people of Ulster. There was a universal perception that solely malcontents in the south of Ireland had planned these actions and people were now in no mood to grant independence to the country.

On the contrary, popular feeling was running high and the part that had been played by the Dublin Fusiliers and other regiments from the South went unnoticed, while it took decades for the British to become aware that the loyalty of the people of Ulster is strictly conditional. No sooner did the proposals for partition become known in Ireland than the Nation League assumed pre-eminence among the number of small political parties that had mushroomed into being. While most of its leaders were members of the IRB, which saw the opportunity to turn the tables presented by the evolving situation, the membership was swollen by those who were disillusioned and no longer trusted the intentions of the British government.

The Irish people were in an angry mood and leaderless, for Redmond's plans now lay in ruins. Thus it was that in September 1916 the League, whose operations had been more or less clandestine since the Rising, and which had been at pains to keep within the law, felt strong enough to come out into the open. At a mass rally held in Phoenix Park, speaker after speaker argued that Pearse and his comrades had been right after all, and that theirs had been the only way open to the Irish people. The effect on the crowd was electric and exceeded the wildest expectations of the organisers. People left the Park cheering the names of the dead leaders of the Rising and cursing that of General Maxwell, who had ordered their execution.

This meeting was to mark the turning of the tide and it was not long before the first tangible results were to be felt. As yet the Nation League, which was an amalgam of a number of smaller parties, had not chosen a formal name and it is interesting to note how it came to acquire the title Sinn Fein. This was, after all, a party that had been the brainchild of Arthur Griffith and had not been republican as such. Griffith had preached a doctrine of self-reliance built on the concept of a semi-independent Ireland, linked to Britain through the person of a joint monarch and, prior to the Rising the party's support had been infinitesimal.

The Irish Parliamentary Party dismissed the whole notion of Sinn Fein as the "hopping of fleas" but the name was adopted by the Republicans, no doubt to deflect attention from their activities. Paradoxically though, the name 'Sinn Fein', meaning 'Ourselves Alone', summed up their objectives. Nevertheless the British, unaware of its meaning and taking their cue from Redmond, dubbed the Rising 'Sinn Fein' in order to show their contempt for it. Griffith himself argued unsuccessfully with the leaders of the Volunteers over the assumption of this title, insisting that it was up to the people to decide what form the new government should take, but the IRB insisted that there was no room for manoeuvre as a Republic had already been declared. Consequently the name stuck.

Thus 1917 saw the emergence of a revitalised Sinn Fein, which in January had an opportunity to flex its muscles when the North Roscommon seat fell vacant. To date the younger section of the population had mainly answered the appeal of the leaders and they had become concerned lest this imbalance should prove detrimental to their interests. They were also anxious to pick a candidate who had a national reputation and appeal.

George Nobel, Count Plunkett, was just such a person. Now in his sixties he had all the qualifications necessary to undertake Sinn Fein's first test of public opinion. Formerly a director of the Science and Arts Museum in Dublin, he and his wife had been deported to Britain following the Rising. In addition his name had been erased from the list of members of the Royal Dublin Society as three of his sons had taken part in the Rising, one of whom had been executed.

His success in the election was such that when the result was read out at the Court House in Boyle, it was evident that not only had he outstripped his nearest rival but that he had secured an overall majority. The seat had proved ideal for Sinn Fein to test its strength. A sleepy country town, Boyle not only had connections with the Connacht Rangers but it had previously returned a succession of Irish Parliamentary Party candidates.

The British authorities, which up till now had been more or less complacent, had been shaken by this totally unexpected result. What had previously been regarded as a safe seat had been overturned and their overreaction was such as to ensure the success of future Sinn Fein candidates. Instead of accepting the democratic will of the people, in which case in the absence of a candidate of similar calibre Sinn Fein might well have run out of steam and this election result been forgotten, the authorities replied with mass deportations. On 22 February British forces arrested men prominent in the national and language movements, among them Sean T O'Kelly and Barney Mellows from Dublin, and Terence Mac Swiney and Thomas Mac Curtain from Cork.

These events only served to spur on the infant Sinn Fein to redouble its efforts and by the end of the month it was given another chance to prove itself. This time the authorities had every reason to be confident, for they had left nothing to chance and their chosen candidate, one Patrick Mc Kenna, was well known in the South Longford constituency where the election was to take place. Furthermore he had powerful connections that had provided him with an elaborate electoral machine and a number of prominent MPs had agreed to speak on his behalf.

By contrast Sinn Fein's nominee, Joseph Magennis, was currently serving a sentence of penal servitude in Lewes Jail and Mc Kenna had every reason to believe that this unknown convict posed no threat. However it was such as close call that two recounts were needed to decide the outcome, when to the consternation of the authorities Magennis was declared the winner. In the normal course of events he would not have stood a chance in the face of such powerful opposition, but what proved decisive for him was the intervention of the Church, then represented by the Archbishop of Dublin, William J Walsh, who wrote a letter to Mc Kenna's campaign directors urging them to act if they wished to prevent the partition of Ireland. Copies of this letter, of course, appeared on posters throughout the constituency. This electoral triumph was repeated almost immediately.

With the support of the Church, Sinn Fein's chances of success had been enhanced, immeasurably, and when a seat became vacant, in East Clare, Sinn Fein nominated de Valera to oppose Patrick J Lynch, KC. Then almost unknown, de Valera, who was to play such a pivotal role in Irish politics, was the last surviving commandant of the Rising and had just been released from jail. Were it not for the fact that he was an American citizen he would have had to face the firing squad with the other leaders of the insurrection.

De Valera agreed to stand for Sinn Fein on one condition – that they allow Eoin Mac Neill to accompany him on the platform. This he stipulated in order to heal a rift in the Volunteers that had arisen following Mac Neill's last minute cancellation of the mobilisation orders for the Rising, which had resulted in its postponement until the Monday of Easter Week. Such was de Valera's victory at the polls that he defeated his opponent by a margin of two votes to one.

Successful as these early Sinn Fein gains were, in one respect they made a bad situation worse. By using the establishment of a Republic and reference to the Rising, which had killed the Home Rule Bill, as a basis for their campaign, they also ended what hopes the more liberal element might have had of resuscitating the Bill. It also lent credence to the more conservative elements across the water, who had been delighted to see its death. Consequently Lloyd George was now at their mercy. Meanwhile de Valera, who was later to become a statesman of international repute, made one of the errors that where to characterise his early career.

Addressing his supporters at the count, he appeared wearing the now banned uniform of the Volunteers, thereby bringing down the wrath of the entire British people on the new movement. Sinn Fein could already smell victory and no good could come of such theatrical posturing; indeed it was to bring misery to the Irish people. It was Sinn Fein's success in Kilkenny, their first attempt at an urban constituency and a city in which they seemed to have no hope of success that galvanised the authorities into action. But now the reaction verged on near panic.

By the time of this election Sinn Fein had gained sufficient experience at the hustings to build a highly efficient electoral machine. The opposition, on the contrary, were if anything apathetic, so convinced were they that they would win the seat. Thus while Sinn Fein canvassed every elector in the constituency, the nominee of the Irish

Parliamentary Party, whose *raison d'être* had ceased to exist, hardly bothered to hold any meetings and chose to rely on the antipathy to Sinn Fein, which appeared to be self-evident in the city. After all, most of the electorate was made up of some 1,200 elderly businessmen, to whom a republican could hardly be expected to appeal.

Sinn Fein were faced with an uphill task, but this time they had an experienced candidate, W T Cosgrave, who had served for a number of years on the Dublin City Corporation. An eloquent speaker, he had no difficulty in persuading the electors that they would be better represented by Sinn Fein than by the Irish Parliamentary Party, which supported a government now committed to partition. His victory was too much for the authorities, who banned a meeting planned to be held in Dublin to celebrate the result. Wholesale arrests followed and the offices of Sinn Fein were raided, but this only created sympathy for the party among Dubliners who, until now, had regarded the movement with hostility.

In June 1917 the British had granted an amnesty to prisoners taken during the Rising, other than those serving life sentences. This apparent U-turn is not easy to explain, for following the amnesty the British Government had appeared to go one stage further and an Irish administration had been set up in Dublin. Had this been so constituted as to be genuinely representative of the Irish people it might have been regarded as a halfway house on the road to Irish independence. However it had been made up of carefully selected nominees, with the object of giving the appearance of self-government while ensuring that this objective would never be achieved. But now the successes of Sinn Fein were being regarded with considerable apprehension by the authorities, who were determined to undermine the new movement if they were unable to crush it.

In September Thomas Ashe, who had received a long prison sentence for his part in the Rising, died in England as a result of an attempt to force-feed him while he was engaged in a protracted hunger strike. Republican prisoners, with no mean success, have used this same weapon ever since. The executive of Sinn Fein decided that this was an opportune time to test public opinion in Dublin and, in order to do so, decided to avail themselves of the people's deep-rooted respect for funerals.

The funeral of Thomas Ashe took place on the 30 September and was preceded by his lying in state at City Hall. Many thousands of Dubliners took part in the funeral cortege, which appeared to be carefully choreographed. It included a number of priests, as well as mayors and their councillors, together with 10,000 trade unionists. It was led by units of the Volunteers and the Citizen Army, while the people of Dublin, who had turned out either in sympathy or from mere curiosity, packed the pavements along the route from the City Hall to Glasnevin. Sinn Fein had planned to stage-manage the funeral to the utmost effect, and those who led not only wore the banned uniform of the Volunteers but also carried what rifles they could procure to make up a firing party.

The organisers well satisfied with this level of popular support now envisaged a plan that was calculated to antagonise the entire population of Dublin against the authorities. To this end it was arranged that their agents would spread a rumour among the crowds, who were not aware that a stop was to be made outside Findlater's Church, that the British army was mobilising there with the intention of stopping the funeral. Consequently, when the cortege made its planned halt, panic swept through the crowd and people began to run in all directions. This instilled such hatred among the people as to make the subsequent war of independence inevitable.

That this devious plan, which was to bring untold suffering to the Irish people, was made in advance is self-evident. On receiving a request from the army for instructions, Dublin Castle had issued strict orders that the funeral should be allowed to proceed without molestation for the sake of public order. In fact after halting at Findlater's Church for a few moments the funeral preceded on its way, undeterred by either the army or the panicking onlookers. Neither was there any sign of disruption at the grave, even after Michael Collins had delivered a brief funeral oration and a volley of shots had been fired over the grave.

The following month saw the October Revolution in Russia, which resulted in the collapse of Connolly's workers' movement in Ireland because Lenin and his Communist co-conspirators attacked not only the Orthodox Church but also religion in general. The Vatican therefore condemned socialism. However Connolly's followers transferred their allegiance to Sinn Fein, thereby eliminating the latent threat of a split in the Republican movement.

As 1917 had seen the birth of a new movement out of the ashes of the 1916 Rising, so 1918 was to prove to be a year of destiny – one that was to prove disastrous in terms of Anglo-Irish relations. Subsequent events were to lend credence to the myths that had become current both before and after the Rising.

The year opened with the defeat of the Sinn Fein candidates in Waterford and East Tyrone. Prime Minister Lloyd George mistakenly believed that the party's luck was running out, whereas the contrary was the case and it was rapidly gaining support throughout the country. Carried along by a false sense of security, he foolishly embarked on a policy destined to turn the entire Irish people, with the exception of the Northern Unionists, against England and lead to a war of attrition between the two countries.

No sooner had the results of these two by-elections become known than he precipitated a crisis by introducing conscription in Ireland. Not only was this measure strongly opposed by the Irish Parliamentary Party, but also the Irish Convention, which he had created, was also highly critical of it, as was illustrated by a report sent to London on 8 April. Lloyd George, however, was insistent and when his proposal became law, Irish MPs at Westminster returned home in a body to join in the resistance of the people. The Lord Mayor of Dublin called a meeting that was so constituted as to be the first meeting of an Irish Government, independent in all but name.

De Valera and Arthur Griffith represented Sinn Fein; John Dillon and Joe Devoy were there for the Irish Parliamentary Party. There were three Labour delegates, while Tim Healy and William O'Brien represented the Independents and the All for Ireland League, respectively. During the ensuing crisis the people came to regard this team as a National Cabinet and it is a tribute to de Valera's negotiating skills that he was able to weld together so many conflicting viewpoints to work as one.

Taking a leaf out of the book of Sir Edward Carson, who had drawn up the Solemn League and Covenant to resist Home Rule, a similar declaration was drawn up to resist conscription and, on Sunday 21 April, no fewer than two million people signed this document and pledged their support. Two days later the trade unions called a general strike that resulted in all work, other than in four counties in Ulster, being brought to a standstill.

Meanwhile, ever since the release of those of their leaders who had survived the Rising, the Volunteers had been training in secret drill halls, in many cases joined by those who were at home on leave from the front. Lloyd George, who was daily becoming more alarmed by reports he was receiving from Dublin Castle, decided on a new tough policy towards Ireland and to this end appointed Lord French, who had been Commander-in-Chief of the British forces in France, to the position of Viceroy. At the same time sweeping changes were made in the Irish military and police forces, while the Chief Secretary, responsible to the British Cabinet, was replaced by Edward Shortt to ensure that the new conscription laws were enforced rigorously.

These changes proved wholly counterproductive and only served to spur the Irish people on to greater resistance. De Valera and John Dillon joined forces and were to be heard speaking at massive meetings organised throughout the length and breadth of the country. £100,000 was collected for an anti-conscription fund and simultaneously the Volunteers concentrated their efforts on obtaining arms, and raids on British army units as well as their armouries became commonplace.

By May Lloyd George found himself in an impossible situation and in desperation attempted to divide the movement by arresting the leaders including de Valera, Arthur Griffith, Maud Gonne, Countess Markiewicz, Count Plunkett and Sean Mac Entee. However, as rumours of the forthcoming arrests had been current for some time, due to the leaking of the imminent publication of details of an alleged 'German plot', Sinn Fein had taken the precaution to appoint substitutes to take over in the event of such an eventuality. In fairness to the British Prime Minister he had good reason to suspect the existence of such a plot and there was no necessity for him to invent it, as some commentators have suggested.

The war was now at a critical stage and there was abundant circumstantial evidence to support the theory that something of this nature was afoot. Not only had Pearse invoked the aid of Germany at the time of the Rising, but also he had received a briefing from his intelligence services that there was some doubt as to the motives of Carson. This followed the discovery that Eoin Mac Neill, among others including Sir Roger Casement, had held meetings in Cork and Galway where support had been voiced for the Ulster Volunteers, who shared their opposition to Home Rule. Consequently not a few in official circles suspected that there was a degree of collusion between the two movements, however incompatible their aims might have appeared at first sight. In addition there was a remarkable similarity between the Larne and Howth gun runnings. Now, with anti-Irish feeling running high, Lloyd George deemed it to be wise to trust no one.

The general public in England, who drew a parallel between Casement's arrival in Ireland aboard a German submarine and the smuggling of Lenin to Moscow in 1917, where he had masterminded the October Revolution, shared his views in this respect. This had resulted in the withdrawal of Russia from the war, thereby releasing the German army to pitch the whole of its weight against the Allies on the Western Front.

Accordingly, coinciding with the arrest of the Sinn Fein leaders, a proclamation from Lord French appeared in the newspapers, announcing that certain elements in Ireland were in collusion with the enemy and that a treasonable conspiracy existed in the country. It went on to call upon "all loyal subjects" to assist in the prosecution of the war by stamping out the plot. The proclamation also proposed that it might be possible to replace conscription with voluntary enlistment.

If Lloyd George had had the foresight to leave well alone, this carrot might well have proved enough for Irish public opinion to swing back behind the war effort, even at this late stage. Instead he chose to employ a mixture of threats and cajolery in an effort to obtain new recruits for the army. Without consulting the House of Commons he instructed his Viceroy to issue a second proclamation, containing the promise that those who enlisted would receive land. This caused uproar; both in Ireland and in England, where angry MPs at Westminster demanded to know what and whose land was to be given away. Lord George was forced into a humiliating climb-down for he had no option but to withdraw the bribe in the face of mounting criticism.

In an article published in the *Morning Post*, the conservatives suggested that the question of land could be settled by confiscating the property of 'Shinners' as a penalty for their treason. But the vacillation of Lloyd George at this juncture had two immediate results, for not only did the Irish people distrust him but he became a prisoner of the conservative element at home. Consequently, as the recruits that he had been anticipating were not now forthcoming, he was forced into another embarrassing volte-face. As his campaign in this respect had proved a complete failure, he sent fresh instructions to his Recruiting Council in Ireland to tell the people that if they did not volunteer they would be conscripted.

Sinn Fein, which had had to face the possibility of a severe setback following Lord French's initial proclamation, was soon once again firmly in control of events. This time it was under the leadership of Fr O'Flanagan, a catholic priest and powerful mob orator who was, in his time, every bit as persuasive as Ian Paisley in his heyday. It was he who engineered Sinn Fein's success at the East Cavan by-election when the seat became vacant. His chosen candidate was Arthur Griffith, then serving a sentence in Gloucester jail, and due to the number of deportations that had taken place from the area he faced a formidable task. Nevertheless, to the consternation of his opponent Griffith was returned with a comfortable majority.

The authorities, now at their wits' end, threw caution to the winds and determined on a policy of repression, which was to lead them on a collision course with the Irish people. Offices were raided, and anyone who was known to be an active member of Sinn Fein, Cumann na m'Ban or the Gaelic League was placed under arrest. As the days passed, the army and police force assumed all the appearances of an army of occupation. On 15 June, sixteen cities and counties were declared Proclaimed Districts and only three days later many other parts of Ireland were scheduled as Special Military Areas. This meant that all meetings within them could be suppressed and even fairs banned in some towns, at the discretion of the local RIC chief.

A further blow was struck on 4 July when it was announced that in future it would be an offence to join any Nationalist organisation. The people, stung by these actions, rallied to Sinn Fein and soon so many seditious meetings were taking place that it became impossible for the army or the police to contain them. Those who had stood for Home Rule were swept aside – some of the Parliamentary Party MPs, for example, still supported the government in its endeavours to gain recruits. Even though they were opposed to conscription they saw, in voluntary enlistment, a possible compromise that, if supported, could strengthen their case for Home Rule. They did, after all, still have the backing of a considerable body of public opinion that remained loyal to the Crown.

When the Armistice came on 11 November, enormous crowds bearing Union Flags assembled in Dublin to celebrate the ending of the war. Feeling was running high and understandably so, for many thousands of Irishmen had lost their lives and limbs at the front, particularly in the terrible battles of the Somme, Ypres and Mons The Irish had earned a reputation for bravery that was second to none. That night a mob wrecked the headquarters of Sinn Fein at 6 Harcourt Street and managed to set the building ablaze. The rioters were joined by a number of soldiers who were at home on leave and the police stood idly by as a running fight developed between the mob and those who were trying to extinguish the flames. This single event, coupled with the inaction of those responsible for law and order, was to have far-reaching repercussions.

Not only was 1918 the year of a general election but it also saw the great influenza epidemic, which cost almost as many lives in England as the war itself. On 9 December, as the election campaign was reaching its height, a young Volunteer, Dick Coleman, died in Usk prison. An inquest was held and it was revealed that the hospital staff levels had been so depleted by illness that many of the Irish internees who had contracted the disease were in danger of death.

Telegrams were immediately sent to the government by horrified relatives, requesting permission to send Irish trained nurses to the hospitals to treat all, irrespective of nationality or the nature of their offence. Their pleas were ignored. The refusal to grant the necessary permits for this mercy mission generated considerable heat among women, who were exercising the right to vote for the first time at a general election.

Sinn Fein, though technically illegal, was allowed to take part in the contest, possibly to demonstrate its electoral weakness. Indeed it appeared to be fighting a losing battle against insuperable odds for, the Irish Parliamentary Party, though largely discredited, held the vast majority of seats and had received a fresh lease of life with the ending of the war.

By contrast over 50 of the Sinn Fein candidates were in jail and, subjected to continual harassment, hardly a day passed without one of their campaign officials or election workers being arrested. This only served to attract the sympathy of women, many of whom harboured memories of the suffragette struggle, and the Sinn Fein election offices were inundated with offers of help from new supporters, many of whom had been loud in their denunciation of the party in the past.

Faced with this new and unexpected threat the Parliamentary Party began to lose heart. The result was a foregone conclusion when Colonel Arthur Lynch, a veteran Home Ruler who had also played a part in the government's recruitment campaign, announced his intention of yielding his seat to Sinn Fein. So great was the backlash that the party, which had stood only an outside chance at the beginning of the election, was found to have captured 75 seats while their rivals totalled a mere 30.

No sooner was the electoral campaign over than Sinn Fein proceeded to represent the result as a victory for the Republican movement. In truth it was a protest vote against the activities of the government during the campaign in general, and against conscription in particular, for the people were voting for peace, not war. Nevertheless

Sinn Fein set about organising massive protest meetings throughout the country to demand the release of prisoners. With the movement now firmly in control of the militants, rather than using their new found power to come to an accommodation with the authorities they set out on a course destined to inflame all who opposed them.

Too late, the organisers discovered that it was easy enough to rouse a mob but containing it was another matter. Following mass rallies in Dublin on 5 January 1919, their supporters made forays into such places as Grafton Street, in the most Unionist quarter of the city, where they inflicted no little damage. When nightfall came they climbed onto the roofs of buildings to rig up banners bearing their demands across the street.

Such was the atmosphere when the Dáil met on 21 June, under the chairmanship of Count Plunkett, an occasion which could have been used to demonstrate to the world that Sinn Fein had the ability to exercise the control and restraint that would be necessary were their efforts crowned with success, but this was not to be. The Unionists, who had been still further estranged from their compatriots by the events of the past fortnight, refused to attend. Cathal Brugha, who had been elected Speaker of the House, having read the Declaration of Independence proceeded to underline the feeling of the meeting when he concluded with the words, "Deputies, you understand from what is stated in this Declaration that we have cut ourselves free from England. Let the world know it and those who are concerned bear it in mind, for come what may now, whether it be death itself, the great deed is done."

The implied threat contained in this statement was not lost on the authorities. For a period confusion reigned in official circles, opinion at Dublin Castle being almost equally divided between those who felt that, whatever their own opinions, the people had spoken and all they could do was make the best of it, and those who considered that the Dáil had no authority to make decisions on the part of the Irish people. After all, its members had been elected to the House of Commons and not to an assembly representing abstentionists who refused to take the seats to which they had been elected. Meanwhile the Irish news media were demanding that firm action be taken by the British Government to restore order in the country, but it was the suspension of Fr O'Flanagan by his Bishop, on account of his association with the most militant faction of Sinn Fein, that provided the government with a much needed excuse to act.

While the fact of the Declaration of Independence is well known, the immediate circumstances surrounding the first meeting of the Dáil are not, and neither is the Democratic Programme that was enunciated during these early proceedings. It may come as an unpleasant surprise to some of Ireland's legislators, past and present, to be reminded that one of the main provisions stated that "Every citizen should be entitled to an adequate share in the nation's labours" and that "No child shall be allowed to suffer from hunger or cold."

In fact, from the foundation of the State in 1921, any hope of the fulfilment of such worthy aspirations was dashed by the endemic corruption of the body politic, further aggravated by a system of proportional representation with multi-seat constituencies, which allows political parties to put up an unlimited number of candidates to fill the available seats. This not only ensures that it is well-nigh impossible to elect a government, unless it is led by one of the two major political parties, which owe their origin to the Civil War, while clientelism at both local and national level causes unsustainable promises to be made in the run up to an election, not to mention the creation of vested interests that use powerful lobby groups to obtain their objectives.

The dangers of this situation did not become apparent until after the demise of de Valera, when they were exacerbated by a growing connection between big business and a number of highly placed politicians. But it was not until 1985 that the resultant scandals saw the emergence of the Progressive Democrats, who were responsible for establishing a number of Tribunals of Enquiry that exposed the extent to which the State had been plundered ever over the decades.

During the weeks leading up to the first official meeting of the Dáil, which the authorities had now decided not to recognise, everything possible was done to hinder preparations. Further arrests were made, the headquarters of Sinn Fein was subjected to constant police raids, and a move to unseat deputies who were still in jail was under consideration. However when the Dáil eventually met in the Mansion House, no attempt was made to disrupt its proceedings other than a refusal to grant parole to those still in jail to attend the meeting.

It was nearly three months before the Dáil met again, an action packed period, during which the shape of things to come began to emerge. In February 1919 de Valera had escaped from Lincoln jail, a feat that had been carefully planned and executed by Michael Collins and Harry Boland, who were waiting for him in the street outside the prison. This event caused a storm in the House of Commons, with angry MPs demanding a strict tightening of security both at home and in Ireland.

However while the repression of Sinn Fein became an urgent priority for Lloyd George, he was determined to find some way of diffusing what had now become a menacing situation. So when Pierce Mc Cann died in prison he decided to release all but a few of the remaining internees. The logic of this was obvious, for by so doing he was hoping to placate popular opinion in Ireland rather than exasperate it by giving way to any further demands of the conservatives at home.

In early March the first batch of prisoners arrived home to a rapturous reception from cheering crowds lining the docks. One man was not with them – de Valera. As he had escaped from custody he was liable to be rearrested and it was essential for him to remain in hiding. He had had not long to wait as he too was pardoned on March 26. Sinn Fein announced that not only was he to return home but that a civic reception was planned for him, to culminate in his receiving the Freedom of the City of Dublin from the Lord Mayor.

Releasing the prisoners was one thing but permitting this ceremony to go ahead was more than the authorities could stomach. In any event, they feared that with the vast crowds that would be attracted to such an event, it would only need a spark to set off mob violence on an unprecedented scale. A prohibition order was issued and troops were sent to Dublin to enforce it.

De Valera was anxious lest a dangerous situation be created and as, in his view, no particular principle was involved, he requested the organisers to cancel the arrangements, stating that if there were to be a showdown, it would be a matter of far more consequence than a mere civic reception for himself. It is quite clear that at this stage he favoured negotiation rather than confrontation, while the reception accorded to him by the people proved that he was their undisputed leader. Now he had once again demonstrated his diplomatic skill in persuading his supporters to call off this potentially dangerous civic reception.

Had the British Government responded by releasing the remaining prisoners, an opportunity would almost certainly have presented itself to arrive at a settlement, thereby avoiding the horrors of the next two years, the subsequent civil war and the bitterness that was to characterise Anglo-Irish relations for decades. But just as Sinn Fein was now hostage to the militants, so Lloyd George had become the captive of the hard-line elements in his administration.

In Ireland passions were riding high and an angry crowd assembled at Tinaheley, County Wicklow, to demand the release of Robert Barton, who had been rearrested on 26 February. In fact, unknown to them, he had already escaped and was lying low. The authorities, however, were left in no doubt that violence would ensue if their request for his release were refused.

Within a fortnight of this meeting a further 20 internees made a spectacular jailbreak from Mountjoy prison in Dublin. This period also witnessed the firing of the first shots in the coming conflict when a number of Volunteers, led by Dan Breen and Sean Treacy, ambushed an unarmed RIC patrol that was escorting a vehicle carrying explosives. A daring and well-organised raid later took place at Collinstown, then an RAF air base, and sufficient rifles and ammunition were taken to arm an entire company of Volunteers.

It was in this tense atmosphere that the Dáil met again, on 10 April. Since the Mansion House meeting it had held a number of private sessions, at one of which a Provisional Government had been elected, led by de Valera. The personnel making up his Ministry had been carefully selected to include moderates as well as hardliners, for he was acutely conscious of the ever-present threat of a split in the Movement. As yet this had not materialised, but there was considerable tension between the two groups that was to surface from time to time, despite his best efforts at diplomacy.

In order to prepare for a public meeting to endorse his proposed government, his first Cabinet included Arthur Griffith (Minister for Home Affairs), Cathal Brugha (Defence), Countess Markiewicz (Labour), Michael Collins (Finance), Laurence Ginnell (Propaganda), W T Cosgrave (Local Government) Eoin Mac Neill (Industry), Robert Barton (Agriculture) and Count Plunkett (Fine Arts).

However when the Dáil met and the Cabinet was endorsed, it became clear that it was the viewpoint of the militants that prevailed and de Valera was placed in a difficult position. Personally he favoured a peaceful solution and it was only subsequent events that led him to adopt a hard line. Nevertheless he was a democrat and to maintain unity he had no option but to bow to the wishes of those who had endorsed his election. But the militants were hell bent on avenging the victims of the Rising.

When he addressed the Assembly a grim-faced de Valera did so in terms that were tantamount to a declaration of war, announcing that the RIC was to be ostracised and treated as part of the British Army of Occupation. He also made it clear that if a war was to be prosecuted, it would be vital for him to secure the support of at least one foreign power, to ensure that the Irish Republican Army would have the advantage of belligerent status. Failing that, prisoners taken during the ensuing battles would have no rights before the law and would be in danger of being treated as common criminals.

He could see no hope of obtaining such support from any of the Great Powers, other than perhaps America, which had a large population of Irish descent. But his appeals to President Wilson, whose aid he endeavoured to elicit by expressing his approval of the American peace proposals at the Paris Peace Conference, as opposed to those of the French President, 'The Tiger' Clemenceau, fell on deaf ears.

He then planned to visit America himself – a secret that was so jealously guarded that his own Cabinet were not made aware of it until he had arrived safely. That day saw the launch of the first Dáil loan of £100,000, half of which was to be raised overseas. The bulk was for the purchase of arms, with a small amount being set aside to cover day-to-day expenses. It was not until 19 June that the Dáil met again and the deputies were informed that de Valera had succeeded in making the journey to America, where he had first made his presence known at a number of press conferences.

Prior to this journey he had first had a discussion with M J Ryan, a banker and leading official in Pennsylvania, whom he had met in Dublin while he was on his way to Paris to press Ireland's claim to be heard at the Peace Conference. Ryan had made De Valera aware of the difficulty he would encounter in floating such a loan in the

United States. As he had explained, American laws relating to foreign loans were so complicated that it would be next to impossible to get any bank to handle such a proposition. But he had suggested that de Valera endeavour to present his case in person to American officials and it was this that had finally decided him to make this journey to the United States, whatever the risk.

De Valera had crossed to Liverpool, where he had remained in hiding, awaiting the first chance to board a boat bound for America. There had been an unexpected delay but he had made the best use of his time in drafting the Constitution of the Self Determination League of Great Britain and Ireland, through which the Irish living in Britain, and later those resident in the Dominions, could contribute to the struggle in their motherland.

While in America he came up against many obstacles, not the least being that his supporters were, as at home, bitterly divided. He therefore set about the task of healing the rifts in the Friends of Irish Freedom, an organisation that had been established after the Rising by the American Branch of the IRB. But it was not until a year later that his efforts were crowned with success, when he founded a new movement to cover all the Irish organisations in the United States. This was known as the American Association for the Recognition of the Irish Republic, which had a combined membership in excess of the numerical strength of Sinn Fein and the Self Determination League, put together and was to form a powerful and influential lobby group. Meanwhile, at home, the war had begun in earnest, for Lloyd George's position had now become untenable. The Irish wanted war and his own people were insisting on a fierce repression.

CHAPTER 7

The War of Independence

Following a number of isolated incidents in 1919, a full-scale war of attrition erupted in 1920. This followed a proclamation confirming the earlier proscription of the Dáil as an illegal organisation, meaning that future meetings had to be held in secret. There was also an order suppressing the publication of any newspaper that published the prospectus of the Dáil loan or contained Sinn Fein propaganda.

Sinn Fein countered with their own clandestine publications. A number of newssheets were produced, chief among which was the *Bulletin*, the first copy of which was published in November 1919. This gave a highly coloured version of the activities of the IRA and details of reprisals by the Crown forces. The location of the offices of the *Bulletin* had been carefully chosen and, despite an intensive search by the army and police forces, it was only discovered, and then almost by accident, on 26 March 1920 at 11 Molesworth Street, in the heart of what was then regarded as the headquarters of Unionism in Dublin.

The *Bulletin* was to become an invaluable weapon in the armoury of Sinn Fein, for not only was it circulated at home but copies were sent to selected MPs at Westminster, where it made a considerable impact by exposing the misdeeds of the Crown forces, which were supposed to be restoring law and order. This led to a furore in the House of Commons, and H Asquith and Sir John Simon, who had so far proved themselves to be no friends Ireland, were to become foremost in their criticism of the authorities.

Following de Valera's proclamation ostracising the police force, the 11,000 members of the RIC had found themselves subjected to long and bitter attacks. Shootings of policemen and attacks on their barracks soon became an almost daily occurrence. A sergeant was killed while leaving the eight o'clock mass at Bandon, barracks were blown up, and the families of serving policemen were intimidated. So vicious were these attacks that, in its edition dated 3 March 1920, the *Constabulary Gazette* warned its readers that "No man going away in the morning can be sure of returning home in the evening." Nevertheless, despite the wholesale murder of their comrades, the intimidation of their families and the ostracism, the majority of the police continued to carry out their duties bravely. Still, the strain often proved too much for those near and dear to them and many felt obliged to resign from the force.

The actions of the IRA were beginning to cause Sinn Fein to lose the support of the ordinary people. Boycotting the police force was one thing, but the average citizen was becoming heartily sick of cold-blooded murder, many of the victims of which had been prominent members of their communities, as well as neighbours for no reason other than that they wore an RIC uniform. Besides, in 1918 they had voted for peace, not war, and their main reason for voting Sinn Fein was to ensure the defeat of any move to enforce conscription, or attempt to introduce partition, by the back door. A sense of disillusion was setting in and was rapidly leading to a feeling of hopelessness and despair.

It was then that Lloyd George's government made it most fatal error. The advent of 1920 had seen Britain facing an unemployment problem of crisis proportions. Those who had returned home from the front, expecting to find a land "fit for heroes", soon found themselves faced with the bitter reality of tramping the streets in search for work and were, in many cases, reduced to begging to keep body and soul together. These men were in an angry mood. It was in these circumstances that the British Prime Minister conceived the idea of finding work for these ex-servicemen in Ireland and a force, subsequently known as the Black and Tans, was recruited in England. The first of these made their appearance in Ireland on 25 March.

Here it is necessary to dispose of a myth that has been perpetuated *ad nauseam* regarding this force. The Black and Tans were not, as many people still believe today, made up of convicted murderers and thieves released from British jails. But they were battle hardened and ruthless troops whose actions were to lend credence to this myth. They had already acquired a fearsome reputation abroad, and had been trained to kill and to expect nor give any quarter. However when they first arrived in Ireland the last thing on their minds was to get involved in another war, particularly with the local people, many of whom had shown themselves to be sympathetic to their plight. Consequently they succeeded in becoming, at any rate initially, more acceptable to the people than the RIC, which resented them.

Indeed at one stage Sinn Fein feared that the existence of such an apparently friendly police force might undermine their campaign. However neither they nor the authorities had counted on the resourcefulness of Michael Collins. He has rightly been credited by Irish historians with being a military genius, but he was also a calculating and ruthless character to whom any means justified the successful prosecution of the war. It mattered little to him what suffering would be inflicted on the hapless civilian population so long as it contributed to the realisation of his aims. Thus he planned to precipitate the Tan war although, in fairness to him, it is unlikely that he would have realised the terror his plans would unleash.

At first carefully selected attacks were made, mainly in remote rural areas close to villages. The object was to cause panic and give the impression that the whole of the people of the area were in collusion with a vast guerrilla force and that no one could be trusted. In fact at this stage the IRA had at most 500 men under arms and, with the drift away from Sinn Fein, it was vital for them to find some way of attracting new recruits.

A typical example of such an attack is to be found in James Gleeson's book *Bloody Sunday*. Apparently the unit of the Black and Tans to which he refers was situated near a river overlooked by a thick briar hedge, and they had the habit of swimming there, leaving their clothes in charge of one of their number. On this occasion they were no sooner in the water than a unit of the IRA opened fire, peppering the water all around them with shots. It would appear that none of them was wounded, apart from being scratched when they were forced to dive naked into the briar hedge. One of them, too scared to go back for his clothes, ran to the nearest cottage in search of a pair of trousers but was met by an elderly woman who explained that she had no such thing and could only give him skirt. Wearing this he made his way to barracks and reported that his unit had been attacked by hundreds of IRA men and, although he hadn't looked back, believed that he might well be the only survivor of the attack!

This panicked the garrison, which fired distress signals that exploded with a deafening roar giving off clouds of smoke, and the military hurried to the scene, only to be regaled with similar stories of an attack by the IRA. Along with its humorous side this action had a grim purpose for it was followed by others, during which a number of casualties were inflicted on the Tans, making them suspicious of the entire civilian population. They also became misled as to the strength of the IRA, which was to have dire consequences, for these men, who had been shunned by the RIC but had made many friends among the ordinary people, were transformed into raving savages. They became a terror force from which no one was immune and the killing of civilians and the destruction of their property was to become a daily occurrence.

Thus began a rampage that continued throughout the War of Independence and spared no one, irrespective of whether or not they were involved in the IRA. As far as the Tans were concerned the local people were Irish, and that fact alone excused whatever action they chose to take against them. Many former supporters of the Irish Parliamentary Party and their families, who had been subjected to such attacks, transferred their allegiance to Sinn Fein. There is little doubt that these outrages had the tacit approval of the authorities, who had planned the murder of selected members of the Dáil. One such victim was Tomas Mac Curtain, who was murdered in his home on 25 March, to coincide with the arrival of the Tans in Ireland.

Completely demoralised by the activities of the Tans, the RIC, who had been opposed to their recruitment in the first place, soon appeared to disintegrate. By the summer it became impossible to man the smaller barracks and the police withdrew from the villages to be quartered only in the larger towns. Provision for such an eventuality had been foreseen by Sinn Fein and, while the IRA set about destroying only those barracks that were likely to be reoccupied, the party made arrangements to establish its own police force, as well as the Republican Courts, in order to counter a new menace. The land hungry, as well a criminal element, were determined to make use of the hiatus caused by the withdrawal of the regular police from the rural areas, and there was fear of a land war developing.

Much has been written about these Courts, but it stands to reason that when they first came into being their effectiveness was limited. They had neither the means nor the manpower to maintain them and the IRA could not supply the personnel to enforce their decisions. They therefore came to be used to prosecute those whose connivance with the British forces warranted it. Nevertheless their propaganda value proved immense.

British intelligence services in Ireland still remained woefully inadequate, otherwise Collins's ploy would have been discovered and the Tans sent home before they could inflict lasting damage. Paradoxically this ineffectiveness was to result in another myth that they had themselves created. In order to sow distrust among the people they had noised it abroad that the failure of past rebellions had been due to informers rather than the incompetence of the rebels themselves. They had hoped this would dissuade people from becoming involved with underground movements or secret societies but having given birth to this myth – which has lasted to this day – they found that when they badly needed inside information it was not forthcoming.

The authorities, faced with what appeared to be a countrywide rising, decided to endeavour to restore order by recruiting an auxiliary police force. Unlike the Back and Tans, the Auxiliaries were seasoned officers who had been unable to settle down to civilian life and were chosen on account of their toughness and battle experience. Lloyd George was convinced that such men would be able to quell the rebellion and ensure that the activities of the Black and Tans were directed solely at known members of the IRA.

The Auxiliaries arrived in Ireland in late July, but instead of taking control of the situation they formed with the Tans a wild, undisciplined terrorist force that was subject to no one, not even the regular army commanders on the spot. They had but one objective – to mount punitive expeditions to seek out and kill not only members of the IRA but anyone suspected of sheltering them. But it was the Black and Tans who were to achieve the greatest infamy, being determined to show these officers that they could outmatch them in ruthlessness and villainy. The Auxiliaries, for their part, would stoop at nothing to obtain information. Consequently many innocent victims, instead of being protected by the Auxiliaries, were seized during their systematic raids and beaten up in police barracks while the Tans, in many cases abetted by these officers, engaged in a campaign of wholesale arson and murder.

In these circumstances it is not unnatural that the IRA should also be guilty of atrocities. One of the worst occurred on 28 November when a number of wounded Auxiliaries were massacred following an ambush at Kilmichael. General Tom Barry, who was in charge of the IRA flying column responsible, was vehement in his denial that any such outrage had taken place, and this incident was ascribed to British propaganda by those who had no first-hand knowledge of the event.

However it is interesting to compare Barry's account with that of Bill Munro, who together with his commanding officer was one of the more responsible Auxiliary officers. They were based at Macroom and like the other members of their unit regarded the activities of the majority of the Auxiliaries with distaste. As they had acquired a reputation for fair dealing, they had become acceptable to the local people – so much so that they had taken to sightseeing rather than conducting the usual patrols. Only one incident had marred their otherwise peaceful mission, and occurred when they surprised a meeting on the Kerry border. Several arrests were made and one man was killed while attempting to escape.

The discovery of this meeting made it necessary for them to resume patrols. When one of them failed to return a search party, of which Munro was a member, was sent out the following morning. When they reached Kilmichael they discovered two burnt out Crossley tenders and the mangled remains of 20 of their colleagues. The town of Macroom was almost as shocked as the Auxiliaries and it was only the intervention of their commanding officer that prevented their enraged men from setting fire to the houses of those in the area believed to be IRA sympathisers.

The peace that had reigned in the area had been shattered and 10 days later it was reported that one or two people in the neighbourhood had been seen carrying pistols in their trousers pockets. The Auxiliaries based at Macroom Castle, who had been unnerved by an experience that Munro described as worse than anything he had seen during the battles on the Western Front, posted a notice in the town to the effect that as they could no longer trust the local people, no males would be permitted to appear in public with their hands in their pockets.

Savage as the Kilmichael massacre and similar events elsewhere had been, it was now clear that both sides were involved in a cycle of atrocities and revenge killings. But to portray the members of the IRA flying column that took part in this event as heroes, as some commentators have done, is an insult to the cause they represented. The shooting of Lieutenant-Colonel Bruce Ferguson Smyth at the Country Club in Cork, less than a month after his announcement of the terms of reference of the newly recruited Auxiliaries there, sparked off a mutiny in the Listowel RIC some 10 days later. This resulted in all hell being let loose in Cork City by the Tans and by the following morning they had killed 40 people.

It was then that the Restoration of Order in Ireland Act was rushed through the House of Commons. As a result of Coroner's inquests on those killed by the Crown Forces were suspended and the normal Courts were replaced by Court's Martial, which sat in secret and had the power to impose the death sentence. A curfew was also imposed on certain areas of the country, which was now, to all intents and purposes, under martial law, although it was not officially imposed until later.

In the early months of 1920 everything was going according to plan for the IRA. Their ambushes and attacks had produced the desired response; as death and terror stalked the land, many who had been determined to have no truck with Sinn Fein had joined the IRA. Still they could not let up in their efforts to win popular support and it would be many months before they could secure the allegiance of the majority of the population, as many still regarded them as being responsible for their plight.

The turning point was to come on Sunday 21 November. Michael Collins had become alarmed at British intelligence, which had proved so inefficient and lacking in cohesion, being reorganised with a highly competent team of operatives. The extent of the threat soon became apparent, with late night raids being carried out by men of a very different calibre from the Tans and Auxiliaries. They relied not on brute force but on expertise to extract information from suspects, who were often allowed to go free to act as unsuspecting decoys.

His first priority was to discover the names and addresses of all undercover agents operating in Ireland and make plans for their elimination. He decided to act in one fell swoop. A Sunday morning was chosen for this action as the streets would be crowded with people going to Mass and the movements of the murder squad would be least likely to attract attention.

How close the British came to discovering this plot can be judged from the fact that two of Collins's key men, Peadar Clancy and Richard Mac Kee, were arrested only the night before the operation. The following morning, as the church bells were chiming, a number of young men made their way to the addresses that had been supplied to them and, by the time Mass was over, 11 officers had been killed in their beds, some in front of their wives. Two Auxiliaries also died in a fruitless endeavour to intervene.

Necessary as it had been for Collins to take such drastic action to remove this threat to his organisation, these apparently cold-blooded murders could have been disastrous from a propaganda point of view. In reprisal the Auxilliaries' infuriated colleagues were considering torching the homes of IRA suspects in Dublin when their attention was drawn to posters advertising a GAA match between a team from Leinster and Tipperary, to be played in Dublin that afternoon. It was known that the proceeds were to go to the dependents of IRA men.

The game was no sooner in full swing than the Black and Tans swarmed into the ground, firing indiscriminately into the crowd. Soon a large number of men, women and children lay dead or wounded, and had it not been for the intervention of a British officer who demanded that the firing be stopped, there is little doubt that either one or both teams would have been lined up against a wall and shot.

While there were a number of IRA men in the crowd, nothing could excuse this senseless outrage. It later turned out that twelve civilians had been killed and 60 injured, and the wave of sympathy that had been building up for the officers who had been murdered in the morning soon evaporated, From this moment on the war became ever more terrible. Until now murders by the Crown Forces had been unofficial, but now official executions began to take place and no one, guilty or innocent, was safe, as long as they were suspected of collaboration with the IRA. With each day that passed the atrocities committed by both sides grew ever more savage, as did the reprisals.

For many months Cork City and County had been the scene of such vicious fighting that it seemed inevitable that some devastating reprisal would take place. This came on 11 December when the Tans, aided by the Auxiliaries, engaged in an orgy of burning, sacking and looting as they set about setting fire to everything in their path. This operation could have been extremely hazardous for the IRA had units stationed in the hills overlooking the city.

Had they taken action the people could have been spared, but instead they chose to watch the burning from their vantage point, overlooking the inferno below, Their hearts were filled with anger, though not unmixed with glee. Once more the British had played into their hands and from now on the fury of the people would know no bounds. The Tans had won the propaganda war for them.

CHAPTER 8

The Truce and the Treaty of 1921

On Christmas Eve 1920 de Valera returned from America after a hazardous journey that involved changing boats in England. He succeeded in evading discovery, despite the fact that both vessels were searched, but he would almost certainly have been captured had it not been for the quick thinking of Billie Humphries, an English sailor, in whose home he stayed while awaiting passage to Ireland. Humphries took a great risk, for the harbouring of Irish fugitives was punishable by death, and it is possible that de Valera's gratitude to him and for the risks he had taken contributed to the shaping of his policies many years later.

As soon as he returned he resumed his functions as President and Chairman of the Army Council. New Year's Day was to witness an ominous turn of events, when rumours that had been sweeping the country were confirmed. An order was issued making all future reprisals official, while it was made clear that all such punitive measures should be limited to the burning of the houses of those suspected of action against the Crown Forces or collusion with the IRA. Furthermore notice should be given to those involved, to enable them to remove personal possessions under supervision.

Until that time, when an attack was launched against the British Forces, massive and haphazard reprisals had followed. These had been undertaken by the Black and Tans or the Auxiliaries, operating from the nearest constabulary barracks, and the subsequent lootings and killings had been subject to no controls. Such reprisals culminated in the burning of the City of Cork, which had given an enormous boost to the IRA's propaganda and had led to questions being asked in England and abroad, as well as in Ireland.

Had this order been effective it might have gone a long way to retrieving the situation, for the IRA was now beginning to suffer serious reverses due to the sheer weight of the forces pitted against them. In the battle following the burning of the Custom House in Dublin on 25 May 1921, their strength in that city was seriously. However the order was ignored for the most part, and the grim competition to see who could inflict the most fearsome reprisals on their adversaries, between the army and the police forces on the one hand, and the Auxiliaries combined with the Black and Tans on the other, continued unabated.

Since November 1920 the crescendo of violence had increased in intensity, and by

March of the following year a new and menacing element inspired by Carson had crept into the equation. This was sectarianism, designed to wean away any Protestants who might have been attracted to the independence movement, by fostering the illusion that Sinn Fein was totally opposed to all his co-religionists A number of murders were carefully planned and carried out, the first being that of Thomas Hoggett, a Protestant Unionist living in Cavan. On 24 July J W Biggs, a popular tradesman in Bantry who had stated publicly that the greatest goodwill existed between Catholics and Protestants in Munster, was lucky to escape with his life when his premises were razed to the ground.

In Derry, where Catholics formed the majority and had control of the Corporation, they worked in complete harmony with the Protestant councillors. This attracted favourable comment in the London *Times* but the article in which this appeared sparked off a vicious pogrom against Catholics living in the city. This was soon to engulf almost the entire northeast of the country, fanned by sectarian propaganda in the Unionist Press of the area, which led its readers to believe that the IRA enjoyed the wholehearted support of the entire Catholic community.

After three months of vicious rioting, during which some 60 Catholics were killed, many injured and thousands driven from their homes, the Ulster Volunteers, formed by Carson, joined the police force to form the infamous B-special constabulary. The pogroms increased in intensity but to suggest, as have some commentators, that the British Government had any hand in fomenting them, is to fly in the face of reason. The one thing the authorities feared most and were most desperately anxious to avoid was the alienation of Catholics, as this could only lead to their being driven into the ranks of the IRA, to whom they would look for protection.

Meanwhile, in order to conceal the heavy casualties that had been sustained, the IRA stepped up its attacks. But the greatest blow to morale came on 22 June 1921, when de Valera was arrested at his home, in Blackrock. To their amazement and relief however, he was mysteriously released the following morning. The reason for this soon became apparent.

The fanaticism of Carson had added a different dimension to the struggle and, following some of the fiercest fighting of the war, as the IRA escalated their campaign Lloyd George realised that he was in a no-win situation and decided to seek a way out of the situation. It was in these circumstances that he wrote to de Valera on 24 June suggesting a meeting; the terms of a truce were agreed on 9 July.

So relieved were the people of Ireland that when the British Commander, General Macready, and the IRA Chief of Staff met at Dublin Castle, a vast crowd assembled outside to cheer all – Irish and British. But the truce was an uneasy one and de Valera was forced to hold a special meeting at the Mansion House to discuss its terms. He had invited five Unionists to attend but only four came. Sir James Craig was conspicuous by his absence, despite an urgent telegram sent to him in the hope that he would change his mind.

Within 48 hours of the truce being signed Belfast became the scene of one of the most violent pogroms, which were to continue for the next two years despite the pleas of King George V. When opening the Stormont Parliament, which came into being following the signing of the Peace Treaty, the King called on his Protestant subjects to show forbearance and conciliation, concluding his address by imploring people to "forgive and forget so as to join in making for the land they love, an era of peace, contentment and goodwill". The so-called Loyalists answered his call by continuing to burn down the homes of their Catholic neighbours, while during the protracted negotiations leading up to the treaty, there were isolated incidents when the IRA broke the truce, and both sides took advantage of the hiatus to regroup their forces.

Following the Mansion House meeting de Valera accepted the British Prime Minister's invitation and the two men met at 10 Downing Street on 12 July. Lloyd George, plainly nervous, was at pains to make his guest feel at home. A Welshman, his opening gambit was to appeal to their common Celtic heritage, but he proceeded to attack the Irish Parliamentary Party and said that he could well understand Sinn Fein's disenchantment with its performance.

This angered de Valera, who instead of trying to find some common ground with his host became truculent and accused him of breaking his pledges to the Parliamentary Party. He seemed to be completely oblivious of the fact that, but for the outbreak of the world War, the Home Rule Bill would have become law long ago despite the efforts of the Unionists to thwart its passage. Neither did he appear to understand the political difficulties with which Lloyd George had been confronted as a result of the 1916 Rising.

Lloyd George, however, remained patient and went on to elaborate on his plans, which would have resulted in Ireland acquiring Dominion status. He stressed that by such an arrangement Ireland could become fully independent and enjoy all the advantages of Australia, New Zealand and South Africa. His proposals also contained provisions that in the event of war, Ireland would agree to make her ports available to Britain.

De Valera, as was proved some years later, would have been quite happy with this arrangement. But the activities of the Auxiliaries and the Black and Tans, with the apparent connivance of the authorities, and those of the Unionists in the North, had resulted in his having become sympathetic to the viewpoint of the militants. The tone of the meeting changed when the vexed question of partition came up for discussion.

Lloyd George insisted that it was necessary, if only as an interim measure, in view of the crisis in northeast Ulster, but on this question de Valera was adamant and was not prepared to listen to Lloyd George's argument that the situation there was such that no other solution was possible. This was despite Lloyd George's assurance that in the event of the division of the country a Boundary Commission could be set up to review the situation.

It was then that a clash of wills developed between the two men, but it was agreed they would adjourn and continue their discussions on 21 July. At the conclusion of the meeting Lloyd George told de Valera that he would make the terms of a draft treaty available to him in advance, so that he would have the opportunity of discussing it with his colleagues before any final conclusion was reached.

On returning from London, de Valera called a meeting of his Cabinet and there was unanimous agreement that he should not compromise on the question of Northern Ireland. It was suggested, however, that partition might prove a solution if it was based on the nine counties of Ulster, in order to bring about a more even balance between the Catholic and the Protestant populations. In the end this suggestion was rejected, as it was clear that any such arrangement could lead to a civil war on an unprecedented scale, which could well result in the contagion of sectarianism spreading to engulf the entire country.

Lloyd George's cardinal error had been to agree to give direct rule to the Northern State without ensuring safeguards to protect the Catholic minority. In the event de Valera rejected the British proposals on his return to London on 21 July. So much has been written about this second meeting with Lloyd George, much of it emotive and making little sense, that it is necessary to present the facts in context. Lloyd George genuinely believed that a rejection of the terms would lead to a resumption of the conflict, for he was under considerable pressure from his Cabinet colleagues. He explained his predicament to de Valera, but his comments were misconstrued as a threat and have been presented as such to this day. Threats there were, but they were to come later from both sides.

Determined to find a way out of this impasse, Lloyd George suggested that they delay publishing a joint communiqué, the normal procedure had they come to an agreement. He put it to de Valera that the Irish people were entitled to know the terms for they, after all, were the final arbiters. De Valera retorted that the manner in which the Irish Government chose to conduct its affairs was none of Lloyd George's business. This reply was extraordinary inasmuch as it betrayed a certain unwillingness to trust the Irish people not to give way on the question of partition, and there can be little doubt but it contributed to Lloyd George's assumption of a hard line in their future discussions. Nevertheless de Valera agreed to take the matter up with his

Cabinet for further consideration, on Lloyd George's undertaking not to make public the terms of any proposed treaty in advance of a final decision being taken.

The republican chronicler David Hogan is insistent that the latter broke his word by enlisting the aid of General Smuts, the South African Premier, who met de Valera shortly before a letter written by Smuts appeared in the British press, extolling the then unpublished British terms. He goes on to accuse Lloyd George, without a scintilla of evidence, suggesting that he, rather than Smuts, was responsible for leaking this information. Not only is it inconceivable that Lloyd George could have withheld from the Prime Ministers of the other Dominions matters concerning the possible admission of a new member, but it would appear that this was either a genuine oversight by Smuts or, more probably, a deliberate attempt by one of Lloyd George's more conservative Cabinet colleagues, unhappy with the way he was handling the affair, to derail any attempt to bring peace to Ireland.

In any event the damage was done and, when the Irish Cabinet met, a decision was taken to reject the terms of the treaty out of hand. A letter was drafted to this effect and conveyed to London by Robert Barton and Joseph Mc Grath. Lloyd George, who was in Paris returned to London immediately and called a Cabinet meeting, at which General Macready was present for consultation. Lloyd George was, however, determined to make some conciliatory gesture in an endeavour to retrieve the situation. This resulted in a statement being issued, aimed at getting the meeting of the Dáil, which de Valera had apparently refused to countenance, off the ground. It read:

"In keeping with the public undertaking given by the Prime Minister that His Majesty's Government would facilitate, in every practical way, the steps now being taken to promote peace in Ireland it has been decided to release forthwith, and without preconditions, all members of Dáil Eireann who are at present interned or who are undergoing a sentence of penal servitude or imprisonment, in order to enable them to attend a meeting of Dáil Eireann, which has been summoned for August. His Majesty's Government have decided that one member, J J Mc Keown, who has been convicted of murder, cannot be released."

De Valera's reply was swift and uncompromising and he issued a statement to the effect that unless General Mc Keown was released, he would not take part in any further negotiations. He was incandescent with rage, for Lloyd George had outsmarted him, leaving him with no option but to call a meeting of the Dáil. However despite his somewhat unpromising response, Lloyd George was determined to show that he was prepared, as far as possible, to meet his wishes and that night General Mc Keown was set free.

On 16 August the Dáil met in full session at the Round Room in the Mansion

House. But de Valera, more intransigent than ever, insisted that he could not and would not accept the terms on behalf of the nation. He went on to refer to the threats that had been worked up by the British media, adding that they had not flinched before when threats had been made against them and they would not flinch now, because more arms were being sent for.

An angry and bitter correspondence then took place between the two Prime Ministers, but Lloyd George eventually succeeded in persuading de Valera to meet him in Inverness on 20 September. In his final letter accepting this invitation de Valera he wrote: "We deem it our duty to reaffirm that our position is and can only be, as stated, throughout this correspondence. Our nation has formally declared its independence and recognises itself as a sovereign State. It is only as the representative of that State and as its chosen guardian that we have any authority to act on behalf of its people."

Harry Boland and Joseph Mc Grath delivered this letter to Lloyd George himself. He read it with ill-concealed dismay, for what de Valera had failed to appreciate all along was the great personal risk that he had taken politically, for his more conservative partners in government could well demand his resignation unless he could persuade de Valera to budge from his uncompromising stance, and it would appear that he had failed. He explained his dilemma to the Irish emissaries and asked them to telephone de Valera and request that he redraft the letter, omitting the final paragraph. Unfortunately the line was so bad that the impression given to Dublin was that he was sending it back. A flurry of diplomatic activity then ensued, and Bob Brennan was sent to London immediately to ensure that the Prime Minister had received the letter.

Now desperate to retrieve his political position, Lloyd George called a Cabinet meeting in Inverness. The fact that it was being held in Scotland, rather than in London, emphasised the gravity of the situation and the ensuing publicity led to the cancellation of the proposed peace conference. Meanwhile he telegraphed to de Valera complaining that he had not "come to meet me by a single step but have merely repeated in phrases of emphatic challenge the letter and spirit of your original claims".

With the cancellation of the proposed peace conference, for which Lloyd George had been so eager, military consultations now took place between the British government and the military authorities and it would appear that all hope of peace had been abandoned.

De Valera's intransigence, coupled with the cancellation of the peace conference that Lloyd George had been endeavouring to initiate, resulted in a spate of speculation. Some of the more hard-line newspapers, in particular, the *Daily Telegraph*, become increasingly hawkish. Meanwhile, although they continued to correspond, such contacts as there were between de Valera and Lloyd George were becoming ever more acrimonious. Eventually, in a final effort to prevent the talks from breaking down,

Lloyd George wrote to de Valera suggesting that they should ignore past statements and communications in order that they might make a fresh start.

In conclusion he wrote: We therefore send you a fresh invitation to a conference, to be held in London, on 11 October, where we can meet your Delegates, as the spokesmen of the people whom you represent, with a view to ascertaining how the association of Ireland with the community of nations, known as the British Empire, may best be reconciled with Irish national aspirations."

This was an invitation with no preconditions, nevertheless in his reply, while agreeing to this conference, de Valera reminded Lloyd George that their respective positions were known and understood. The Irish Cabinet met in preparation for the coming peace talks and, after some discussions, Arthur Griffith, Michael Collins, Edmund J Duggan and George Gavan-Duffy were appointed plenipotentiaries to seek "a treaty or treaties of settlement, association and accommodation, between Ireland and the community of nations known as the British Empire".

De Valera who did not take part in the treaty negotiations signed this authorisation. The reason for this has remained an unanswered question. Several possible theories have been advanced by various commentators, perhaps the most plausible being that he considered that the chances of the negotiations reaching a successful conclusion would be better without his presence, as he had crossed swords with Lloyd George on every occasion on which they had previously met.

However on being shown the letter he had sent in reply to Lloyd George's invitation to the peace conference, the Irish delegates made it clear to de Valera that, if they were to be successful, they must be free to exercise their negotiating powers without interference, insisting that any statements of an inflammatory nature, emanating from de Valera could well imperil any chance of a settlement. De Valera initially refused but, on being reminded that his not-an-inch stance had already proved counterproductive in that it had delayed the calling of the peace conference, he eventually agreed provided that he was kept informed of the progress of the negotiations. In particular he insisted that he should be made aware of all matters of importance before any agreement was reached, and it was therefore agreed that Erskine Childers accompany the Irish delegation as secretary.

Irish historians would have us believe that the members of the Irish delegation were overawed, or intimidated, by their unfamiliar surroundings. Although it is true that they lacked experience of diplomacy, whereas their British counterparts were skilled negotiators, De Valera who, apparently without reference to his Cabinet, contented himself by making provocative statements from Dublin compounded their difficulties.

This placed the Irish plenipotentiaries in an impossible position, for when the more delicate stages of the negotiations were reached and the question of the future function of the British monarch came up for discussion, de Valera issued a strongly worded instruction that "There can be no question of our asking the Irish people to agree to any arrangement which would make them subject to the Crown or demand from them any allegiance to the British King." He ended this message by stating that "If war is the only alternative, we must face it and the sooner the other side is made to realise it the better." This statement angered the Irish delegation and in reply they reminded him of his promise not to interfere with their ability to exercise their negotiating powers, concluding with a request that all future instructions to them should have the written authority of the entire Cabinet.

Yet we are given to believe by Irish chroniclers that Lloyd George was alone in endeavouring to influence the course of the negotiations. Conveniently, however, they overlook the appointment of Erskine Childers as secretary to the delegation. He was clearly de Valera's emissary, sent to ensure that his will would prevail in any decision taken during the talks.

So much did Arthur Griffith distrust Childers that he would not even bother to read the memoranda prepared by him. Robert Barton was persuaded to write them, on Childers' behalf, in order to deceive Griffith. Surprisingly Childers never reported these differences to Dublin, nor did he give de Valera any warning of the delegation's eventual decision.

When the question of partition came up there can be no doubt that Irish delegation's negotiating position had been seriously eroded. Not only had the implementation of the Home Rule Bill now become politically impossible as a result of the 1916 Rising, but following the War of Independence what hope they might have had of securing independence for the whole of Ireland had evaporated because of the situation in the north. The Unionists, who had already rejected home rule, were determined to resist, with force if necessary, any settlement that would see their incorporation in any Independent Irish State. With the Great War over this was no idle threat, for many of them were spoiling for a fight.

It was, in these circumstances that Lloyd George presented what was then the only possible compromise to prevent a war of unimaginable proportions breaking out in Ireland. He proposed the division of the country into two States, with the Free State comprising 26 counties and Ulster, reduced to six counties to ensure that the continuing violence there was confined to the northeast, continuing to be a province of the United Kingdom. At the same time he proposed the creation of a Boundary Commission that could examine the possibility of the gradual reunification of the two parts of the country when the situation in Ulster permitted.

After some discussion a pragmatic decision was taken by the Irish delegation to accept the temporary partition of Ireland. But it was not envisaged by either side that the Boundary Commission would be rendered inoperative by a civil war that would engulf the Free State following the ratification of the treaty in Ireland.

The treaty also provided for tax being levied on British goods by the new Irish State and it was agreed that it would have a share in its own defence, although Britain would be allowed to make use of Ireland's strategic ports in time of war. The Oath of Allegiance was to be modified in such manner that it would eventually become meaningless, other than as a mere matter of form. With these terms agreed the delegates undertook to take the treaty to Dublin for ratification.

On their return from London an angry De Valera confronted them. Erskine Childers, who had absented himself from the final sessions of the conference on the plea that he was indisposed, had not informed him of their decision. Both Cathal Brugha and de Valera demanded to know on whose authority they had accepted the terms without first referring them to Dublin. De Valera in particular was prepared to accept neither partition nor the watered-down form of the Oath of Allegiance. He was convinced that he would secure the support of the Cabinet for his stance, but when it met three of its members were in favour of accepting the treaty while three others were equally opposed to its ratification. This left W T Cosgrave, on whose support de Valera was counting, to ensure its rejection.

However following a stormy meeting between the two men Cosgrave declared his intention of siding with the signatories of the treaty. De Valera, extremely despondent at his failure to carry his Cabinet with him, now fought desperately to find a solution to the problem. Finally on 13 December, the day before the Dáil was due to discuss the ratification of the treaty, he conceived the idea of presenting them with an alternative draft that would ensure the rejection of the one accepted by his delegates. Known as Document 2, it was so hastily prepared that it contained many important omissions, and when he presented it to the Dáil in a secret session it was incomplete. After an unpromising discussion he withdrew it, saying that he would submit a revised text on 4 January. But it was the original defective draft of Document 2 that was released to the press on that date.

Much has been made by republican commentators of the poor reception given to this draft by the newspapers, which they allege to have been anti-Sinn Fein. While this may have been true of some journals, it is interesting to note that one of the most outspoken advocates of the treaty, as negotiated by the Irish delegation, was the Belfast daily nationalist newspaper, and the Church was unanimous in its support for those who counselled its acceptance.

The treaty debates, which were held in the Council Chamber of Trinity College, Dublin, lasted for three weeks, interrupted only by the Christmas holidays. On

7 January the Dáil finally ratified it by 97 votes to 64. De Valera resigned, but not before he made a powerful speech insisting that "The Republic still goes on until the nation has disestablished it." Arthur Griffith succeeded him as President of the Provisional Government of the Free State. The treaty was subsequently endorsed when the people voted by a substantial majority to accept it, first on 18 June 1922 and again the following year, which saw the establishment of Cumann na n'Gael as the main political party of the new state. Public opinion, however, was bitterly divided as were the members of the new Dáil, This led to the growth of two separate armies, one supporting the Free State while the other, or Irregulars as they were then called, demanded a Republic. The spectre of division that had haunted the independence movement ever since its inception was becoming a reality, as daily the situation grew ever more menacing.

CHAPTER 9

The Civil War and the Fascist threat to Ireland

Frantic efforts were made by both Michael Collins and de Valera to avert the coming catastrophe, but in the end their efforts proved to be to no avail. De Valera withdrew his forces to the Four Courts and civil war, which many had foreseen, became inevitable when on 28 June 1922 the Free State army bombarded his headquarters using artillery left behind by the departing British forces.

Nothing short of a miracle could have averted the outbreak of this conflict, which was to drag on, but for a brief ceasefire, until 1926. Such were the disparate factions making up the independence movement, and so great were the tensions between them, that only the War of Independence and the diplomatic skill of de Valera had held them together. But the instability of this alliance was put to the test at the time of the treaty.

To further exacerbate the situation a potentially dangerous ambiguity had arisen, inasmuch as the powers and capabilities of the President had never been clearly defined and it was open to question whether de Valera should be regarded as President of the country or simply of Dáil Eireann. He regarded the former to be the case and consequently felt free to reject the treaty, which he regarded as being invalid as it had been signed without his consent.

Such was the hatred the conflict engendered that some commentators accuse him of fomenting it, while others blame the British, the Free State army or the treaty itself; Irish chroniclers have tended to brush it out of history. However of one thing there can be no doubt: de Valera would have been prepared to do anything to stave off the looming disaster, short of sacrificing what he regarded as an inviolable principle, but the plain fact is that the country, like the army, was split down the middle and he believed that it was facing the establishment of a right-wing dictatorship.

He made a tragic mistake when he withdrew his supporters in the army to set up the Irregulars, based in the Four Courts, for the new Free State government had received an apparently overwhelming mandate from the people, who had voted for the treaty in a general election only 12 days before. In doing so he had misjudged the strength of their support for they had voted for peace, not war, but the shelling of the Four Courts by the Free State forces was the signal for thousands who had endorsed the treaty to switch their allegiance to the Irregulars.

This was to lead to a chain reaction, the repercussions of which were to last to the present day, with the Irregulars and not the men of 1916 becoming the precursors of the IRA, as we know it. Hence the distinction that is made today between the old IRA and the new, which first saw the light of day in 1926. But as the shells rained down on the Four Courts the militants were baying for blood and crying out for action against the 'Free Staters' brother's hand was raised against brother. Michael Collins now replaced Arthur Griffith as President of the Provisional Government and Commander-in-Chief of the Army, for he had more experience, while Cathal Brugha assumed command of the Irregulars. But within two months both men lay dead, Brugha being killed on 5 July during the evacuation of the Hamman Hotel, near Marlborough Street in Dublin, and Collins at Beal na Bliath in County Cork the following month.

The Four Courts surrendered two days after the bombardment took place and a number of prisoners were taken, including Sean Lemass. This was the second time he had been arrested, the first being during the 1916 Rising when, then aged 15, he was caught carrying a rifle. On that occasion he was released, having been cautioned, by the officer in charge, but this time he was not so fortunate and was lucky to escape with his life. The Irregular leaders, however, had escaped to the Hamman Hotel, which served as a temporary headquarters, and when this was attacked they reached safety through the Hamman Street Post Office, which was under the control of Sean Mac Entee.

A few days later their strongholds in Upper O'Connell Street were captured, but nobody of any note was found among the many prisoners taken. Meanwhile Oscar Traynor sent couriers to the country with the aim of raising 10,000 Irregulars for a march on Dublin. Only 100 turned up, but as the war spread like wildfire through the Provinces some hundreds of thousands became engaged on one side or the other.

One of the many notable actions that took place was the siege of Enniscorthy in County Wexford, where some 200 Irregulars attempted to starve the garrison into surrender. As it gathered momentum, the Civil War was to subject the country to a calamity, the evils of which far surpassed any it had suffered during the War of Independence, as the list of executions and reprisals grew ever more staggering. So great was the bitterness it engendered that it became commonplace for each side to execute four prisoners for each one of their own taken. There can be no doubt that the normally fun loving and welcoming Irish people had been brutalised by their experiences at the hands of the Black and Tans and the Auxiliaries.

Some of the worst outrages took place in the southern counties. In Ballyseedy, County Kerry, nine young men were tied to a bomb; only one, who had a miraculous escape, survived. In the same county, according to an eye witness, a successful operation by the Irregulars, in which they inflicted numerous casualties on the Free State forces, earned a terrible retribution when in a follow-up attack the government troops set fire to a barracks in which a number of Irregular prisoners were being held.

Millions of pounds worth of damage was done, particularly to crops and livestock, and before the carnage came to an end, many whose names were household words had been slain by their former comrades. Among their number was Erskine Childers, who was executed by Free State forces on 22 November 1924.

One of the most lasting effects of the Civil War was the emergence of two conflicting versions of the struggle. This is due to its origin being directly linked to the causes of the 1916 Rising, which was precipitated by the adherents of two conflicting, extremist, ideologies. One was nationalist, right wing and fought for the independence of Ireland and against Home Rule; the other was internationalist, left wing and regarded the revolution as a prerequisite to the establishment of a worldwide socialist order.

However Irish historians are perhaps wise to play down the Civil War period of Irish history, for fear of reviving memories of the internecine strife that tore the country apart. Those who do refer to it tend to be so biased by their own experience, or that of their families, as to make an objective analysis extremely difficult, if not impossible. Nevertheless it is possible to give the lie to some of the myths that have been perpetuated and reveal some little-known facts.

Even today there are many who still believe that de Valera was directly responsible for the death of Michael Collins. That this is patently untrue is proved by the account given by Ned Horgan, who took part in the ambush in which Collins was killed. According to him it was prepared on hearing from a scout that a strange lorry, believed to belong to the Free State forces, was approaching his area. On seeing it they opened fire as soon as it came within range, Neither Horgan nor his companions had any idea who was travelling in it and were amazed to find Collins among the dead. Within weeks of the war breaking out Collins, determined to find a way of ending the strife, had arranged to meet de Valera secretly to see if they could find a means of resolving the impasse. But as a result of this incident the Civil War, rather than ending, increased in intensity.

The story of Frank Aiken, which is unique but not generally known, is well worth recounting, particularly in view of the part he was to play in ending the Civil War and the considerable influence he was to have in the evolution of Irish politics. A man of peace, he did not believe that the problems between the two sides were insoluble, and ever since the outbreak of hostilities he had been endeavouring to bring about a truce.

Initially an officer in command of a unit of the Free State forces, he had succeeded in keeping his unit neutral as well as establishing himself as an intermediary by setting up a line of communication between General Mulcahy, who was Minister of

Defence in the Provisional Government, and Cathal Brugha, who was in command of the Irregulars.

Following the attack on the Four Courts he visited the former in an endeavour to persuade him to declare a truce and recall the Dáil. As his efforts proved fruitless he went on to Limerick, where a local ceasefire had been arranged between Commandant General Michael Brennan, who had charge of the Free State forces there, and Liam Lynch, Commander-in-Chief of the Irregulars. But this proved to be short lived and he returned to Dublin only to discover that his own men were under orders from Beggar's Bush Barracks, then the Free State Army Headquarters, to mount an attack on the Irregulars stationed in the neighbourhood.

He called a meeting of his officers and it was decided that they would take no further part in active operations unless the Republicans were first offered an honourable way out of the conflict. He then reported the outcome of these deliberations to General Mulcahy, explaining that it was essential that he retain a neutral stance, or his credibility, as a go-between would be fatally compromised. However some of the latter's entourage suggested his arrest and, it being so ordered, he was taken the following day to Dundalk jail.

While there the Republican prisoners elected him as their spokesman although he was still regarded with some suspicion by the Irregular leaders outside the jail, many of whom felt that he might well be a spy. It was then that he planned and executed a successful jailbreak, which resulted in the freeing of 120 Irregular prisoners. No sooner had this been accomplished than he reorganised them and took part in one of their most vital operations during the Civil War, in which the town of Dundalk was occupied. In a further effort to make peace he called on the people of the town to cease all hostilities, but Free State forces that were sent to recapture the area thwarted this attempt. There can be little doubt, however, that his conciliatory gestures were to have a considerable effect on de Valera's thinking both then and in future years.

It was in September 1922 that de Valera asked Aiken to become a member of the Executive of the Irregular Forces, but true to form he refused unless it was agreed that Sinn Fein set up a civil authority. De Valera demurred at first, but eventually agreed. From that moment a close relationship was established between the two men that was to lead to Aiken's becoming de Valera's closest confidant. This may well have led to the latter's policy of neutrality but, paradoxically, it was Aiken who prompted de Valera's secret support for Britain during World War Two, having been the first to recognise the menace of Fascism in Italy and Nazism in Germany. This threat was confirmed when the Irish Blueshirt movement endeavoured to stage a *coup d'état* in Ireland.

The first fruits of Aiken's influence were to be seen when the political wing of Sinn Fein was revived and a Republican Cabinet formed while elections were held in those areas under their control. However with the continuing unrest they were unable to take part in any decision on a national level and later, when this became possible, many of those eligible refused to take their seats in Dáil Eireann, which they refused to recognise as the national parliament.

Early in 1923 Aiken summoned a meeting to be held in the Nyre Valley of the Comeragh Mountains in County Waterford. This remote location was chosen because many of those invited to attend were men on the run, including members of the Republican Executive and the Republican Cabinet. The meeting lasted from 16 to 23 March and the following motion was proposed: "That, in the opinion of the Executive, further armed resistance and operations against the Free State will not further the independence of the country." As the motion was only defeated by one vote it was decided to adjourn the meeting and reconvene it at a later date.

Meanwhile the Irregulars suffered further setbacks, suffering heavy casualties to their already depleted forces, and only a few hours before the second meeting was due to take place it was discovered that their chosen rendezvous was surrounded by thousands of Free State troops. That morning Liam Lynch, who had become commander of the Irregulars, was killed in a running gun battle and it took eight days for the leaders, aided by members of the Tipperary Brigade, to elude their pursuers and reach safety.

Finally, on April 28, the Executive met at Mullinahone, County Tipperary, and Aiken succeeded Lynch as Chief-of-Staff. It was decided that the Republican Movement should make peace, provided that the other side agreed to the ending of the partition clauses in the treaty. However W T Cosgrave, whose newly formed Cumann na n'Gael party had taken over the civil administration of the state, rejected these terms. Aiken, undeterred, having consulted with de Valera, announced a unilateral ceasefire on 28 May. In July he attempted to bring together the remaining members of the Irish Republican Brotherhood, which had been split in two as a result of the Civil War with the object of disbanding that organisation, but these overtures met with no response and the government continued its mopping up operations against the now hopelessly outnumbered Irregulars, in the course of which de Valera was taken prisoner.

During the ensuing year the government escalated its attacks with a view to wiping out the remaining pockets of resistance, but war weariness was setting in and in 1924 a minor mutiny occurred in the Free State Army. A decision was then taken to call a halt to large-scale operations. De Valera once more found himself a free man when an amnesty followed, but sporadic actions continued to be fought throughout the country. Sinn Fein split when a new radical group was formed that refused to accept the Dáil as the government of the country and announced its intention of continuing to fight against partition.

The situation remained unchanged until 1926, when de Valera announced his intention of breaking with the militants and forming a new republican party, Fianna Fáil, which would enter the Dáil and fight its battles by constitutional means. The reverberations of the Civil War continued for many years, as it became the main factor in politics, particularly in rural areas. In the cities even as late as the 1950s, some deputies continued to go about their business carrying handguns and others, including Dan Breen, employed bodyguards for protection.

Despite the continuing strife, W T Cosgrave's Cumann na n'Gael administration, which had taken over from the Provisional Government in 1923, made considerable strides in building up Ireland's shattered economy. In this he had the aid of an efficient Irish civil service, which he had inherited from the British. On the political front he proceeded carefully with the construction of a new Constitution to ensure that there could be no confusion or possible misinterpretation of the functions of the various bodies and personnel that made up his government, in particular as regards the extent of de Valera's power as President.

Thus provision was made for the creation of the Office of President, as distinct from that of Taoiseach, or Prime Minister, of the Dáil. In 1938 Douglas Hyde following an agreement with De Valera's Fianna Fáil party assumed this function. The judiciary was afforded a special position as distinct from the legislature and Gavan Duffy was given the task of establishing a new Irish police force, the Garda Siochana, or Civic Guards.

The task of rebuilding the economy was daunting for there was a lack not only of managerial but also of engineering skills. Nevertheless by the end of his term in office, Cosgrave was to leave a visible monument of achievement in the form of the Shannon hydroelectric scheme. He did, however, labour under a number of disadvantages from the outset, being faced not only with the continuing strife during the early years of his term, but also its aftermath. Despite the normalisation of politics that had taken place in 1926 with the creation of Fianna Fáil, he was forced to take draconian measures to restore order.

In the same year the murder of Kevin O'Higgins, Minister for Justice, by the newly constituted IRA saw a renewal of civil war passions due to the steps taken to maintain public order. Consequently the IRA became increasingly active and a fascist element among Cumann na n'Gael was soon to make itself evident.

Cosgrave's government was also in some difficulty in his negotiations with Britain to solve the vexed question of partition. He had been cautiously exploring a means whereby the treaty could be used as a means to ensure the fulfilment of the national aspiration to unity but the Civil War had placed an insuperable obstacle in his path. In 1925 the British government had informed him that, due to the continued unrest, in the south they saw no useful purpose in continuing with the Boundary Commission and that it was being wound up.

Cosgrave was innately conservative and it was his failure to make any headway on the question of partition that was to make it possible for de Valera's Fianna Fáil, then in a minority, to gain power in 1931 with the help of votes from the Labour party, led by William Norton, who was to prove invaluable to him over the next 12 months. Meanwhile in 1931 de Valera had established a daily newspaper, *The Irish Press*, in opposition to the more conservative *Irish Independent* and the *Irish Times*. His party then went from strength to strength, making it possible for him to remain in power as the head of a Fianna Fail government for the next 16 years. In the light of all that had occurred the smooth change from vanquished to victor after a hard but cleanly fought election campaign was remarkable. But the early years of de Valera's administration saw it confronted with well-nigh insurmountable economic difficulties that were aggravated by his attempts to unilaterally revoke the provisions of the treaty relating to partition, and further exacerbated by his subsequent refusal to honour the land annuities.

This was followed by the so-called economic war, though it was and still is widely regarded as an act of retaliation by the British government, which was in reality the result of factors affecting world trade. Britain had been badly hit by the world recession in 1929, as a result of which the government had initiated a Buy British campaign. Posters bearing this message appeared throughout the length and breadth of the country, while the Empire closed ranks and pulled together as a single trading block.

As a consequence there was a switch in import policy to member countries that supplied agricultural produce, much of which was formerly sourced in Ireland. The fact that the Buy British campaign coincided with a period when there were strained relations between the Irish and British governments lent credence in Ireland to the belief that an economic war was being waged.

If de Valera had to contend with considerable economic difficulties, these were nothing when compared with the political problems he faced. Like his predecessor he had to grapple not only with the continuing activities of the IRA, following his break with Sinn Fein, but also with a number of militants within his own party. And now a new and even more sinister threat emerged, on this occasion from the right wing Cumann na n'Gael party, with the emergence of the unmistakably fascist Blueshirts.

Organised and led by General Eoin O'Duffy, it was not long before the menace of a new civil war reared its head for O'Duffy was convinced that he had the support of the army. Therefore in 1934 he planned a march on Dublin with the object of staging a *coup d'état* and the overthrow of the elected government.

However in the meantime Frank Aiken, who was Minister for Defence in the Fianna Fáil Cabinet and had been observing with apprehension the rise of European Fascism, set about forging links of mutual trust between the army and the government. Earlier that year he had also established a volunteer force to assist in combating the dual threat posed by Sinn Fein on the one hand and the Blueshirts on the other.

Broadcasting to the nation on Radio Eireann on 24 February that year, he made a strongly worded warning against the fascist threat and appealed for recruits for the new force, which was later to be called the Local Defence Force. He said: "The times we live in are full of violence and confusion. Long-standing governmental institutions are crashing all over the world. Above the wild fury of this upheaval we must keep our heads cool. The threatened fury of these mad and barbarian ideas must be turned back from our shores." Having issued this strong condemnation of the use of force to gain political ends, he concluded by adding: "There is only one way, particularly in our situation, to choose our leaders and our policy and that is by the free vote of the people."

In the event, to the consternation of O'Duffy, the army stood loyally behind the elected government and such was Aiken's success that the threat of a *coup* soon receded. It is interesting to note that the Commander-in-Chief of the army was none other than Michael Brennan, the Commandant General of the former Free State Forces, whose acquaintance Aiken had first made when he was in Limerick on a peace mission.

The government's firm handling of this situation had prevented the IRA from becoming a force of any real importance, but the reality of the fascist threat soon became apparent to de Valera when Blueshirt thugs attempted to break up his own political meetings, and this was to play a decisive role in the shaping of his future policies and actions. He was to become Ireland's representative at the Geneva Conference of the League of Nations, where he exhibited statesmanlike qualities that few had thus far recognised. He established himself as a formidable opponent of European Fascism, as a result of which he was eventually elected President of the League.

In 1935, despite the traditionally friendly association between Ireland and Italy, he called on all nations to support him in his call for sanctions against that country, following Mussolini's invasion of Abyssinia. The following year he was no less forthright in announcing his qualified support for the Spanish government in its struggle against Franco's Phalangists.

When calling for sanctions against Mussolini he spoke for the whole free world and, in exhorting his listeners to take up the same definite attitude, he made an impassioned plea for the Great Powers of the world to come together, ending with the words: "A terrible menace can be warded off by making a tenth of the sacrifice now that would have to be made in the event of war."

This stand greatly enhanced his stature and prestige and, for the first time, he found himself propounding the principle of collective security that had resulted from

THE DOMINIONS OF
THE ANGEVINS

North Sea

ULSTER
Armagh
Dundalk
Drogheda
CONNAUGHT
Dublin
LEINSTER
Limerick
Cashel Wexford
MUNSTER Waterford

Irish Channel

Perth
Stirling
Edinburgh
Alnwye
Newcastle

York

Anglesey
Chester
Newark
WALES
Powys
Leicester

Milford
Gloucester
Oxford
London
Bristol Windsor Rochester Canterbury Bruges
Oaksbury Clarendon Dover
Exeter Southampton Winchester Hastings Calais
Boulogne Flanders Verdun

English Channel

THE EMPIRE
FRANCE

Cherbourg
Havre Harfleur Aumale
Caen Rouen Andeleys
NORMANDY PARIS Champagne Burgundy
Avranches
Brest BRITTANY Dol
Rennes MAINE Le Mans Orleans
Quimper Angers ANJOU Blois
Nantes Tours Touraine
Fontevrault
Chinon Berry
Poitou
Marche
Limoges
Lyons
AQUITAINE Auvergne
C. of
Maurienne
Bordeaux

Bay of

Biscay

GASCONY
Toulouse Arles Avignon
COUNTY OF TOULOUSE Provence
Marseille

Wolfe Tone

Daniel O' Connell

Charles Stewart Parnell

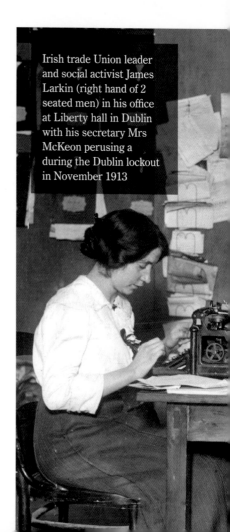

Irish trade Union leader and social activist James Larkin (right hand of 2 seated men) in his office at Liberty hall in Dublin with his secretary Mrs McKeon perusing a during the Dublin lockout in November 1913

Michael Davitt

William Gladstone

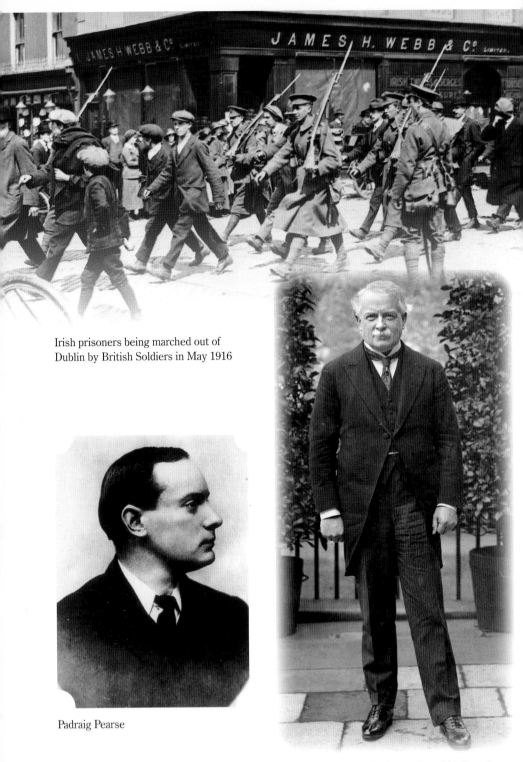

Irish prisoners being marched out of
Dublin by British Soldiers in May 1916

Padraig Pearse

David Lloyd George in the garden of 10 Downing
Street in October1922

Meeting of Sinn Fein delegates led by Michael Collins (seated centre) at the Anglo Irish treaty negotiations in London. Other people in the picture are: J.Chateris, Gavan Duffy (bearded), Erskine Childers, RC Barton (seated left), EJ Duggan and Arthur Griffiths (seated far right), October 1921

Eamon de Valera leaving 10 Downing Street in London after signing the Anglo-Irish Trade Agreement in April 1938

Sean Lemass centre, Frank Aiken (head bent right) (Photograph Courtesy of The Irish Times)

Sean Macbride (Photograph Courtesy of The Irish Times)

Jack Lynch (Photograph Courtesy of The Irish Times)

Garrett Fitzgerald (Photograph Courtesy of The Irish Times)

Charles Haughey with
Margaret Thatcher,
May 1980

IRA
sympathisers
supporting
hunger
striker Bobby
Sands, during
a march in
May 1981,
London

The Irish Council state meeting group December 2004 back row Fr L to R, Albert Reynolds, Enda Marren, Professor Denis Moloney, T.A.Finlay, Mary Davis , Anastasia Crickley, Senator Martin Mansergh, Dr Garrett Fitzgerald, Ronan C. Keane , John Bruton, Colonel Harvey Bicker, Daraine Mulvihill and Liam Cosgrave. front row Mary Robinson, Rory Kiely (Cathaoirleach) Rory O'Hanlon (Ceann Comhairle) Mary Harney (Tanaiste) , Taoiseach Bertie Ahern, President Mary McAleese, Justice chief Justice Murray, President of High Court Justice Finnegan, Attorny General Rory Brady and Patrick Hillery

Bertie Ahern with
Brian Cowan

a British initiative. However though he had the backing of Britain and France, the other Great Powers turned a deaf ear to this proposition and it was this that made him decide that, in the conditions of the 1930s, small nations such as Ireland had no option but to remain neutral. Nevertheless he never regarded neutrality as a pious aspiration or an end in itself, but simply as a matter of necessity in the circumstances. Later however, under pressure from his own Fianna Fáil party, he included a clause in his 1937 Constitution providing for neutrality.

The new situation dictated a change in de Valera's policy. While not diluting any of his demands, unlike many of his own supporters, he was no longer prepared to adopt an anti-British stance as a matter of principle. Thus when King Edward VIII abdicated in 1936 many in Ireland regarded it as an ideal opportunity to set up an All Ireland Republic, thereby overturning the 1921 treaty. But to the surprise of some and the consternation of others de Valera chose to use the situation to achieve a compromise designed to ensure that Ireland remained within the Commonwealth.

This was enshrined in his External Relations Act, which reads as follows: "It is hereby declared and enacted that so long as Saorstat Eireann is associated with the following nations, that is to say Australia, Canada, Great Britain, New Zealand and South Africa, and so long as the King, recognised by those nations as the symbol of their cooperation, continues to act on behalf of each of those nations (on the advice of the several governments thereof) for the appointment of diplomatic and consular representatives and the conclusion of international agreements, the King so recognised may and is hereby authorised to act on behalf of Saorstat Eireann for the like purpose, as advised by the Executive Council so to do."

A great step forward in Anglo Irish relations, this Act was the cause of considerable controversy at home. Nonetheless he succeeded in overcoming criticism, no doubt due to the fact that he had achieved a steady, though restricted, programme of social and economic reform despite the world recession and his star was on the rise.

Meanwhile the opposition party in the Dáil, Cumann na n'Gael, formed the basis of a new political party that emerged with the title Fine Gael. This organisation was very much inclined to the right and originally included the remnants of the Blueshirt movement as well as a number of independent deputies. In later years it became responsible for the foundation for the recovery of the economy, which had been destroyed by the Civil War. Meanwhile both main political parties became involved in auction politics, at election times, which resulted in tax and spend policies that led to the country being on the verge of ruin by the late 1950s.

Following de Valera's anti-fascist stance in Europe and his siding against Catholic Italy, as well as those whom his opponents regarded as the saviours of Catholicism in Spain, a determined attempt was made to influence the Church against him. This could have been a serious threat as he was regarded with ill-concealed dismay by various members of the hierarchy, some of who went so far as to express the view that he had gone soft on communism. De Valera, however, immediately set about assuaging their fears by promulgating his 1937 Constitution, which remained unaltered for many years.

This pragmatic move, designed to silence his critics, was a masterpiece of diplomacy as a clause was inserted that afforded a special position to the Catholic Church. On the face of it he had created a Catholic State for a Catholic people, but this was unavoidable given the circumstances and, with the ending of the Cold War between the USSR and the West, this section was deleted in 1972 after a referendum.

Among other provisions in the Constitution was one concerning the right to own private property, in order to counteract the fears expressed by some that he might embark on a socialist agenda. Subsequently it was used on to protect unscrupulous land speculators on the one hand, and on the other by local interests to obstruct the construction of vital infrastructure by involving the state in costly litigation regarding planning permission. Nevertheless this Constitution succeeded in its objective of reassuring de Valera's critics.

They were finally confounded in 1938 when he met the British Prime Minister, Neville Chamberlain, and secured an agreement that not only revoked Clause 7 of the 1921 treaty, which afforded Britain the right to use Irish ports in time of war, but also wrote off the Land Annuity debts and reaffirmed Ireland's position as a full trading partner.

While the negotiations were taking place, however, the IRA did everything in its power to disrupt them and prevent any possibility of an accord. Bombs were placed under railway bridges in London in an endeavour to stir up public opinion against Ireland, but as the clouds of war between Britain and Nazi Germany gathered de Valera kept in constant contact with London. He had made up his mind on a definite course of action in the event of war but, remembering what he had experienced during the treaty negotiations, he decided to tread warily as he could not trust his own people with the exception of a few chosen confidants.

CHAPTER 10

De Valera's War against Fascism

It has often been said of de Valera, by those who did not know him well, that he was a very aloof man. It would be truer to say that he was very lonely and that his apparent detachment was due to the fact that, unlike most of his contemporaries, he fully appreciated the significance of the events that were taking place abroad and the potential menace of the Nazi threat to Ireland. But, being a pragmatist, he realised that the course on which he was about to embark could never become known if he were to survive politically.

He was in a unique position to evaluate the threat posed by Hitler as he had had experience of the operations of fascists in his own country. They had been a mainstay of the opposition and he had seen his own political rallies broken up by Blueshirt rowdies in much the same way as Hitler's Brownshirts had dealt with their opponents.

The 1930s had seen the world paralysed by the threat of Soviet Communism to the extent that a blind eye had been turned and even tacit approval given to the activities of Hitler, Mussolini and Franco. The Roman Catholic Church, among others, had been prepared to give active support to the fascists, as they seemed to be the only bulwark against a system that had persecuted its priests and destroyed its churches.

However, de Valera had learnt from his diplomatic experience that the non-aggression pact signed between Nazi Germany and the Soviet Union had, in all probability, been entered into by Hitler in order to enable him to unleash his European war of conquest. In any event the two 'isms' were equally evil. Later his assumption was to be proved correct when, without warning, Germany invaded the USSR.

Following his discussions with Chamberlain, his mind was made up on the course he had to take. But criticism of his policies had reached its peak in 1936 when General O'Duffy had sent his Blueshirts to Spain to fight for Franco with the blessing of the Church. De Valera had become aware that many of his own supporters were to be found in the International Brigade, which was made up of social democrats as well as communists pledged to defend the Spanish Government.

This had also confirmed the suspicions of his opponents that he had gone soft on Communism and led to the promulgation of his 1937 Constitution, with its provision for Irish neutrality. This was another stroke of genius for while neutrality might apply to a dispute between two foreign nations, de Valera never intended that the state should stand idly by in the event of a threat to its integrity, which would almost certainly occur should Britain be invaded. Nevertheless it appeared to be a sop to Hitler.

This proved useful, for in the highly charged atmosphere neither he nor the Irish Government could be seen to side openly with Britain. As well as part of the IRA there was a sizeable body of opinion in Ireland that was sympathetic to the Nazis and, in the event of an invasion they would have provided a formidable fifth column, little realising that this would have seen the destruction of the Irish State and the imposition of a dictatorship.

Above all he decided that not only his opponents but also his own Fianna Fáil Party must be kept in the dark as to his intentions. Although the party had a reputation of unswerving loyalty to its leader, had his plans been leaked the ensuing dissention would have be such that not only would weeks of careful planning be undone but also the very future of Ireland as a nation would be imperilled. Furthermore his experience during the treaty negotiations had taught him that he would have to act with only a few carefully chosen confidants if Ireland was to be saved from Hitler's plan to dominate Europe.

When World War Two broke out in September 1939 he therefore took immediate steps to counteract this menace from within and without by invoking the Offences against the State Act. This gave the army and the police wide powers to arrest and search the homes of IRA supporters and their Blueshirt colleagues. Action against both groups was confined, at any rate initially, to surveillance, but meanwhile selected officers were sent to England to be trained by MI.5. This led to the creation of the highly efficient Intelligence and Counter Espionage Service, known as G2, which was made up entirely of Irish personnel under the command of Captain Liam Archer. This was to act later in collaboration with Captain Grieg, the British naval attaché

Such was the efficiency of this organisation that when de Valera initiated a full-scale crack down on the IRA most of its leaders found themselves behind bars and their replacements proved to be more of a liability than an asset to the German Abwehr, due to their clumsy attempts to pass on information to German spies operating in Ireland and Britain. This led to the interception and arrest of more than a few key German personnel by G2 as well as MI5 and, by 1940 the IRA bombing campaign in Britain had been brought to an end.

It had never occurred to the German spies operating in Ireland that they had anything to fear from de Valera or that anything unusual was taking place, due to his government's much publicised refusal to accede to Britain's request to expel Dr Hempel, the German Ambassador. However the newly formed G2 was given strict instructions to keep a strict watch on the embassy and it was not long before it unearthed sufficient evidence to give the Irish government legitimate grounds to protest about the use to which it was being put. Consequently not only were the embassy's telephone links to the continent cut off, but its short-wave transmitter was seized. The excuse was made to the embassy that similar action was being taken against all the belligerent nations, whereas this was in fact not the case.

Thus, unknown to the embassy, G2 mounted an offensive that effectively neutralised the entire German espionage network in Ireland. When Winston Churchill replaced Chamberlain as Britain's wartime Prime Minister, it was arranged that he and de Valera would begin a war of words to cover his activities. Consequently, when he repeated his predecessor's demand to the Irish government, that Hempel be expelled, he knew full well that the subsequent rejection would dispel any lingering doubt in the German Ambassador's mind as to Ireland's neutrality.

In August 1940, following the loss of France and the British withdrawal from Dunkirk, General Leonard Kaupisch, who had charge of the fourth and seventh German Army Corps, was ordered to prepare for the invasion of Ireland, an amphibious landing being envisaged as a diversionary tactic while plans were finalised for the invasion of England. This would result in Britain being isolated having been cut off from any supplies it was receiving from America, and she could be starved into submission in the event of her failing to capitulate.

The proposed military occupation of Ireland, codenamed Fall Grun, made provision for an initial force of 3,900 men to set out from the French ports of St Nazaire, Lorient and Nantes to establish a bridgehead between Wexford and Dungarvan. This was to include Panzer and other motorised units as well as infantry and artillery. Meanwhile a meeting of the newly formed Werwirmachtshaftstab England (English Military Economic Staff) took place at the beginning of September and Dublin was featured as one of the six proposed German administrative headquarters to be established once the invasion of the two islands had been completed. It was intended that the invasion of Ireland begin just prior to the assault on Britain, which would be preceded by heavy air raids on London and other cities. However while it was expected that the British might try and resist, the subjugation of Ireland was thought to be a foregone conclusion.

Both De Valera and Churchill had anticipated this very situation as early as the spring of 1940. Consequently on 24 May the first of a number of top-secret meetings took place in London between Captain Archer, Joseph Walshe and a number of British Navy, Army and Air Force commanders, at which it was agreed that direct liaison between Dublin, London and the General Officer Commanding in Northern Ireland be established immediately. That afternoon Archer and Walshe, together with Lieutenant-Colonel Dudley-Clarke, a military adviser, flew to Belfast in Churchill's private aircraft for talks with Sir Hubert Huddlestone.

This was followed by two further meetings that took place in a conference room under government buildings in Dublin's Kildare Street. Arrangements were made for the Irish and British forces to fight shoulder to shoulder to repel any attempt by the Germans to invade Ireland. Such was the secrecy surrounding these meetings that not only did the military personnel attending them travel in mufti, but they made use of an underground passage to reach the room set aside for the conference. General Mac Kenna explained the delicate political situation in Ireland and it was agreed that the British would hold back until the eleventh hour, when it had become clear that an attack was imminent and that the German invasion force had been assembled in preparation for the landings.

Meanwhile the relevant Irish army commanders would be warned of such an eventuality. It was arranged that any initial German thrust in the southeast would be engaged by General Michael Costello's 1st Division, stationed in Cork and the 2nd Division, under General Hugo Mac Neill. On receipt of a signal the British forces stationed in the North would cross the border and race to the aid of the Irish troops defending Dublin. In the interim G2 would endeavour to identify any subversives, IRA or otherwise, and make arrangements for their arrest if need be.

Only four days after the evacuation of the British Expeditionary Force from Dunkirk, the instructions given to General Laupitch were revealed in reports emanating from espionage agents operating in Germany and the Irish army was placed on the alert to repel any invasion from whatever quarter. An air raid warning system, which had already been installed, was updated. The previous system, although it had been recently augmented by an emergency military radio, had relied on a telephone call from England.

On 21 June Churchill sent Malcolm Mac Donald to Dublin as his special emissary to discuss the unfolding situation with de Valera. It was then that the first suggestion was made to solve the problem of partition and establish a united Ireland that would continue, in normal circumstances, to remain non-belligerent and whose integrity would be guaranteed jointly by Britain and America. However this proposition proved impractical due to the refusal of the American government to agree to send military aid to Ireland should it be necessary.

All this was to change the following year with the Japanese attack on Pearl Harbour. Later Churchill had to intervene to restrain the Americans, who were anxious to invade Ireland in order to make use of its ports during the Battle of the Atlantic. Mac Donald then suggested that there should in principle be a United Ireland and that it should enter the war on the side of the Allies. De Valera might have favoured this plan but he realised that it would mean taking his Cabinet into his confidence. He also doubted that he could persuade them to take this course unless a Constitution for a United Ireland were first drawn up and published by both governments.

Mac Donald could well understand de Valera's difficulty and suggested that they go ahead with the preparation of a constitutional framework. Any such proposition was fraught with difficulties, not the least being the attitude of Lord Craigavon, the Prime Minister of Northern Ireland. In view of the possible dissention that might arise, it was decided not to proceed when the paramount interest of both Ireland and Britain was the successful prosecution of the war against Hitler.

It was then that a secret pact was made with Churchill to devise a scheme whereby Ireland could play a vital role in winning the war while maintaining all the outward appearance of non-belligerence. It was also agreed to send troops to Ireland's assistance should its role result in any danger to the country. It all meant that cordial relations were established between the two men, who were to meet on a number of occasions.

This pact was one of the best kept secrets of the war and this state was preserved by public utterances that were aimed at protecting de Valera from the wrath of his electorate should the truth become known. Naturally security dictated that the people be kept unaware of German plans to invade Ireland. Nevertheless as the British, with the backing of America, gradually recovered their military strength and succeeded in fighting off the German air offensive, increased provision was made for the protection of Ireland. During the next year stringent precautions were introduced to protect the Irish coastline, for although the danger of invasion had receded there were several false alarms caused by low-flying German reconnaissance aircraft. In March 1940 a plane flying over Dublin came under heavy anti-aircraft fire, while another that crash-landed was found to be carrying photographic equipment. It is a matter of conjecture whether the bombing of Dublin's North Strand was accidental or – as appears more likely – that it was a reprisal for Irish attacks on German aircraft overflying the country.

Meanwhile Captain Archer had been promoted from the command of G2 to the position of Chief of Staff of the Irish Army. At G2 he was replaced by two men, Dan Bryan and Richard Hayes, whose expertise in deciphering codes was to result in the organisation becoming one of the most efficient intelligence gathering organisations in the world. Initially the brief of G2 had been to watch the west coast to ensure that no spies were landed from the U-boats operating in the area, but this role became extended to plotting the positions of enemy submarines, which made a habit of surfacing there, as they felt free from attack.

During the Battle of the Atlantic this task was taken over by General Archer when he was still at G2, and instructions were given to the Western Command to monitor U-boat movements and report to him. This information was relayed direct to the British Admiralty, enabling it to sink countless German submarines and helping to secure the Atlantic Corridor, without the Germans being any the wiser as to how their positions had been discovered.

The Americans, who were not aware of the part that Ireland was playing, were becoming restive and anxious to force the issue of the Irish ports. But Churchill, who was more than satisfied and of the opinion that Ireland's apparently neutral role had proved of infinitely more value than any overt action, refused to sanction anything that could endanger his secret collaboration with de Valera.

Meanwhile many thousands of Irishmen had joined the British forces, with some becoming household names. One such was Paddy Finucane, a Kerryman, who was not only awarded the DSO but also the DFC with two bars and was one of the heroes of the Battle of Britain. When he eventually met his death, having taken on hopeless odds, this greatest of all fighter pilots was mourned by the entire British nation, in particular the people of London, where flags were lowered to half mast.

As D-day approached, arrangements were made for the Allied Commanders to make use of the Irish meteorological services to ensure the most accurate weather forecast for this hazardous operation. As it turned out, without this cooperation the Normandy landings could well have ended in disaster. In addition de Valera gave his approval for close liaison between G2 and the American secret services and two Americans joined Colonel Bryan's staff to ensure that every loophole in the intelligence chain was closed.

When the war ended, de Valera kept up the façade of neutrality by making a courtesy call to the German Embassy to express his condolences on the death of Hitler. This has often been misrepresented but was simply a shrewd move to gauge public opinion for he knew that many, including a majority of his own supporters, still harboured pro-German sympathies. Anything less would only have added to the suspicion, which was beginning to grow, that some of his actions had been anything but neutral. Nevertheless it was necessary for him to test the temperature before putting into action his plans to arrest and deport all German internees wanted by the Allies for questioning.

In the Irish media the reaction to this visit was positive. On the other side of the water, where the public were wholly unaware of de Valera's lone stance against Hitler's Germany, the reaction was understandably hostile. In these circumstances de Valera contacted Churchill, who was planning to make a broadcast expressing his appreciation of the part that Ireland had played in the winning of the Battle of the Atlantic, and explained that any admission of de Valera's role in the British war effort would be disastrous to him.

Churchill, who was every bit as devious as de Valera, realised that the only way of preserving the Taoiseach's political integrity was to continue with the war of words that they had used so successfully to give the appearance Irish neutrality. He therefore broadcast a scathing denunciation of de Valera, for they were both aware that any praise coming from him would put an end to the delicate behind-the-scenes negotiations between them on the question of Irish unity.

A general election was in the offing in both countries and prudence dictated that they keep up the appearance of antagonism until they were both safely returned to office. However both men were surprisingly defeated in the ensuing contests and their carefully laid plans, which were to have seen Churchill's announcement of his government's intention to introduce legislation that would pave the way for a united Ireland, were thwarted by both incoming governments.

No one had suspected a wartime pact with England. The only existence of such an alliance was contained in the reply to a question in the House of Commons when, in typical British understatement, Emrys Evans the British Undersecretary of State for Dominions, stated that there were "no grounds for suggesting that the Irish Government has committed un-neutral acts to Britain's disadvantage".

Nevertheless it soon became clear how thin the ice was on which de Valera had been treading; some of his more draconian, though necessary, wartime measures were now being brought into question in Ireland. Not only had his government interned the Blueshirts and the IRA but also he had ordered the execution of a number of members of the latter organisation. Considerable retrospective sympathy now made itself felt and public opinion began to swing against him. This manifested itself in the growth of a number of new political parties, chief among which was Clann na Poblachta, an ultra-republican left-wing organisation led by Sean Mac Bride, who had formerly been Chief of Staff of the IRA. Unlike Sinn Fein, however, this party was committed to pursuing its aims by peaceful means.

Unswerving supporters of Tone's dictum that England's difficulty was Ireland's opportunity, Clann na Poblachta were insistent that aid should have been given to Germany during the war. With their strong appeal for the immediate ending of partition and the severance of all remaining links with England, they soon began to make serious inroads into the support for de Valera's Fianna Fáil party.

While they were not in a position to form a government on their own, they joined ranks with the right wing Fine Gael party and, when the government fell in 1948, became a powerful constituent of the first Inter-Party Government under John A Costello. The main achievement of this administration was in the field of health but one of its first acts, under pressure from its Clann na Poblachta wing, was the introduction of legislation to repeal de Valera's carefully worded External Relations Act, designed to keep Ireland in the Commonwealth, and replace it with the Republic of Ireland Act (1949). This finally severed all remaining links with the British Crown and declared Ireland's status as a Sovereign Republic outside the Commonwealth. In so doing they rendered the achievement of a united Ireland that much difficult, but the

Act itself might not have proved such a barrier had it not been for the fiery rhetoric that accompanied it.

Clement Atlee, the British Labour Prime Minister, responded by enacting the Government of Ireland Act in the same year, in order to reassure the Unionist majority in Northern Ireland that Britain would not countenance any attempt to coerce them into a united Ireland. In Ireland this was seen as the permanent enshrinement of partition and resulted in an all-party, anti-partition campaign. Internationally the effect was insignificant. Nonetheless the concept of collective security, which de Valera had propounded so successfully prior to the war, was replaced by a refusal to consider joining NATO unless the six counties of Ulster were re-united with the remainder of the country. The main effect of this decision was to encourage the IRA to resume their attacks against the border.

In 1951 the Inter-Party Government fell from office over the Mother and Child scheme, introduced by Minister for Health Dr Noel Browne. It was a bold and imaginative plan aimed at introducing a National Health Service, but it was strongly resisted by the medical profession, which regarded it as being the beginning of socialised medicine. Costello decided to consult the Archbishop of Dublin to seek his support for the proposed legislation, but he too declared his opposition to it unless provision was made for a means test.

This case became a *cause célèbre*, inasmuch as it appeared that there had been direct interference by the Catholic Church in the government's conduct of affairs, but in fairness to the Church it should be stressed that Costello had invited this intervention. However as a result Mac Bride forced Costello to demand Noel Browne's resignation and the government went to the country.

Clann na Poblachta was annihilated at the ensuing election, for already an outcry had been caused following the revelation of the horrors of the Nazi concentration camps and their mass genocide of the Jews as well as others. Consequently the people had become increasingly alienated by the party's pro-German sympathies.

De Valera was returned to power and immediately set about repairing the damage that had been done to Anglo-Irish relations by the previous administration. His thinking on European defence had already been spelled out in a speech he made in Sligo on 20 May 1945, on the occasion of his receiving the Freedom of that city. He told his audience: "We must set about placing our defences on as solid and permanent foundation as we can and must never allow a crisis like that of September 1939 to come upon us without being prepared to meet it quickly and with all the energy that the nation can assemble."

In furtherance of this policy de Valera sent Aiken to London to discuss the strengthening of Ireland's anti-aircraft defences, but before these negotiations could be completed, his age, coupled with the fact that he was now almost blind, forced him to retire from active politics. Of particular significance was the first public announcement by Winston Churchill, made during a speech in Washington in 1952, that he favoured the creation of a united Ireland despite the actions that had surrounded its withdrawal from the Commonwealth by the Inter-Party Government. It was Churchill, also, who successfully overcame fierce resistance by Soviet Russia to Ireland's admission to the United Nations.

However, the damage had been done and ever since successive Irish governments have made neutrality the cornerstone of their foreign policy. They have also remained oblivious to the fact that such a stance, like freedom, can only be bought at the price of eternal vigilance, which entails the provision of a defence mechanism capable of repelling any potential invader.

De Valera's contribution to Ireland had been enormous. As well as his achievements abroad, his successive administrations had made steady progress towards revitalising the domestic economy. It is not generally appreciated that prior to 1931 Ireland had been a net importer of dairy produce. Indeed, in that year the agricultural sector had sunk to such a low ebb that the country was importing more bacon than it was exporting. When the Fianna Fáil party was returned to power in 1932 one of its first actions was to take steps to redress this situation and others affecting farm incomes. The success of the administration's policies can best be judged from the statistics.

In 1932 only 20,000 acres were devoted to wheat production, but within two years this figure had been trebled and 10 years later stood at 480,000 acres. A tillage drive was initiated and agricultural grants were doubled. Large-scale peat production was commenced and a sugar beet industry was developed. The results of this policy speak for themselves. Between 1932 and 1942 the acreage under tillage increased from 1,425,000 to 2, 424,000 acres and during the same period sugar beet production rose from 5,012 to 80,000 acres, sufficient to keep three new factories in full-time production and supply the entire home market with sugar.

The emphasis placed by de Valera on the need to increase agricultural output has led some to come to the erroneous conclusion that he was oblivious of the requirements of the urban areas. While it is true that priority was given to establishing a solid foundation for an agricultural economy, he was acutely aware of the needs of all his people, particularly those living in the cities. His successive administrations concentrated on the provision of new housing to replace the slums, augmenting the health services, considerably increasing old-age pensions and introducing a system of widows and orphans pensions.

Today it is difficult to visualise the plight of the needy in the 1930s. It was such that when de Valera first came to power he found it necessary to introduce a system of free food vouchers, free fuel and even free boots to supplement the unemployment benefit. De Valera was a controversial figure throughout his political life. An idealist he was subjected to much unwarranted criticism by the ill informed, but what errors he may have made were far surpassed by his service to Ireland. On his retirement in 1959 he was elected President – a well-merited distinction from a grateful people. Sean Lemass, who showed great promise as a junior minister and had been selected as Tánaiste by De Valera, succeeded him as Taoiseach.

CHAPTER 11

After De Valera

Lemass's administration is best remembered in terms of the industrial progress he initiated. As this took shape and more people found themselves in much needed employment, his government enjoyed an upsurge in popularity, as Ireland appeared to have entered a new era of prosperity. Prior to his coming to power Ireland's economy had relied to a large extent on state subsidies. As an economist Lemass realised that this would lead to stagnation and that sustained growth could only be obtained by the injection of private capital. Ever since his appointment by de Valera as Minister for Industry and Commerce, he had introduced bold and imaginative schemes. Some were later to attract severe criticism regarding the operation and make-up of the boards controlling them.

The Fianna Fáil party then consisted of a left and a right wing, so his elevation to the position of Taoiseach was welcomed equally by the trade unions and venture capitalists. He set out to unite the party by maximising support from both factions. In order to placate the left he established a network of semi-state enterprises; granting monopolies to such large, privately owned companies as Cement Roadstone Limited, assuaged the misgivings of the right. But his greatest achievement in the economic field was the establishment of Aer Lingus, the state-owned national airline; an initiative that was greeted enthusiastically by all.

He then set out to achieve maximum industrialisation, in order to provide the optimum employment, in continuation of a programme he had begun prior to becoming Taoiseach. He extended the number of semi-state companies and enticed foreign investors to set up in Ireland with promises of grants, tax concessions and an abundance of cheap labour. As more jobs were created, the popularity of his government grew. However a note of warning had been sounded earlier regarding the creation and management of some of the new public sector undertakings.

This was contained in a report by the Commission on Vocational Organisation, which complained that some of the Corporations or Boards that had been established were "merely notional or fictitious companies, in which the State has the sole controlling interest, while others are incorporated under the Provident and Friendly Societies Acts". The report then went on to state that "in many of these companies, the possibility of profit is so remote as to preclude the investment of capital by the public". In other words the public was being forced to support these companies through exchequer grants. The report continued with a damning submission relating to some of the personnel on these Boards, stating that political pull or party affiliation, rather than ability to do the job, appeared to be the main qualification for those seeking senior appointments.

This criticism was well founded, for in the 1950s and 1960s, so tough was the competition for such coveted positions that it became the practice for those seeking preferment to elicit the intervention of their elected representatives, who were more often than not members of the party in government, in support of their applications. The exposure of this political patronage revealed that the corruption that had been endemic since before the foundation of the State was alive and well.

The benefits that had accrued from the introduction of a mixed economy, while undoubtedly benefiting a sizeable minority, had resulted in the rich becoming richer while the poor grew poorer. This situation was aggravated by Lemass's promise of an "abundance of cheap labour" to those industrialists who proposed to set up in Ireland. It was further exacerbated by the emergence of a group representing the nouveau riche, as the private sector became ever more dominant. The results soon became evident in the corruption of the body politic itself.

Both the main parties had been forced to look outside their membership for financial support and, as the private sector increased, the main opposition party, Fine Gael, had been forced to vie with Fianna Fáil for the same source of finance. But as both parties developed similarly right wing polices, though maintaining their ideological differences, the politics of promise became predominant in local and national election campaigns.

In the past the electorate had tended to select candidates, within the party of their choice, who were local personalities. This resulted in the creation of a Dáil made up of doctors, publicans and prominent members of the GAA, whose prowess on the playing field, with one or two notable exceptions, was not reflected by their political acumen. Now, the electorate had Hobson's choice at the polls as the gap between the policies of Fianna Fáil and Fine Gael narrowed.

This was to result in both the main parties engaging in shameless horse-trading for votes, and in later years even resorting to buying the support of their natural opponents when the result of a major contest appeared to be in doubt. This was done by agreeing to include some aspect of the opposition's policy in their own programme for government, whether or not it was sustainable. Successive administrations became increasingly vulnerable to powerful pressure groups representing outside interests, not to mention the involvement of senior politicians with big business interests.

While a Labour party had existed since the foundation of the State, it had failed to make the best use of what opportunities presented themselves. Fragmented between social democrats and more doctrinaire socialists, though later it severed links with the latter, it finally lost whatever chance it might have had by entering into a coalition arrangement with Fine Gael. In addition the careful distinction that had been made in the Constitution between the Executive and the Judiciary had to some extent been eroded, because the government appointed the latter and, all too often, those elevated to the bench owed their preferment to their party affiliation. There is no doubt, though, that most Irish Judges carried out their duties in an even-handed manner.

De Valera, who had effectively been removed from the political arena by virtue of his office as President, was powerless to intervene. Those succeeded him set about prostituting the provisions relating to private property that he had so painstakingly drafted when preparing his 1937 Constitution. Time was to prove that the social doctrine enunciated by Pearse in his Declaration of Independence was to become as meaningless as the Democratic Programme produced by the First Dáil.

The next three decades were to witness the establishment of laissez-faire capitalism at its worst. This in turn was to see the growth of an equally unscrupulous and self-serving trade union movement. Provided that its members themselves were in receipt of a comfortable income, many were not prepared to take up issues on behalf of the lower paid. Labour unrest became commonplace and the country was from time to time paralysed by strikes, a high proportion of which were unofficial.

Lemass had succeeded in achieving his main aim of bringing both industry and employment to Ireland, but the price that had to be paid due to his failure to heed the advice of the Commission on Vocational Organisation was to result in unrestricted private enterprise, although this did not immediately become apparent. His government continued to enjoy popular support as it was unforeseen that the very momentum of its achievements would lead to an era of exploitation, and that future generations would be faced with economic disaster.

Meanwhile the immediate effects began to be felt by the poorer sections of the community living in the cities. Faced with exploitation and the return of landlordism they had no one to turn to. Tenants Associations were formed but these, unlike the Land League that had been founded by Michael Davitt to curb the worst excesses of the British landlords, had no power to protect their members from the ravages of the new Rachmanism. Although the League was reactivated by small farmers it had little or no political muscle, as they tended to support one or other of the smaller parties that pledged to protect their interests and thus posed no threat to the establishment.

This resulted in increased support for Fianna Fáil, to which many trade unionists still looked to further their interests in view of that party's erstwhile left-wing tendencies and Lemass's commitment to the establishment of public sector enterprises. In years to come Fianna Fáil endeavoured to increase its hold over the trade unions through the introduction of a number of National Wage Agreements, but while these bought industrial peace, the differentials built into them simply lead to leapfrogging. When a well-deserved pay rise was given to workers in a lower-paid sector, a similar percentage increase was given to every salary earner irrespective of their income. This was reflected in the cost of living and those who applied for the original increase were back where they started. As prices grew, the cycle of wages chasing prices began all over again. Ireland finally priced itself out of the market, resulting in the economic crash of the 1980s.

While the country enjoyed a period of industrial peace, the underlying problem of labour unrest remained unresolved. This was reflected in ever-increasing pay awards that were passed on to the consumer, resulting in spiralling costs and renewed wage demands. It could be said that Ireland's current problems – though they can be attributed to the negative attributes of the globalisation that resulted in Ireland, like other countries throughout the world, being affected by the high-risk strategy adopted by the banking and financial corporations, particularly in the USA – was also due to other factors that are entirely home made, including the actions of speculators and the dishonest politicians with whom they were involved.

Lemass, by failing to take heed of the warnings issued by the Commission on Vocational Organisations, had unwittingly laid the way for the corruption to follow. While his economic policy saw the beginnings of a new prosperity in Ireland through the introduction of a vibrant free-enterprise sector, no steps were taken to control the misuse of this freedom. Instead of enjoying steady progress, Ireland was to be subject to long periods of boom followed by painful recessions.

There can be no question that Lemass had Ireland's best interests at heart, but he lacked his predecessor's wisdom and foresight. This was to lead him to make a number of basic errors, as his judgement appears to have been impaired by his anxiety to make progress. This was demonstrated by the events surrounding his much heralded visit to Captain Terence O'Neill, Prime Minister of Northern Ireland, whom he had previously met when Ireland had been invited to send a representative to attend Commonwealth conferences, following de Valera's return to office on the defeat of the Inter-Party Government.

As a result of discussions between them, Lemass had been invited to a private meeting in the North. This might well have brought about a historic breakthrough for there can be little doubt that O'Neill had been impressed by the Irish government's decision to send a fleet of fire engines to the North, during the War, following a particularly vicious air raid on Belfast. A veil of secrecy had surrounded the preparations for this meeting, due to the tense political situation, but on his return Lemass was convinced that he was on the verge of an agreement and could not restrain himself from announcing that the conference had taken place. This sudden revelation and the attendant publicity it generated undoubtedly contributed to O'Neill's downfall, but had the meeting remained secret it might well have served to initiate a dialogue with the Northern administration.

While Lemass is still remembered in terms of the industrial progress he initiated, during his term in Office, by far the most lasting achievement of his administration was that of his Minister for Foreign Affairs, Frank Aiken who conceived and piloted the Nuclear non-Proliferation Treaty (1961) through the General Assembly of the United Nations. It greatly lessened the risk of a thermo-nuclear world war and became the basis of future negotiations between the Great Powers, in particular between the USA and Soviet Russia, which were to end in an agreement that paved the way towards the end of the Cold War. Like de Valera before him, Aiken was to become a statesman of world stature and make Ireland's voice respected among the nations.

Jack Lynch, who succeeded Sean Lemass, pursued the same policy as his predecessor. Undoubtedly one of the most upstanding men to have held the office of Taoiseach, he was hugely popular. Unfortunately his very popularity and innate decency was the source of his greatest weakness and was to result in his downfall, for he was surrounded, with one or two notable exceptions, by dishonest men, some of whom he had included in his Cabinet.

For a period nothing of any importance took place, for the people of Ireland were more concerned with bread and butter issues. But the corruption that had become manifest prior to his period in office became rife throughout the country. This was evident in both main parties, as wholesale bribery was used to obtain votes in elections, particularly in the rural areas where farmers were offered unconditional grants in exchange for their support. This led to the demoralisation of the farming community and resulted in many becoming more interested in the vast profits to be made from selling their land to speculators rather than in farming it.

The unconditional grants they received were to prove illusory when the government introduced a programme, initially confined to Dublin, to provide much needed employment by expanding the suburbs. It also set about completing the programme to re-house the slum dwellers. Many agricultural workers deserted the land to take up more lucrative employment in the building trade in the city, and so began the drift from the land. However far-reaching changes were also made on the industrial front and reforms covering a wide aspect were introduced, among them being a revision of the educational curriculum. The Irish language was dropped as a compulsory subject, although it still continued to hold a position of prime importance as extra marks were awarded to students who presented their examination papers in Irish. Knowledge of the language still remained an essential qualification for any position in public service.

Meanwhile trouble was brewing with a threatening situation that had developed in Northern Ireland, where the flagrantly sectarian nature of the government and the gerrymandering of constituencies by the Unionist Party had given rise to many injustices. Not the least of these being that it was possible for a Catholic majority, in certain local government areas, to be controlled by a Protestant and Unionist Council. Previously the 1920s had seen the outright persecution of Catholics living in Protestant areas, who had been driven out of their homes with the active connivance of the authorities.

In the 1960s, however, with the emergence of the Social Democratic and Labour Party, which was non-sectarian and open to both sections of the community, the power of the Nationalist Party waned rapidly. But Catholics were still subjected to unconcealed discrimination when it came to obtaining employment in the then flourishing shipbuilding and textile industries that have seen such a sad decline in recent years. Not only did applicants for jobs have to declare their religion when seeking the most menial posts, but also in nearly every case promotion was open only to Protestants.

Nevertheless Catholics and Protestants both stood to gain economically by remaining in the Six County State, for the Southern State was still comparatively underdeveloped and could not match the social welfare system that was enjoyed in the North, due to the subventions the Province received from the British Government. In these circumstances the SDLP decided to shelve the national issue, to which they were committed, and concentrate on obtaining civil rights for their supporters. Thus the long-term objective of obtaining a United Ireland by peaceful means was temporarily put aside.

In order to achieve their aims they founded a civil rights movement and so began an era of agitation that was to see a new and alarming development in the South. Throughout the years Sinn Fein, through its military wing, the IRA, had continued to carry out sporadic raids on the Border but had had little political impact. Since the 1940s, no doubt due to its wartime involvement with the Germans, the party had to all intents and purposes been regarded as redundant, and for some time the socialists among its membership had been complaining about the party's abstentionist approach to politics. Consequently in 1969 a meeting was convened at which party leader Tomas Mac Giolla, who was himself a socialist, proposed that the IRA cease all further military action and that the movement should become totally committed to constitutional politics, pursuing its aims by peaceful means.

To this end the abstentionist policy was to be abandoned, the institutions of both the Southern and Northern States were to be recognised and the position of the Westminster government acknowledged. This proposition was accepted by the vast majority of those present but totally rejected by the minority, representing the more militant faction. This group left the hall as soon as the result was known and set up the national socialist Provisional Sinn Fein organisation with its military wing, the IRA. History had repeated itself and Sinn Fein had split into two factions, just as it had when de Valera had founded his Fianna Fáil party, but this time into Officials and Provisionals.

Later, in order to emphasise his break with Sinn Fein, Mac Giolla formed the Workers' Party, but as it appealed to the more fundamental aspects of socialism it met with limited electoral success. Other former Sinn Fein members broke away from this party to form the Democratic Left, which eventually joined the Labour Party. Such was their success that many years later Pat Rabbitte, who had once been one of the leaders of Sinn Fein, was to become the Labour Leader. Meanwhile the Officials were to play their part, together with the SDLP, which had replaced the conservative Nationalists in the North, in furtherance of the cause of the growing civil rights movement.

The activities of this movement were highlighted by bloody clashes when supporters of the Reverend Ian Paisley, who was determined to ensure the maintenance of the status quo, broke up their marches. In this they were often aid by the police, in particular the B-Special Constabulary. These events were seen on television screens in millions of homes, not only in Ireland but also throughout the United Kingdom. The British public, who had previously been unaware of the denial of civil rights in Northern Ireland, were informed for the first time of the extent and bitterness of the sectarianism that existed there. Paisley himself had formed the Democratic Unionist Party in order to obtain civil rights for workers who were members of the Unionist Party and had thus succeeded in introducing an active working-class element into Unionism. This group found particular comfort in his sectarian outbursts, for while Protestant workers enjoyed certain privileges, particularly in the field of housing and employment, they were otherwise no better off than their Catholic compatriots, and in order to safeguard what benefits they enjoyed they had been forced to lend their support to the Unionist establishment.

Paradoxically, such was the nature of politics in the Province, that the Protestant workers were even more vehemently pro-Union than the Establishment that had exploited them. Paisley's oft-repeated incitements to violence, contained in the *Protestant Telegraph*, which he edited, served to bring home to the British people the extent of the cancer that existed in Northern Ireland. This prompted Captain Terence O'Neill, who was only too aware of the impending threat to the State and who feared civil war, to make his famous television address in which he appealed for calm and hinted that change must come.

His warnings, however, went unheeded by his own supporters, who would not countenance any liberalisation of the regime and who had been openly critical of him ever since his meeting with Lemass. But to the consternation of his supporters he lost his seat to Paisley at the next general election, largely due to the fact that he had underestimated his opponent. Despite his deeply held and often vehemently expressed religious views, Paisley was an excellent constituency worker and had done more to ensure that his Catholic constituents were not discriminated against when it came to allocating housing than his Unionist opponent had ever done. As a result he enjoyed a substantial vote from that community.

This was a time when the British government was becoming seriously concerned at events in the Northern Province and when Bernadette Devlin (now Mc Aliskey) made her maiden speech in the House of Commons she electrified the nation. Her impassioned plea for action on behalf of the minority community, which was widely reported in the media, captured the imagination of the British people and it was not long before they added their voices to the demand for action.

As a result Foreign Secretary James Callaghan ordered troops to be sent to Northern Ireland to protect the Catholic community and immediate steps were taken to disarm the hated B-Specials. In September 1969 Callaghan was rapturously received when he paid a visit to the Bogside district of Derry, which was later to become the scene of some of the bitterest fighting of the ensuing decades.

Nevertheless there were still some areas in the Catholic ghettoes that were not willing to accept policing by the RUC, which years of bitter experience had left them unable to trust. The authorities therefore decided to allow the people living in these districts to form their own volunteer police force. This duty initially fell to members of the Official IRA, which since the split in Sinn Fein had continued to keep its own close-knit organisation to protect itself from attack by the Provisionals. But during the 1970s the Officials were again divided, with one section remaining militant and forming the Irish Republican Socialist Party, with its military wing the Irish National Liberation Army, and the other becoming the more moderate constitutional socialist party known as the Workers' Party, which severed all its paramilitary connections.

The Officials had the respect of the Catholic community, for they had thrown the whole of their weight behind the civil rights movement, while popular support for the Provisionals had diminished. Nevertheless, in order to re-establish themselves as community leaders their members were anxious to be seen to be taking part in this peacekeeping operation. To start with the two factions worked together and so successful were their efforts that they received a favourable mention in the Compton Report, but an uneasy truce existed between them and the Provisionals were restless and anxious to go on the offensive. It only needed a small spark to set fire to hidden tinder and this was provided by one of the most cynical plots in modern history.

CHAPTER 12

Charles Haughey and the Arms Plot = The Violent Seventies

Southern politicians watched events in the North with ill-concealed trepidation as there was talk of the British Government conceding a United Ireland. Since the death of de Valera many had come to accept the existence of the Border, although political necessity had dictated that they keep up their ritual denunciation of it. Now an entirely different situation existed with the possibility that the civil rights movement might succeed in translating their publicly expressed aspirations into reality.

Some people had actually gained by partition and they feared, not without good reason, that the largely left-wing civil rights movement, which had already captured the imagination of the people, would sweep throughout the entire country with the consequent overthrow of the laissez-faire capitalism that had served a corrupt Establishment so well.

Such was their alarm, at any threat to their entrenched position, that they were determined to discredit the civil rights movement at all costs. The question was how to go about the task. The Irish electorate was fully behind the movement, as was public opinion in Britain, and it would be political suicide for anyone to voice an opinion against it. But one of their number, Charles Haughey, a government minister who represented those in Fianna Fáil who still harboured radical republican views and sympathised with the nationalist aims of Sinn Fein as distinct from their political objectives, took the decision to provide them with arms. Ostensibly this was to enable them to protect the Catholic community, but in reality the purpose was to stir up sectarian strife and dupe the Catholics into coming into conflict with the British army.

Haughey and those who were involved in the arms plot were wholly undeterred by the suffering that such action would bring to both communities in the Province, so long as they succeeded in bringing the civil rights movement into disrepute in the eyes of both British and Irish people. This would end all hope of a United Ireland until the threat of socialism had been had been eliminated.

Captain Kelly, an Irish intelligence officer, was sent to Belfast where he made contact with the IRA and arranged to supply them with arms. But this initial meeting was premature, inasmuch as it took place with Sinn Fein in the summer of 1969, prior to the split in that movement and the establishment of the Provisionals. Following the

Officials' rejection of force as a means of solving the national problem, they published a warning in the *United Irishman*, a Sinn Fein journal, to the effect that plans were afoot to send arms to Northern Ireland. It gave the names of prominent people involved in this bizarre enterprise, including those of Cabinet ministers, among whom was Neill Blaney. The article concluded with an exhortation to the people of the North to have nothing to do with arms or the plotters.

As the *United Irishman*, had a circulation that was limited almost exclusively to members and supporters of Sinn Fein, the general public remained unaware of what was taking place. Feelings were running high at the time, due to events in the North, and Jack Lynch found himself caught in a cleft stick. This caused him to make a number of unwise decisions, as illustrated by his creation of a special sub-committee, to which sweeping powers were delegated, following a crisis meeting of the cabinet in mid-August 1969. Appointed to this sub-committee were Charles Haughey, then Minister for Finance, Jim Gibbons, Minister for Defence, and Neill Blaney.

This was strange in view of its brief, which was to deal with contingencies that might arise from the Northern situation. But it would seem that Lynch was anxious to distance himself from any decisions it might take, because earlier a fund had been set up for the Relief of Distress in Northern Ireland, and when it was suggested that money should be released from it for the production of a newspaper to be entitled *The Voice of the North*, he had shown himself to be unequivocally opposed to any such proposition. Now, unknown to him, the plotters and their accomplices were making this fund available for the purchase of arms by the IRA, with whom they were secretly negotiating. The full extent of the involvement of leading members of the Southern administration may never be exposed. Nevertheless the revelations that appeared in *Magill* magazine, which have never been denied, are a sufficient indictment of the principal participants. In addition, sufficient facts are known from the transcript of evidence at the subsequent trial of the conspirators to make it clear that Captain John Kelly made a number of visits to the Continent in connection with the purchase of arms, and the results of these visits were reported to Haughey in February 1970.

Haughey then informed Kevin Boland, a ministerial colleague who supported the plan to import arms, and, as Captain Kelly's negotiations were proving protracted and none too successful, Haughey arranged for a shipment of arms to be landed at Dublin Docks on 25 March. A further supply was flown to Dublin Airport. In the meantime Gibbons had arranged for men from Derry to be trained at a camp in Donegal and in February he authorised the movement of arms to Dundalk.

The rest of the Cabinet knew nothing of these plans and care was taken to keep Lynch in the dark. When he first became aware what was afoot, in April, he found himself in an invidious position. Feelings were running high and at first he tried to delay making any decisions by announcing to his Cabinet, on May 1, that the matter had indeed come to his knowledge but, as there was no proof of the allegations contained in the *Magill* article, he considered the matter closed.

Six days later, however, the evidence that had been gathered against the conspirators proved to be incontrovertible and he was left with no option but to act. Haughey and Blaney were dismissed on the spot, followed by the sacking of Gibbons, while Kevin Boland resigned. Meanwhile the success of their efforts to foment violence in Northern Ireland was daily becoming more apparent.

Christmas 1969 saw the end of the honeymoon that had existed between the Catholic community in the North and the British army. Until then, so successful had been their peacekeeping operation that the possibility of a reduction in the size of the garrison had been under consideration. But the turn of the year was to witness an entirely different situation. January and February 1970 saw fierce clashes between youths in the Bogside area of Derry and the British army. These continued unabated and in April a number of troops were injured in fierce rioting, which had by then spread to Belfast.

On 3 July a bomb wrecked an Army Information office in Belfast and by 5 August it had become clear that the Provisional IRA was provoking these attacks. The suggestion that young people were being forced into battle at gun-point might have seemed far-fetched, but was later shown to have more than a grain of truth when it was discovered that young girls in the Ardoyne district of Belfast were being forced to plant bombs.

The riots in the North were accompanied by a skilful propaganda campaign in Southern Ireland, where the rioters were represented as freedom fighters, and this resulted in a growing groundswell of public opinion in their favour. So strong was this that considerable sympathy became apparent for Haughey and his fellow conspirators. This became particularly evident when the Arms Trial opened, as arranged, in September.

Haughey protested his innocence of any involvement in the affair, insisting that the arms were imported for the sole use of the army. Yet strangely enough neither the army nor the police intelligence services had been informed of their importation. Furthermore, as Minister for Finance it is difficult to understand why he should have chosen to keep the government in the dark as to these additional defence appropriations.

How he and his companions succeeded in avoiding conviction, despite a retrial that commenced at the beginning of October is a matter for conjecture. It is of course possible that they owed their acquittal to the fact that crimes committed in furtherance of the national objective were still countenanced by the courts. It is, however, clear from the depositions that Haughey was prepared to jeopardise his co-defendants to save himself.

It is also known that only a fortnight before his second hearing he had a lengthy meeting with the Minister for Justice, who remained unconvinced by his protestations. He then turned his attention to Colm Condon, the Attorney General, who, according to his wife Stephanie, was subjected to considerable pressure to drop the case. In the event the case against the defendants was dismissed, but the luckless Captain Kelly, who had been under the impression that he was carrying out government orders as was his duty as a soldier, whether he approved of them or not, was made a scapegoat for the politicians and convicted. In 1975, on being reinstated to the front bench of Fianna Fáil, Haughey promised to give a full account of the events surrounding the Arms Trial but this has never been forthcoming.

The discovery of the arms plot and the failure of the courts to convict the conspirators caused considerable public unease. Many felt that it was stretching the bounds of credibility to expect them to believe that both the Minister of Finance and the Minister for Defence had been involved without the entire Cabinet, including Lynch himself, being in some way aware. Others felt, equally strongly, that the plotters should never have been arrested in the first instance, and denounced Lynch accordingly.

The result was that a constitutional crisis was precipitated, aggravated by the fact that there were a number of defections from Fianna Fáil and more than a hint of a general election in the air. However the government's hand was strengthened by the success of its candidates in the Donegal and South County Dublin by-elections.

Meanwhile the changing pattern of events in the North was giving cause for grave concern, for the British army had become weary of presenting a sitting target for the IRA and gangs of stone-throwing youths. By November 1970 they were talking in terms of taking offensive action. The SDLP decided to boycott a planned civil rights march, for it was becoming clear with every day that passed that the Provisional IRA was bidding to dominate that movement and it could only be a matter of time before it had effective control.

On 4 December internment was mooted for the first time, not by the Northern government but by the Southern. This news came in the form of an announcement that evidence of a conspiracy to kidnap prominent persons had been discovered and that as a result the measure was under consideration. James Chichester-Clarke, who had succeeded O'Neill as Prime Minister of Northern Ireland, then stated that he would not stand in the way of internment being introduced there. However it was to fall to the lot of his successor, Brian Faulkner, to put the policy into effect. But such was the level of violence that erupted in the first two months of 1971 that these facts tended to become obscured, as did statements made by political and Church leaders.

As the violence increased, the IRA was condemned by the Catholic Bishop of Down and Connor, and in February the civil rights movement, which no longer had any control over the excesses of its supporters, decided to abandon its appeal to the European Court of Human Rights. However despite the appeals of the Church and the elected representatives of the Catholic community, the troubles continued to escalate and, on 6 March, a sizeable quantity of arms and ammunition was discovered in the Falls Road and other Catholic districts of Belfast.

On 20 March, Chichester-Clarke was forced to resign following strong differences of opinion that had arisen within the ranks of the Unionist Party regarding his handling of the security situation. Brian Faulkner replaced him as Premier of Northern Ireland. In the South, Lynch added his voice to the call for an end to terrorism and, having condemned the murder of British soldiers, offered to lend a hand to the new Prime Minister. He immediately set about rounding up IRA suspects, but once again found himself threatened with a no-confidence vote.

Those ministers who had been forced to resign due to their complicity in the Arms Plot spearheaded the attack on Lynch. To their dismay, however, when the vote was taken Haughey decided to support the government. This certainly seemed strange at the time, but subsequent events have proved that this was simply a pragmatic move on his part and that he was biding his time to wrest control of Fianna Fáil from Lynch.

By late August internment measures that had already been announced had been introduced, and a prison camp had been established at Long Kesh. This was probably the most fatal error made by the Northern administration, for it provided a rallying point for the civil rights movement, which had now become little more than a front for the Provisionals. Sweeping powers of arrest were given to the police in an endeavour contain the violence, much of which had now taken on an ugly sectarian aspect. Indeed, a number of Protestant paramilitary organisations had come into being, the most prominent of which were the Ulster Defence Association and the Ulster Volunteer Force.

But so widespread were these arrests that a number of people, completely innocent of any paramilitary involvement, were caught up in the net and found themselves behind bars together with IRA, UDA and UVF activists. This measure thus proved counter-productive and resulted in many who had not as yet been involved, turning to or lending their support to one or other of the terrorist groups.

Simultaneously Lynch's administration, which had survived, was intensifying its drive against known terrorists in the South. But it was internment without trial in the North that was attracting the most publicity and resulted in a public outcry.

In January 1972 a march was to be held in Derry, in protest at internment without trial. It was sure to attract a large crowd and the army would be on patrol in strength, to prevent the riots that so often took place following such demonstrations despite the peaceful intent of the protestors. Little did the marchers who set out on that Sunday afternoon, thereafter to be known as Northern Ireland's Bloody Sunday, expect what was in store for them.

No sooner was the procession well under way than a shot rang out from somewhere behind and the army returned fire – despite orders shouted by their commanding officer that they were not to shoot unless they could identify their targets. But it was too late. Already a number lay dead or injured and the crowd in the ensuing panic and confusion would not have heard his orders. It appeared that the army had opened fire on a peaceful protest by civilians.

The events that occurred that day have never yet been satisfactorily resolved, but actions other than those of the army require some explanation. Few concrete facts are known, other than that a single shot rang out from somewhere close behind the protestors and that the army undoubtedly over-reacted. However there is another scenario that would account for events. Was a shot fired into the air from a hidden position behind the crowd by a member of the Provisional IRA, with the deliberate intention of provoking a response from troops who would fear that they were under attack? What other purpose could have been served by firing such a shot, other than to give the impression that the army had opened fire indiscriminately on an unarmed crowd?

The propaganda effect of such a ghoulish deception would have been enormous and in the event, whatever the truth, the result from the point of view of the Provisionals was an unqualified success. The Southern media fell into the trap that would seem to have been prepared for them. Scathing articles appeared in the newspapers, denouncing the actions of the British army, and soon feelings were running so high that when a large mob descended on the British Embassy in Merrion Square, Dublin, and proceeded to set it ablaze with petrol bombs, the police did little or nothing to interfere. Anglo-Irish relations reached a low ebb but this setback was short-lived, despite the widespread indignation that greeted the publication of the Widgery Report.

The findings of this report into the Derry massacre were that a lone gunman had opened fire on the army, which had panicked and retaliated, resulting in the marchers being caught up in the crossfire. The soldiers were exonerated from all blame in the affair. This conclusion, though it caused considerable anger in Ireland, was borne out by a newsreel of the event that showed the commanding officer frantically endeavouring to prevent his men from firing their weapons. This clearly gave the lie to the Provisionals' propaganda that it was an unprovoked attack on an unarmed crowd.

March 1972 saw the abolition of the Stormont government by the British authorities and the Province was placed under direct rule from Westminster. But the outrages and sectarian murders instigated by the paramilitaries on both sides of the sectarian divide continued unabated, as the reign of terror the Provisionals had instigated was intensified by a systematic bombing campaign. They stepped up their propaganda in the South and it seemed that nothing could end the cycle of violence, despite the strenuous efforts that were being made by the British and Irish Prime Ministers.

Dublin was also to receive its baptism of fire. Following a number of bombings that had taken place in other parts of the country during 1972, a car bomb exploded in Nassau Street, in the centre of the city, during the evening rush-hour. Two people were killed and 50 passers-by were injured, Responsibility for this and other, mainly fire-bomb attacks, was claimed by Protestant paramilitaries, but it was suggested by a group of journalists that the Nassau Street outrage had been carried out on direct orders from the British army, as a reprisal for the carnage that was taking place in the North.

It is doubtful if there is any truth in this allegation, but it cannot be denied that such a reprisal had been invited by those who had taken part in the Arms Plot and the failure of the Southern government to take any effective action to prevent the country being used as a base for the IRA's attacks on the Northern Province. May 1973 saw a general election, in the South, which resulted in the Fianna Fáil administration's defeat. A coalition government composed of Fine Gael and Labour Deputies replaced it, but a pact was established between the outgoing and incoming governments regarding policy on Northern Ireland, which resulted in a bi-partisan approach to the problem.

The new Prime Minister, Liam Cosgrave, lost no time in establishing contact with Edward Heath, his opposite number in England. This led to a number of meetings with Brian Faulkner, in search of a peaceful solution. Their discussions soon bore fruit and a conference was held at Sunningdale in the autumn of 1973 to discuss the possibility of setting up a power-sharing administration, to be composed of elected members of both the majority and minority communities. The proposed Assembly would replace the Stormont government.

Faulkner's action in coming to this accord was immediately condemned by Ian Paisley and the more extreme elements in the Official Unionist Party, who had made their displeasure felt as soon as it became known that talks were taking place with Dublin. They now endeavoured to delay the implementation of the accord by procedural wrangles, and when the Executive at last took office, set about its systematic destruction. Initially their actions were limited to disrupting meetings of the Assembly, but the deathblow was struck by the Ulster Workers' strike in 1974. This strike was called by the Ulster Workers' Council, operating from Paisley's power base in the Protestant ghettoes of Belfast. Not only did it have the support of the

Protestant paramilitary organisations but also that of the Provisional movement, which was equally opposed to the formation of any such Executive.

Whether this strike would have succeeded without the massive intimidation that took place – at least 1,700 cases were reported – is a matter for conjecture. But once the workers at Ballylumford power station downed tools, the Province was paralysed and the downfall of the Executive assured, because military intervention on a sufficient scale could not be mounted due to the security situation. It took place when the once monolithic Unionist Party was in the process of fragmenting into factions, while Paisley's Democratic Unionist Party was emerging as a potent political force.

Following successive electoral triumphs over the years, the Democratic Unionists came to represent a very real threat to the old Official Unionist Party – so called to distinguish it from other groups that came into being during this period – although for some years it continued to speak as the main party representing the majority in the North. In the South some questioned the wisdom of power sharing, as it relies on a balance of power being struck between the majority and minority communities, and it could be argued that such an arrangement would tend to enshrine sectarianism.

With the demise of the Executive, direct rule returned and the IRA campaign was stepped up anew, Soon the hideous tale of bombings and sectarian assassinations, by paramilitaries on both sides of the political divide, became an almost daily occurrence and received extensive coverage in the media on both sides of the Irish Sea. During this period the situation was further aggravated by the emergence of a number of splinter groups, such as Saor Eire, but by far the most dangerous of these was the Irish National Liberation Army, the military wing of the Irish Republican Socialist Party.

The IRSP had come into being following a further split in the Official Sinn Fein, which had retained a military wing, the Official IRA, to protect it from assaults by the Provisionals. However it was no longer prepared to support the Official Sinn Fein's call to pursue its aims by peaceful means. Like the Provisionals, the IRSP shared the same aims, using physical force to achieve its objectives, and one of its leading members was responsible for the murder of John Taylor, MP. The only difference between the Provisionals and this new movement was that the former was more nationalist than socialist and the latter was more socialist than nationalist.

Public opinion had undergone a complete change in the South since the collapse of the Sunningdale power-sharing Executive. In 1976, when the Provisionals attempted to hold a mass rally in Dublin following the official celebrations to commemorate the 1916 Rising, the meeting was not only banned by the Minister for Justice but riot troops were brought into the city to ensure that the ban was strictly enforced.

Ever since the Nassau Street and Monaghan bombings, steps had been taken in Dublin to tighten security. Despite this, on 26 July of that year the British Ambassador,

Christopher Ewart-Biggs, was murdered by the IRA who placed a bomb in a culvert close to his home in Sandyford. This event was greeted with universal horror and when Fianna Fáil was returned to power following the 1977 general election, one of the first actions of Jack Lynch, who again became Taoiseach, was to re-affirm the bi-partisan policy towards the North by reiterating that there would never again be an attempt by any Irish Government to coerce the majority in the Northern Province into accepting a United Ireland. Plans were evolved for economic – as distinct from the purely military – cooperation that had been established between the two States.

The election itself had been a landslide victory achieved by the Fianna Fáil central office, which presented a programme of promises to a hard-pressed electorate. These included the abolition of domestic rates and motor taxation, which could not but ensure the party's return but which was to have a devastating effect on the economy. Lynch was to find himself in charge of a party where the rift that had existed since the Arms Trial had now widened into a gulf.

Of the original plotters only Blaney, who was now an independent deputy, continued to give open support to the Provisionals; Boland had retired from politics following his unsuccessful attempt to found a new political party – Aontacht Eireann. Consequently, in an endeavour to restore party unity, Lynch reinstated Haughey to his former position on the front bench. Haughey, however, determined to wrest control of Fianna Fáil from Lynch and the moderate wing of the party, immediately set about undermining Lynch at every possible opportunity, with the eventual result that he had no option but to resign in 1980.

This period saw the beginning of Ireland's economic decline. Fianna Fáil's demonstrably dishonest 1977 election manifesto had relied heavily on foreign borrowing, but the promises it contained were bound to appeal to an electorate hard-pressed by the austerity measures which Fine Gael had been forced to introduce in an attempt to counteract the worst effects of an international financial crisis brought about by the increase in the price of crude oil. This had resulted in a dramatic rise in the cost of manufacture and transport of nearly every commodity, with constant demands on the consumer in the form of increased prices in the shops.

At first it seemed that George Colley would succeed Lynch, but a coup had been carefully organised by Haughey that resulted in him becoming leader of the party and Taoiseach. But the fact that he had been one of the leading figures in the Arms Trial was the cause of no small trepidation in the country at large, and alarm was expressed that his appointment might herald a reversal of the policies of his two predecessors. These fears were rapidly dispelled, for during his first year in office he appeared to be as determined to combat terrorism as his predecessors. Unfortunately his profligate spending policy added to the difficulties already facing the economy and it was not long before his name became a by-word for corruption. After all, he was a career politician who saw power as a means of manipulating events for his own and his cronies' financial gain, and it is probable that at this stage he had come to fear the Provisionals even more than he had the civil rights movement.

There followed a period of instability in the South, as violence spilled over from the North, and Haughey's first year as Taoiseach saw the murder by the IRA of Lord Mountbatten, a retired British admiral, whose only 'crime' was that he was the Queen's cousin. His murder while on holiday in County Sligo destroyed any latent sympathy there might have been, in England, for the cause the IRA purported to represent.

In Ireland the effect was equally dramatic. Lately support for the Provisionals had been dwindling and it now only found expression among a small but vociferous minority. Otherwise a feeling of revulsion swept the land and the people felt a sense of shame that such a cowardly murder should have been committed in their midst. Mountbatten had been a popular figure, particularly among the villagers of Mullaghmore, who looked forward to his frequent visits there.

This sense of outrage translated itself into political action and Anglo-Irish relations improved to such an extent that Haughey was able to take the unprecedented step of inviting the British Prime Minister, Margaret Thatcher, to Dublin for talks. This was a huge breakthrough and her subsequent visit was widely acclaimed, as was the communiqué that was issued following their meeting. This announced the establishment of a new Dublin-London dimension, which would have as its ultimate objective the formation of a Council of Ireland.

The fact that a man responsible for the Arms Plot could come to terms with Margaret Thatcher might seem paradoxical, but in fact it was wholly in keeping with the character of Charles Haughey. While he felt threatened by the civil rights movement when there was a Labour government in England, he was well aware that he could rely on a no-nonsense Conservative Prime Minister, who was totally unaware of the motive that had dictated his apparent U-turn, not to give in to the Provisional IRA and their followers.

Coinciding with these developments, the fortunes of the republican movement reached an all-time low. Change was in the wind and it now seemed to be only a matter of time before a new arrangement could be concluded between Britain and the Southern government. While such an arrangement could well have thwarted the plans of the Provisionals, it was equally distasteful to the extreme Unionists, in particular Ian Paisley's DUP. This party regarded any constitutional or institutional change affecting Ulster as a sell-out and resented the involvement of the Dublin government in any discussions regarding the present or future affairs of the Province. Both factions were equally anxious to discover some means of disrupting talks between Dublin and London, but it was the Provisionals who came up with a scheme, which, combined with a skilfully planned and carefully executed propaganda campaign, could be counted on to restore their lost fortunes.

It is useful to record the subsequent events as they took place, for not only do they reveal the true nature of the Provisional Sinn Fein but they expose the naked intimidation of the IRA that enabled that organisation to hold sway over one section of the community while demanding and obtaining unquestioning obedience from its membership.

It was just prior to Christmas 1980 that the public first became aware of a situation that the IRA was to use to set in motion a horrific chain of events. Bobby Sands, a prisoner at the Maze Prison in Northern Ireland, had infuriated the Provisional leadership by taking part in discussions that had led to the termination of a hunger strike, in which he and several of his companions had been engaged with the aim of securing better conditions

The prisoners' demands had been fair and reasonable and concessions were in the course of being made, despite subsequent propaganda to the contrary. While the European Court of Human Rights had rejected their original request for political status, it had indicated that there should be more flexibility in the regime governing their detention. But there had been a hitch in implementing the new agreement, which at first sight might appear to be a mere technicality but in reality involved an important principle.

The prison authorities had agreed to allow internees to wear their own clothes. It was, nevertheless, ruled that they would have to be ordinary civilian items in order to remove the possibility of paramilitary uniforms being brought into the prison. This would have been undesirable for obvious reasons, but especially as not only republican but also loyalist prisoners were housed there.

Following the collapse of the first hunger strike, the Provisionals had ceased to allow their internees in the Maze to elect their own representatives from within the prison population. They were quick to seize on the opportunity presented by the delay in giving effect to the agreement and ordered Sands to commence a fresh hunger strike. They anticipated that it would reach its zenith by Easter, to coincide with the anniversary of the 1916 Rising, an emotive a sate for republicans as 12 July is for Unionists.

That this unfortunate young man should have been singled out to die was of no consequence, for a blood sacrifice was needed to inject new life into the Republican movement. The Provisional leadership were well aware that they were committing an act of cold-blooded murder against one of their own but they set out to give the impression that the demands of Sands were minimal. However their real intention was to insist on political status, which in view of the ruling of the European Court, the British government could not concede any more than could the government of Southern Ireland, for IRA terrorists being held there. Such a concession would mean recognising the entitlement of anyone who committed murder, in pursuit of a political objective, to receive privileged treatment. Such a principle would undermine basic international law.

Easter came and went and Sands still lived. In the South scant attention had been paid to the hunger strike, despite demonstrations being held in Dublin, by busloads of Provisionals and others who were more concerned with saving their intended victim's life. Most of those taking part came from the North and if anything, due to the disruption they caused, these meetings tended to be counter-productive. But fate was yet to play into their hands.

With the death of Frank Maguire, a Nationalist M.P at Westminster, the Fermanagh-South Tyrone seat became vacant and the SDLP agreed not to oppose his brother Noel. But the Provisionals decided to enter the now dying Sands to contest the election. At first this attracted little attention for the general opinion was that he could not be expected to pick up more than a handful of votes, but subsequent events were to provide the Provisionals with the biggest boost since internment began.

Bobby Sands was to become front-page news for weeks, but it was recognised that as a Sinn Fein member he would not take up his seat even if elected to the Westminster Parliament, so it should have been clear that some ulterior motive lay behind the decision to nominate him. This was lost sight of, as Maguire's brother was a particularly strong candidate whose election would have been assured in the normal course of events. At the eleventh hour, however, he was visited by members of the IRA and to the consternation of the SDLP withdrew his candidature.

What happened at that fateful meeting is not difficult to surmise. He has since disappeared from the political scene and the only statement he made seems to confirm that he was put under pressure. Indeed any other conclusion is inconceivable for he was a man of character who would never willingly have been a party to any breach of his pact with the SDLP, particularly in such a manner, which would lay him open to a charge of fraudulent manipulation.

In any event his withdrawal from the contest was so timed as to make it impossible for his party to select and nominate a new candidate. Thus the only opponent of Sands was Harry West, an Official Unionist, who was not only extremely unpopular among the Nationalist community but his candidacy had also been trenchantly denounced by Paisley. The Provisionals also had the advantage of a well-orchestrated propaganda campaign, which led the electorate to believe that a vote for Sands was a vote to save his life.

The result was a foregone conclusion, but it is interesting to note that in this constituency, which normally returns a nationalist of whatever hue with an overwhelming majority, Sands was elected by a mere 1,000 votes, notwithstanding a near record turnout. But in the aftermath of the election and the undoubted shock it gave to all shades of moderate opinion, the only interpretation given to this vote by the media was, paradoxically, that of Paisley and his followers – namely that every Catholic in Fermanagh-South Tyrone had voted for Sands.

This was demonstrably untrue for not only had there been blatant instances of intimidation during the election campaign, but there were numerous spoiled votes and closer examination of these revealed that a number of Catholics voted for West. There was also no doubt that the share of the vote received by Sands was augmented by some of Paisley's supporters, who had voted for him partly because of the latter's denunciation of West but also because the fortunes of the DUP rose in inverse proportion to those of the Provisionals, as both placed their reliance on an appeal to sectarian tribalism. Hence an entirely different conclusion from the generally accepted one can be drawn, which would explain the narrow margin of between the two candidates.

The media's failure to analyse the results before rushing into print gave an added boost to the already great propaganda advantage now enjoyed by Sinn Fein. Sands, the unknown hunger striker, had failed to excite the public imagination but Bobby Sands, MP was a different proposition. That he had failed to die at Easter mattered little now. Alive, he would serve Sinn Fein's purpose well; dead he would prove invaluable. True to type, they ensured that no amount of pleading on the part of the Commissioners of the Court of Human Rights would succeed in persuading their proposed martyr to give up his fast. When it was first suggested that representatives of the Court visit him in the Maze, his election agent issued an abrupt statement to the effect that such intervention would not be welcome. Then came the ultimate hypocrisy. The Papal Envoy was invoked to give the impression that no stone was being left unturned to save his life, but it soon became clear that neither the Court of Human Rights nor even the Pope himself would be allowed to intervene.

Had those on hunger strike been given the option by their masters of availing themselves of mediation by either of these sources, it would have been possible to arrive at a compromise solution. But the Provisionals were not to be denied their blood sacrifice. By insisting on their demand for political status, which could not be granted, they could be assured of one or more martyrs whose death would be perceived as being at the hands of the British Government, and the political advantage to Sinn Fein would be such as to restore them to a powerful position.

Meanwhile a smokescreen of five, at first sight apparently innocuous, demands was used to cover their real intentions. These were voiced by the H-Block Committees, which Sinn Fein succeeded in establishing throughout the entire country and to which many were drawn out of sincere sympathy for Sands; little reasoning that they had become unwitting accomplices in what was no more than a cynical plot. In the emotive atmosphere that had been generated, it was not generally recognised that none of these demands, nor even all five put together, justified a fast to the death.

As will appear obvious on closer scrutiny, the first of these demands, 'Freedom to wear one's own clothes,' had already been conceded subject to limitations consistent with maintaining discipline among the internees. Indeed there is no question that some of the requests could have been granted but the Provisionals could not be trusted to abide by the conditions that would have had to be imposed, as is illustrated by an examination of each of these requests in turn.

There might been some room for flexibility on the demand for 'Freedom of association,' but care would have had to be taken to ensure that no advantage was taken of such a concession, for example to plot further acts of terrorism or to organise disturbances within the prison. The next demand was for 'Freedom to refuse work.' This is to some extent a contradiction of the last demand for, by its very nature, work implies some degree of association. This was particularly true in the Maze, where work was geared to rehabilitation and prisoners were free to receive vocational education. On the other hand nothing is so debilitating to the psyche as long periods of unemployment. The final two demands concerned full remission of sentences and the question of letters and food parcels. Certainly the former could have been granted conditionally, subject to the future good behaviour of those released. The matter of letters and food parcels could have been examined and any inadequacy it could have been addressed, provided steps were taken to ensure that no arms were smuggled into the prison.

Sands himself faced an impossible choice. Disobedience to the leadership meant death and it was better to die a 'hero' rather than be found shot in the back and branded a traitor on his release. In addition he feared for his relatives, as he was only too well aware that any prevarication on his part would place them in jeopardy. His erstwhile colleagues were quick to deal with any waiverers among their supporters. In the final analysis it can be said that of Sands that he did in fact die a hero, for he died not so much for the false image of socialism, as projected by the Provisional Sinn Fein, but rather to ensure the safety of his relations, in particular his mother and sister, both of whom had pleaded with him to give up his fast.

The Sands case is a classic example not only of the ruthlessness of the Provisionals but also of their ability to sow dissention and inflict the maximum damage on relations between the British and Irish peoples. The leadership had accurately gauged the response of the British Prime Minister, Margaret Thatcher. Indeed in her attitude lay the key to the success of their whole campaign. Her period in office had been punctuated by a succession of confrontations at home, while the death of two of her best friends at the hands of the IRA, Lord Mountbatten and Airey Neave, could be counted on to ensure that she remained intransigent.

If de Valera had been prepared to allow IRA hunger strikers to die, she could hardly be expected to relent, but the words "murder is murder", coming from her lips, did not have the same impact as when the Pope made a similar declaration on his visit to Drogheda. What she said on this occasion was perfectly correct; it was what she omitted to say that mattered. Had her refusal to give way been tempered with compassion for the predicament of Sands, and had she explained why her government was prepared to go no further rather than her adoption of a "not an inch" stance, with all the posturing that typified so much of her dealings with her own people, the Provisionals would have been denied their propaganda victory and the lives not only of Sands but also of a number of his companions could have been spared.

The death of Sands set the tribal drums beating and, as one by one the hunger strikers fasted to their deaths, a massive build-up of Sinn Fein propaganda flooded the South. Meanwhile rioting, such as had not been seen for a decade, enveloped the North and for the first time it spilled over to Dublin. Fortunately the only damage was to property but many feared that the Provisionals were only biding their time and that worse was to come. However it was not long before they were to make some costly errors that were to alienate much of the sympathy they had succeeded in building up in the South.

Following an explosion at the Sollum oil refinery in Scotland, during a visit there by Queen Elizabeth, not only did the Irish Republican Publicity Bureau claim responsibility but also their statement ended with the words, "Had we managed to place the bomb close enough to the British Queen, she would now be dead." True or false, it was clear that this claim had been deliberately made with the intention of further heightening community tension in the North. But with few exceptions the Protestant majority showed commendable restraint in the face of this nerve-wracking provocation, while in the South it showed that the men of violence were prepared to justify any crime, however heinous, as long as it provided them with a spectacular.

This, together with other actions threatened by them – their constant disruption of life in Dublin, enormous protest marches, their adamant refusal to allow any intervention to save the lives of Sands and his companions – combined to lead to a growing sense of disillusionment with the hunger strike and those who had brought it about. Later, when an attempt was made to march on the British Embassy, riot police several of whom were injured by missiles dispersed the protestors, the disillusion turned to anger.

The British government's initial mishandling of the situation may have given the Provisionals a temporary advantage, but it was now appreciated by many that this was largely due to the complexity caused by a number of legal problems that had been dismissed as of no importance when the Provisional campaign was at its height. As well as the international complications, which made it impossible to afford political status to convicted terrorists, there was a further problem in that what is known as Special Category status had already been granted to both republican and loyalist internees in the Maze. Many of these were young people serving long prison sentences and it had seemed that there might have been extenuating circumstances surrounding their cases. But as sectarian murder followed sectarian murder and the violence escalated, it was found necessary to abolish this preferment and tighten up the prison regime.

As British law, in common with most European law, does not act retrospectively, those convicted when internment was first introduced were not affected by this amended legislation and continued to enjoy privileges that newcomers were denied. The government was therefore faced with a dilemma: either it would have to dispense with the new legislation, which was plainly undesirable in view of the nature of the crimes now being committed, or it would have to withdraw the privileges enjoyed by the first batch of internees, who for the most part had been convicted of lesser offences. This would not only be illegal but could only precipitate further trouble.

The problems facing the authorities were further aggravated by the introduction of the Diplock Courts, which were presided over by three judges without a jury. This was an essential measure due to the widespread intimidation of jurors and witnesses. They were, in fact, less severe than the Special Courts that had been set up in the South, where a conviction could be secured on the uncorroborated evidence of a single police officer.

John Hume's suggestion that some of the privileges demanded by the H-Block committees could be granted without prejudicing the legal obligations of the government, and extended to all prisoners irrespective of whether their crimes were politically motivated or otherwise, was rejected. In any event it would not have been acceptable to the Provisionals, who were not interested in compromise.

Those who considered that it should have played a more active role in endeavouring to bring the hunger strike to an end levelled some criticism at the Catholic Church. Certainly an unequivocal warning that by taking their own lives the hunger strikers were committing suicide might have served to dispel the charges of ambivalence that were being made against the clergy. But in view of the refusal by the Provisionals to accept papal mediation it is a matter of conjecture as to whether intervention would have served any useful purpose.

The extensive coverage that had been given by the media to the events surrounding the hunger strike tended to cloud the memory of important political decisions taken in 1980 and 1981. Following the failure of previous Secretaries of State for Northern Ireland to find a formula on which to build a new administration to replace the Stormont Government and the ill-fated Power-Sharing Executive, James Prior was sent to the Province to replace Humphrey Atkins.

His brief was to prepare a plan that would allow for fully representative, devolved, government and he devised a scheme that came to be known as "rolling devolution". He envisaged an Assembly that contained an element of power sharing and would be given more executive functions as time progressed.

To this end, discussions took place between the two governments throughout 1980 and the early part of 1981 in an endeavour to reach an agreement. But from the outset these talks ran into serious difficulties and meanwhile the violence continued to escalate. The Official Unionists and the DUP convinced that a sell-out was being planned behind their backs and that Prior's initiative was simply a device to resurrect the Power-Sharing Executive, which they had rejected, dismissed the matter out of hand. The SDLP remained silent and offered no practical suggestions but later, when asked if they would settle for a modicum of power sharing for the time being, in order to assuage the fears of the two Unionist Parties, they announced that they would have nothing further to do with the proposals.

A parallel conference was then formed between the SDLP and the Alliance Party but eventually both called for the talks to be wound up. Meanwhile in the South Haughey, now Taoiseach continued to pour scorn on the new initiative and Prior found himself trapped in a difficult situation. On one hand the Unionists, who suspected that a determined attempt was being made by the British Government to undermine the Union, were vilifying him; on the other the Nationalists were equally convinced that an attempt was being made to cement it. Consequently the talks had dragged on until the Alliance Party eventually indicated its willingness to participate in the proposed new Assembly.

However the SDLP appeared to be influenced by Haughey's intemperate pronouncements and decided to adopt an abstentionist policy. This left the way open for the Unionist Parties to take control of the new body and, in the circumstances, despite their previous reservations, they agreed not to stand in the way of its formation. The legislation required to establish it was then introduced into the House of Commons and elections to it took place in 1982.

The election result could have been very different had it not been for the decision of the SDLP to opt out of the deliberations of the Assembly. By so doing they had forfeited the veto they would have had over its proceedings in all matters affecting the minority community, and their presence would have ensured a measure of power sharing, inasmuch as all matters would have required their approval before they could be passed into law. Consequently their electorate felt betrayed and while some of their supporters feared that their action foreshadowed the breakdown of constitutional politics, many more switched their allegiance to Sinn Fein, which they now felt should be given a chance.

In the event, from that day forward the SDLP lost considerable ground to a now powerful Sinn Fein, which gained control of the nationalist movement in the North. The only other voice was the newly formed Irish Independence Party, which was short-lived and consisted in the main of former members of the defunct Nationalist Party.

The Assembly elections were followed by a general election in the United Kingdom. Margaret Thatcher was again returned to power but in Northern Ireland the SDLP suffered further serious setbacks. Gerry Fitt (later Lord Fitt), who was by far the most outstanding of their representatives, lost his seat in West Belfast to Gerry Adams, the leader of Sinn Fein who some believed to be chairman of the Army Council of the Provisional IRA, although he has consistently denied having held any such position.

The Provisional Sinn Fein was, if anything, a greater evil than the IRA itself as its leaders stood aloof while encouraging young men, many of them teenagers, to risk their own lives in committing unspeakable acts of violence. This contrasts sharply with the actions of those who took part in the 1916 Rising, who were for the most part honourable men.

In the South it had become evident that the economy was in serious trouble and Haughey decided to hold a general election in a bid to maintain power before the extent of the crisis became known to the public. He therefore dissolved the Dáil and went to the country in the summer of 1981. While the existing malaise had been partly precipitated by the world recession, it was largely the result of the mismanagement of the economy and the corruption that had crept onto Irish politics since the Lemass era. People demand honest politics and looked to Dr Garrett Fitzgerald, the leader of the Fine Gael Party, to provide it.

Fine Gael, however, was unable to obtain an overall majority and looked to the Labour Party to join them in coalition. This was eventually arranged, after a lengthy meeting of that party, but many of its supporters, among them some sitting deputies, including Michael D Higgins, doubted the wisdom of such an arrangement, which relied for its success on its ability to persuade the predominantly right wing Fine Gael Party to adopt a moderate policy.

During his first term in office, which proved to be short-lived, Dr Fitzgerald's most notable contribution was his announcement of a constitutional crusade, aimed at involving Belfast in the Dublin-London talks, that had been initiated by the previous administration, His government floundered, however, as a result of its failure to get agreement from its coalition colleagues, following the introduction of its first budget. In 1982, therefore, the country found itself back at the polls, but following the general election Fianna Fáil found itself in a position where it was unable to form a government.

The country now witnessed some of the most shameless horse-trading for votes since the foundation of the State. While Lynch's government had endeavoured to implement de Valera's re-housing policy, his successors had allowed Dublin's inner city to decay almost beyond redemption, while free rein had been given to developers to disfigure the countryside with sprawling suburbs. This period had also seen the growth of land speculation and the re-zoning of agricultural land for profit, which was to result in the widespread corruption of politicians, both local and national, but it also saw whole working class communities being broken up while those left behind continued to eke out an existence in unsavoury slums.

Having succeeded in gaining the support of the two Workers' Party deputies, Haughey turned his attention to Tony Gregory, a young Independent Deputy who had been elected for a constituency covering the North Inner City. His youth and inexperience, coupled with the determination to improve the lot of his constituents, was to lead him to agree to support Haughey in his bid for power, on his promise to make funds immediately available for inner-city regeneration and make 1a start on a rebuilding programme.

Haughey was well aware that however wise this plan might be from a social point of view, its immediate implementation would only add to the burden on the economy, which was on the brink of collapse. But Gregory's support and that of the Worker's Party, which although its deputies were prepared to vote for his nomination as Taoiseach had strong reservations as to the extent they would prepared to support him in government, were essential if he was to secure however tenuous a majority. Haughey therefore determined to buy Gregory's vote whatever the cost to the country.

Needless to say a government brought into being in such inauspicious circumstances could not last long. The bankruptcy of its policies was soon exposed, but not before the new Minister for Finance, Ray Mac Sharry, had promised to replace the gloom of which he accused the previous administration with boom, a remark that was to cost him his seat in November when the government was forced to resign on a vote of no confidence in its economic plans.

Once again the country was back at the polls and the election that followed was unusual, if not unique, in the annals of any State. The moment of truth had arrived and no party could promise anything but a programme of austerity if it were to retain any credibility with the electorate. So chaotic was the state of the country's finances that the government had no option but to make the Book of Estimates for the forthcoming budget available to the opposition during the course of the election campaign. This unprecedented step made the public aware, for the first time, of the extent of the wastage of resources that had taken place over the years, but it also ensured that Haughey would not be faced with having to take the measures to correct the problem.

These events precipitated a crisis in Fianna Fáil and it was anticipated that Haughey would be forced to stand down following an emergency meeting of the Fianna Fáil Party. But true to form he brazened the matter out, blaming the media for his predicament. Ray Burke succeeded in persuading the meeting that he would be prepared to stand down provided that he was afforded the opportunity of doing so in his own time – time that he would use to plan a comeback.

CHAPTER 13

Garrett Fitzgerald and the Anglo Irish Agreement

A Fine Gael-Labour coalition came to power in November 1982 under Dr Fitzgerald, this time with a small but working majority. It was, however, in an unenviable position, for faced with horrendous economic problems, due not only to the profligate spending of the Haughey government in its attempt to meet the unsustainable promises made in Fianna Fáil's 1977 election manifesto, but also to the additional burden of meeting Haughey's obligations to Tony Gregory.

Fitzgerald was forced to embark on a number of unpopular measures and falling living standards, factory closures and industrial unrest marked his period in office. This was in part due to the failure of the Trade Unions to face up to the realities of the situation, as a result of the false expectations that had been generated over the years by past administrations.

He realised that a programme of spending cuts was essential if the situation was to be brought under control, but when Minister for Finance Alan Dukes announced in a radio interview that the budget deficit for 1983 would have to be cut from £900 million, as proposed in Fianna Fáil's estimates for that year, to £750 million, he was met with a rebuttal by his Tánaiste, or deputy prime minister. Dick Spring, who issued a statement to the effect that there had been no agreement between the coalition partners as to the size of the deficit.

Fitzgerald was inclined to believe that Dukes had overstated the problem and, as he could not afford the political risk of allowing the pressure that was building up between the coalition partners to grow further, he decided to take the unusual step of having the figure checked by New York consultants and discovered that the markets were anticipating a deficit of £900 million, rather than the £750 million announced by Dukes. He therefore issued a statement to the effect that it was government policy to aim at the £750 million previously mentioned by Dukes, but that this was a provisional figure and that no firm policy decision had yet been taken in the matter.

The government was now at a crossroads and Fitzgerald was forced to settle for a policy of containment with regard to public finances and increased taxation, rather than a reduction in expenditure, a policy that resulted in costs spiralling out of control. In order to avoid further conflict with his coalition partners he turned his attention to devising a scheme to end the mindless cycle of violence that had brought daily bloodshed and mayhem to the streets of Northern Ireland, as a result of the terrorist campaign waged by the IRA, which had continually increased in intensity since the beginning of the decade.

To this end he established the Forum for a New Ireland and invited all parties on the island of Ireland to attend, to discuss the problems affecting them with a view to devising an agreed political solution. But the Unionists boycotted the Forum while Sinn Fein was excluded due to its involvement with the IRA. Consequently the deliberations came to be regarded as a means of bringing about a purely nationalist constitutional settlement to the problem.

Haughey agreed to participate but insisted that only Fianna Fáil's republican view of a unitary State would provide a solution to the problem. Eventually he agreed that while this was his preferred option, he would be prepared to accept a federal solution or joint sovereignty if it proved unattainable. But no sooner was the report of the deliberations of the Forum made public, in May 1984, than he reversed his position and to the dismay of Fitzgerald, Dick Spring and the leader of the SDLP, John Hume, declared that only a unitary State would bring peace to the North.

Senator Eoin Ryan, a leading member of Fianna Fáil, also expressed his disquiet at the manner in which Haughey had decided a matter of policy without any reference to his Cabinet or the Parliamentary Party. This was a flagrant breach of party rules and Ryan demanded a full meeting to discuss the issue. After some delay the meeting eventually took place but there was overwhelming support for the Haughey line. Following the meeting Desmond O'Malley, who had served as Haughey's Minister for Industry and Commerce until his resignation due to irreconcilable policy differences between them, denounced Haughey for stifling debate within the party.

Haughey responded by demanding that the whip be withdrawn from O'Malley. A motion to this effect was carried, thereby ensuring that dissent within the party was silenced. This was confirmed by P J Mara, the party's press secretary, in his briefing to political correspondents when he stated that there would be "Uno Duce, una voce." If Mara had set out to illustrate the direction in which his boss was leading his party, he had certainly succeeded in making it clear that Haughey would not tolerate dissent.

Though labouring under considerable difficulties, the Fine Gael-Labour administration introduced not inconsiderable progressive legislation, starting with the Family Planning Bill, which was introduced by the labour Minister for Health, Barry Desmond, and passed in 1985. A bill to allow for a referendum to remove the ban on divorce followed this. This liberal measure, also introduced by Desmond, followed a 1985 report by an Oireacthas Committee that had been established by Fitzgerald. It was supported not only by an overwhelming number of deputies from his own party but also by the majority of rank and file members of Fine Gael. A vocal minority were opposed to this change, but the newly formed Progressive Democrats also supported the measure.

These three parties, unlike Fianna Fáil, which was vehemently opposed to the proposal, had a free vote on the matter and a 'Yes' vote was confidently predicted. That is, until the Church weighed in behind the opposition, with the result that the referendum produced an overwhelming 'No' when it was held in 1986. No doubt the proposers had not counted on the farce of van-loads of nuns turning up at polling stations to vote against a measure that could hardly affect them. Haughey, the most vehement and vociferous opponent of divorce, was absent from the debate on the motion and was believed in political circles to be in Paris with Terry Keane, the wife of a respected High Court Judge, with whom he later made no secret of having an extra-marital affair. The divorce referendum bill finally made it, in the teeth of fierce opposition, in 1996,

Given the circumstances and the unwillingness of his coalition partners to countenance spending cuts, Fitzgerald's government had made the best of a bad job. But by November 1986, faced with an unemployment rate of 20 percent and emigration once more on the rise, the country was facing bankruptcy. Fitzgerald realised that it would be necessary to introduce strict austerity measures if the national debt was to be kept under control, for so deep was the crisis that there was even talk of intervention by the International Monetary Fund.

Spending cuts were inevitable and his Minister for Finance, John Bruton, was instructed accordingly and introduced a budget so stringent that it even included a tax on children's shoes. Not only was this extremely unpopular but it led to the resignation of four Labour ministers. Fitzgerald realised that he could no longer rely on his coalition partners and a split was emerging in his own party, with some members urging that he jettison Labour and forge an alliance with the newly formed Progressive Democrats, whose economic policy was not dissimilar to that of Fine Gael. He was unwilling to take this step and had no option but to go to the country and a general election was called – but not before he had signed the Anglo-Irish Agreement, the outstanding success of his administration. It was a triumph not only for his party but also for the whole country.

Fitzgerald might have been disappointed at the initial reaction to the New Ireland Forum Report, but whatever misgivings there might have been regarding its historical analysis, the importance of the decisions taken during its deliberations cannot be over emphasised. Despite the fact that the debate had been confined almost exclusively to members of the constitutional nationalist parties, they had set about the task of redefining their position and, for the first time, the legitimate rights of Unionists as well as those of Nationalists were fully examined and afforded due recognition.

Thus section 4 paragraph 3 states, in relation to any new arrangement that might evolve, that "The civil and religious liberties, at present enjoyed by Northern Protestants, will be fully guaranteed." The next paragraph stressed the need for a new Constitution that would ensure that the needs of all traditions were fully met. Never before had such an unequivocal recognition of the Unionist position been made, on their behalf, by those representing all shades of constitutional nationalism, To this extent the Report represented a milestone in modern Irish history and as such it was to become a valuable discussion document in the forthcoming Anglo-Irish negotiations.

The document ended by proposing three options. The first was the establishment of a unitary State, in which those who were British citizens would continue to enjoy British citizenship without prejudice to their new status as Irish nationals. This was to be brought into being following a constitutional conference. The second suggested a federal or con-federal arrangement, comprising the two States, each of which would have a measure of autonomy within an all-Ireland framework. Each would retain its own parliament and administration and be able to retain the many laws and practices that had developed separately, in the Northern and Southern States, since the country was partitioned.

Under this arrangement Unionists could maintain their special links with Britain and mechanisms would be brought to bear to ensure full Northern participation in the federal or con-federal administration. The central government would have responsibility for its internal and external security, foreign policy and the administration of law and order, while there would be a federal or con-federal supreme court to interpret the Constitution and rule on any conflict of jurisprudence between the two States. The third option was joint authority, whereby the Dublin and London Governments would share equal responsibility for the administration of the Northern Province.

Finally, steps were to be taken to ensure the cultivation and promotion of the distinct character of the two communities in Northern Ireland, while British citizenship would be automatically conferred on all Irish citizens living in the Province, in accordance with their expressed wishes, while a comprehensive non-denominational Bill of Rights would be promulgated to ensure that individual rights and communal freedom of expression was maintained for both communities.

This solution was aimed at creating a climate of normal political life. Until this had been achieved, new security measures were to be developed that would gradually have the support of both sections of the community, as the alienation of the Nationalists from the forces of law and order was gradually reversed.

However no sooner had the ink dried on the Report than Haughey, to the consternation of his co-signatories, denounced it insisting that he and his party would only be satisfied with a unitary State. On the other hand, Fr Denis Faul in the North stated that whatever attractions the ideal of a unitary State might appear to have, it would not be acceptable to most Catholics in the Province, let alone the majority of Protestants. He pointed out that it was inconceivable that the Unionists, who were not even prepared to make submissions to the Forum debate, could be prevailed upon to take part in the proposed Constitutional Conference.

In the welter of accusation and counter-accusation that took place following the publication of the New Ireland Forum Report, and the fact that Haughey, though now leader of the opposition was set to become the next Taoiseach in light of the difficulties besetting Dr Fitzgerald's government, it is hardly surprising that when the first, much heralded, meeting between an Irish Prime Minister and Mrs Thatcher took place in Downing Street it had had all the signs of being a fiasco. Ultimately there was considerable dismay occasioned by her now famous "Out! Out! Out!" dismissal of the options contained in the Report, at the press conference that followed their meeting. Her actions were undoubtedly prompted by Haughey's earlier intervention and tended to obscure and divert attention from the very real progress that had been made at the meeting.

As Fitzgerald had been at pains to point out on numerous occasions, the Report was to be considered an agenda from which a policy could be developed. This was made manifestly clear by section 5 paragraph 10, which stated, in simple and unambiguous terms, "The parties to the Forum remain open to other views that may contribute to political development." The shortest paragraph in the document, its length belies its importance. When Thatcher and her advisers came to study the Report it became clear to them that the options suggested in sections 6, 7 and 8 were impractical in the light of the existing opposition to them, but that section 5 paragraph 10 offered an escape route whereby the dialogue could be continued.

Though naturally disappointed that he was unable to return to Dublin having had one of the three options in the Report accepted, Fitzgerald was nevertheless encouraged by the interest that Thatcher had shown in the work of the Forum and impressed by her determination to arrive at an acceptable solution that they could sell to their respective governments. But Unionist fears, though temporarily allayed by her apparently outright rejection of the Forum's conclusions, were soon to resurface when it became clear that a series of meetings between ministers and civil servants, from both governments, was to take place in preparation for a further summit.

No sooner had these started than a further difficulty became apparent and they were forced to proceed cautiously in order to avoid arousing suspicions on one hand, and false hopes on the other, as they began to prepare the framework for a new agreement. Either they could keep the Unionists informed of progress, in which case certain elements could be counted on to adopt disruptive tactics, or they could continue their negotiations in secret until such time as an agreement had been reached, in which case there was always the risk of leaks. In the event, they chose the latter course.

Meanwhile the IRA intensified its campaign, this time in mainland Britain, where numerous attacks took place. These culminated in the attempt to assassinate Thatcher and her entire cabinet by means of a bomb at their hotel in Brighton, where they were attending the Conservative Party Conference. This attempt to stir up hostility between the British and Irish peoples, however, proved futile despite some natural reaction from the media.

In the immediate run-up to the signing of the Anglo-Irish Agreement a number of leaks gave rise to intense speculation as to the venue for the meeting of the two Prime Ministers and the extent to which the Dublin Government might be involved in the future running of Northern Ireland. By the time it had been concluded, at Hillsborough, near Belfast, on 15 November 1995, the two Unionist parties had banded together to oppose it. While their pique at being kept in the dark is understandable, the vehemence of their protests and their determination to resist the accord at any price made no sense. Not only did it have the overwhelming support of the British Parliament and the Irish people, but it had also been given a warm welcome by the United States and by Ireland's partners in Europe.

The Agreement between the two neighbouring islands represented a historic breakthrough, for it had established a framework whereby the two countries could work together at all levels. To this end a Secretariat, consisting of civil servants attached to both governments and headed by Tom King, the British Secretary of State for the North, along with the Irish Minister for Foreign Affairs, was established at nearby Maryfield. It was agreed that the Irish Government should have a direct say in decision-making, regarding the role and composition of all bodies appointed by the Secretary of State.

An Inter-Governmental Conference was to be instituted that would be concerned with political matters, security and related issues, including the administration of justice, relations between the security forces and the community, prison policy and the harmonisation of the criminal law, to the benefit of both countries. The Conference would also promote cross-border cooperation and arrangements would be made to involve the minority community in the RUC. A complaints procedure would also be set up.

It was agreed that any change in the status of Northern Ireland could only come about with the consent of the majority of the people living in the Province and it was recognised that at present the wish of the majority was for no change. It was agreed, however, that Britain would give effect to legislation to establish a United Ireland should the situation change. The significance of this agreement is undeniable for it was to be the cornerstone of the Belfast Agreement, signed on Good Friday 1998.

Yet Haughey spurned this milestone in Anglo-Irish relations, which had secured an institutional role for the South of Ireland in the running of the North's affairs. He immediately sent Brian Lenihan to mobilise Irish-American opinion against it and leaders of that community, including Tip O'Neill, the Speaker of the House of Representatives, were approached. They treated this attempt by Haughey to undermine an international treaty, which had been signed by the government of his Country, as an act of treachery and gave it the contempt it deserved. Nevertheless, on Lenihan's return to Ireland Haughey made it clear that he would tear up the treaty, on his return to power.

CHAPTER 14

The Decline of Fianna Fáil
sees the Rise of a New Party

In the 31 years that elapsed since the fall of the Inter-Party Government in 1951, Fianna Fáil enjoyed absolute power except for a few spells, some lasting only a matter of months, when they were replaced by a coalition of Fine Gael and Labour deputies. In 1982, faced with the prospect of a protracted period in opposition, they had to contend with a number of scandals involving the Minister for Justice, Sean Doherty, the Attorney-General and Haughey himself. Michael Mac Arthur, then wanted by the police and subsequently convicted of murder, was not only found hiding in a luxury apartment owned by the Attorney General, but was also seen travelling in a state car, believed to be that of the Minister for Justice.

Haughey described this event as being grotesque, unprecedented, bizarre and unbelievable. So too was his mention of Mac Arthur as a "murderer", even though he had been neither tried nor convicted. This was no doubt a slip of the tongue, when Haughey's concentration was taken up with dissociating himself from the affair, but it prompted the first heave against him, by Charlie Mac Creevy, who tabled a motion of no confidence in October 1982, just before Fianna Fáil lost office.

This was a solo run that was both ill timed and made without consulting his potential supporters in the party. It was doomed to failure, for although both Des O'Malley and Martin O'Donoghue resigned their posts as Minister for Justice and Minister for Health in order to vote for him, his move was disorganised and he had not counted on the culture of fear that had been introduced into the party by Haughey, who had come to regard himself as the Juan Perón of Irish politics.

The scenes that greeted Haughey's victory more than justified the charges of intimidation that had made against him in the past and would be made again in the future. A mob of fascist-type hoodlums descended on his opponents and a fierce fracas developed within the precincts of the Dáil when Mac Creevy and others, including Jim Gibbons, the son of a former Minister, were physically assaulted and could well have sustained serious injuries had it not been for the intervention of the Gardai and Dáil ushers who enabled them to escape.

Following the election of a Fine Gael government, Michael Noonan, who had succeeded Doherty as Minister for Justice, was able to confirm the veracity of the rumours that had surfaced prior to the general election concerning the tapping of the telephones of two of Ireland's most respected political journalists, Geraldine Kennedy and Bruce Arnold. Even more sinister was the disclosure that Garda equipment had been used to make secret recordings of conversations between Martin O'Donoghue and Ray Mac Sharry on the orders of Sean Doherty, the Minister for Justice.

With these revelations the discontent that had been smouldering within Fianna Fáil, regarding the actions of its leader and his conduct of affairs, boiled over. The once proud party founded by De Valera was torn by dissention and, in the coming weeks and months, the corruption that many already suspected had eaten into the body politic was exposed. Yet it was not until the 1990s that the full extent of the rot, involving not only some of his closest associates but Haughey himself, became known.

This dissention resulted in heaves against the leader, but they all failed because of widespread intimidation and the fact that, in addition to his supporters in the Parliamentary Party, many in the constituency organisations shared his diehard republican views. Others admired Haughey's form of 'stroke politics', and he saw to it that loyalty was well rewarded, ensuring the support of backbenchers. Nevertheless the most successful of these attacks against Haughey was that mounted by Des O'Malley.

Once regarded as a potential leader of Fianna Fáil, O'Malley was Minister for Justice at the time of the Arms Trial, when he had refused to entertain Haughey's plea for intervention on his behalf. A strong supporter of Jack Lynch, he had nevertheless served under Haughey. A vocal and fearless critic of the policy adopted by Haughey in opposition, O'Malley had incurred his wrath by voting for the Anglo-Irish Agreement and the Divorce Referendum, as well as Barry Desmond's Family Planning Bill. He made a strong speech advocating a pluralist State and attacked opponents of the Agreement, whom he accused of having a partitionist mentality.

The major clash between O'Malley and Haughey occurred following the publication of the New Ireland Forum Report in May 1984, when after initially giving support to its conclusions Haughey had reversed his position to outright opposition without any reference to his party. It was this defiance of the rules of parliamentary procedure and the snub to his Cabinet that had prompted Senator Eoin Ryan to call a meeting of the Parliamentary Party at which O'Malley, having accused his leader of stifling debate within the party, had been deprived of the whip, in a unanimous roll-call vote. This was against party rules, which required all such votes to be taken by secret ballot, but such was the culture of fear that despite the fact that many shared O'Malley's views, the motion was passed by an overwhelming majority.

Though the whip had been withdrawn from him, O'Malley still felt that he had a future in the party until, following his speech on the Family Planning Bill, he was summoned to its headquarters on 26 February 1985 to face a vote calling for his expulsion. He faced a packed meeting and asked for a secret ballot but, true to form, Haughey refused, being determined to rid himself of the man who had taken part in three attempts to oust him. He realised that the gathering included some of O'Malley's supporters and demanded a roll-call vote, which he insisted should be unanimous. This led to the collapse of the anti-Haughey faction and the nine members who had had the temerity to oppose the motion were afterwards subjected to treatment reminiscent of that meted out to the supporters of Mac Creevy on the defeat of his challenge to the leadership.

As yet O'Malley had not considered forming a new party, but following his loss of the whip and final expulsion from Fianna Fáil he had time to stand back and re-assess the Irish political scene. He realised that the two major parties, which had their origin in the Civil War, were mutually destructive inasmuch as their policies were still governed by the attitudes they had assumed in the 1920s. Consequently they had become hostage to sectional interests with the result that both his own and the main opposition party were now riddled with corruption and it seemed clear that Haughey was hell-bent on establishing an authoritarian State in order to enrich himself and his cronies.

However it was with some reluctance that he turned his back on a party in which he had held high office and of which had been a member for the better part of 20 years. When at last he decided to form the Progressive Democrats he first turned his attention to those in Fianna Fáil who were opposed to Haughey. These included the likes of Seamus Brennan, the party's General Secretary, on whose discretion he could depend. Later, however, following reports that neither Brennan nor any of the other leading figures he had hoped to attract, such as David Andrews, would leave the party, he became hesitant. In fact he might well have abandoned the project in September 1985 were it not for Haughey's opposition to the Anglo-Irish Agreement.

During the ensuing debate Mary Harney, a Fianna Deputy for Dublin South West, with whom O'Malley was already in discussions regarding the possibility of forming a new party, was refused time by Haughey to speak in favour of the Agreement. When the vote was taken she therefore joined O'Malley in the division lobby supporting the Fine Gael-Labour government's motion. Needless to say she was also expelled from the Parliamentary Party, on 17 November 1985, and from that day forward O'Malley's mind was made up.

CHAPTER 15

Fianna Fáil's Decline sees the Rise of the PDs

As long ago as 1982, following the watering down of Alan Dukes's budget proposals at the behest of Dick Spring, Garrett Fitzgerald's right hand man, Michael Mc Dowell, a lawyer who was fast making a name for himself, had predicted the demise of the Fine Gael-Labour coalition unless Fitzgerald took a firm hand with his labour colleagues and began a radical programme aimed at tackling the fiscal and unemployment problems facing the country. Mc Dowell made no secret of his views among his friends in the Law Library where he discussed the matter with, among others, Michael O'Leary, TD, who had quit the Labour Party in 1982 to join Fine Gael, having voiced his opposition to Labour's policies.

By 1984 it had become clear that Fianna Fáil was in a position to gain a landslide victory at the next election and, judging by Haughey's performance to date, it was easy to imagine that party emerging as Fianna Fáil the Fascist Party, rather than as a constitutional republican party. It was this that persuaded Mc Dowell to contact Des O'Malley with a view to discussing the formation of a new party that would break the mould of Irish politics by ending the stranglehold of both Fianna Fáil and Fine Gael. They felt that both were relics of the Civil War and that replacing them with a new policy-driven party, would look to the future rather than the past.

At about the same time, O'Malley received a letter from Paul Mackay, an accountant and long-standing member of Fianna Fáil who had been party treasurer in Haughey's Dublin North-East constituency, but who had had a dispute with Haughey regarding access to donors to the constituency party's funds, the names of which he refused to reveal despite intimidation. Like O'Malley he had been unceremoniously dismissed from the party and offered to lend his support, as well as that of his friends, should there be any truth in the rumours now abounding that O'Malley was considering founding a new political grouping.

Initially O'Malley had hoped to recruit Seamus Brennan, who had resigned as general secretary of the Fianna Fáil Party, David Andrews and other prominent members who shared his fears at the direction being taken by Haughey, to form the nucleus of the new party. But having considered the matter they came to the conclusion that they would be in a stronger position to control events from within the party than by joining a new, untried, party made up of what would be perceived as dissidents opposed to Haughey. They were, however, prepared to collaborate in the formation of such a party and there can be little doubt that their help proved invaluable. A similar invitation had been made to members of Fine Gael but had been rejected due to fears that the position of that party would be undermined by the emergence of a new party.

O'Malley and Mary Harney were therefore joined by Mc Dowell and Paul Mackay, as well as Michael O'Leary and two Labour senators, Helena Mc Auliffe and Timmy Conway. Charlie Mc Creevy also joined the group, although he was not yet prepared to commit himself to the new venture. The new colleagues set about laying the foundations of the Progressive Democrats, or PDs as they became known. The composition of the new party was such as to diffuse early criticism that it had simply been created with the object of serving the interest of the better off, or any other vested interest for that matter. O'Malley already had strong support in Munster, particularly in Cork, where both Pearse Wyse, a Fianna Fáil deputy, and Councillor Marin Quill had expressed an interest in joining his new party. By spring 1985 considerable progress had been made in establishing a party that would be representative of all shades of pluralist opinion.

The party's plans were ambitious. They would set out to end the sleaze and culture of fear that had become a feature of Irish politics and present a new face, free of the baggage of the Civil War that had produced inertia and corruption, and tackle the economic problems facing the country by replacing the tax and spend policy of previous administrations with tax cuts to stimulate the economy. They would also break the mould in Irish politics by establishing coalition rather than one-party rule as the norm rather than the exception, thereby ending Fianna Fáil's monopoly of power when in office.

They also saw the necessity of cutting down on public expenditure in order to reduce the national debt to manageable proportions. It was the policy of the PDs to deregulate state owned industries that could be run more cost effectively and efficiently by private enterprise, and reduce costs by making such industries competitive while opposing public and private monopolies. Self-reliance was to replace institutional dependence, although care would be taken to ensure that social services were improved. Their policy towards the North would be one of conciliation and would stress adherence to true republican policies rather than nationalistic myths.

The launch of the party, on Saturday 21 December 1985, had been carefully planned, received considerable media attention and caught the political establishment by surprise. Fianna Fáil appeared not to be shaken but Haughey was furious and issued a statement to the effect that no member of Fianna Fáil would join the new party. Fine Gael was similarly incensed at the prominent role played by Michael Mc Dowell. However so successful was the launch that in response to an advertisement that appeared on 1 January, over 700 calls were received at the party's headquarters in South Frederick Street from those interested in joining the party, and sufficient money was pledged to more than cover the party's initial expenses. The following week, when the first public meeting was held at the Marine Hotel in Sutton, loud speakers had to be rigged up in the car park to manage the traffic jams and the crowd of 2,000 that had arrived for the meeting.

On 17 January an IMS poll commissioned by the *Sunday Independent* showed that the PDs stood to gain 19 percent of the vote; an MRBI poll, published in the *Irish Times*, gave the party 25 percent. Translated into seats this would have seen the election of anything between 20 and 30 Progressive Democrats. There followed a number of mass meetings during the ensuing months that saw a large number of Fianna Fáil activists desert that party to join the PDs. These meetings had now assumed a countrywide aspect, the first regional one taking place at the Metropole Hotel in Cork City on 20 January.

This meeting, which was so large that it overflowed into the street outside, was of particular significance in that Pearse Wyse jumped ship and joined the PDs, despite the fact that one day before the meeting Haughey had sent Bobby Molloy, one of his most able politicians and a member of his shadow Cabinet, to persuade him to remain in the party. Only three days after the meeting, however, Molloy himself shook Fianna Fáil to its roots by resigning to join the PDs.

Having no doubt what Haughey's reaction would have been if he had known about his intended departure in advance, Molloy had taken care to tell no one of his intentions. He simply left a letter in his filing cabinet stating that after 20 years of service to the party he had become totally alienated from the direction it was taking. Others, including David Andrews, were now rumoured to be on the brink of leaving Fianna Fáil and he confirmed to O'Malley that it was his intention so to do, on his return from a brief visit to Paris.

What caused him to change his mind has never been explained. Was he subjected to threats or did he, like so many potential supporters of the PDs, decide that he would be in a better position to oppose Haughey, if he remained in Fianna Fail? How else can Andrews' overnight decision be explained? Mc Creevy, who had all along been unwilling to commit himself to the new project, decided to return to Fianna Fáil.

The meeting in Cork was followed by other massive affairs in Galway and Dublin, and the first national conference of the party was held in May at Dublin's National Stadium. It was televised by RTE but it was prevented from giving a live presentation of Des O'Malley's keynote address, despite the party's opinion poll ratings, due to a rule proscribing RTE from so doing for any party that had not received five percent of the vote at the last election. Nevertheless the film was featured on news bulletins and received extensive publicity in the national media.

By 1986 the party was making nationwide inroads into Fianna Fáil territory and several household names joined the party. Frank Aiken, son of the co-founder of Fianna Fáil, joined the ranks of the PDs in Louth; Martin Gibbons, son of Jim Gibbons, stood for the party in Kilkenny; Maureen Quill, a close friend of Jack Lynch, became the PD candidate for Cork North Central; and Peadar Clohessy, a former Fianna Fáil TD, stood for Limerick West. Dotted around the country a number of new names joined the growing list of potential candidates who were to make their names at the forthcoming election.

Inroads into the support for Fianna Fáil also took place in the capital, particularly in the South, Southeast and Dun Laoghaire constituencies. High-profile personalities such as Anne Colley, the daughter of George Colley; Geraldine Kennedy, the *Irish Times* columnist; and Michael Mc Dowell were all returned at the general election to represent their constituencies. When the votes were counted, on 18 February 1987, the PDs had gained 14 seats, representing 12 percent of the vote, while many of their candidates topped the poll. The only error made was to fail to put forward sufficient candidates to take full advantage of their support.

However while the party went on to celebrate its twenty-first birthday, such were the vicissitudes that assailed it, due to personality clashes and policy differences, that its momentum gradually faded over the years, and following errors of judgement during the 1989 election the party dropped 8 of its 14 seats. Among the high-profile candidates that lost were Anne Colley, who had topped the poll in Dublin South the last time out, Geraldine Kennedy and Michael Mc Dowell. Among those who retained their seats were Des O'Malley, Mary Harney and four former members of Fianna Fáil, including Marin Quill who held her seat in Cork North Central.

The party appeared to have recovered in 1992. Michael Mc Dowell and Martin Cullen regained their seats while Liz O'Donnell and Helen Keogh replaced Anne Colley and Geraldine Kennedy. Pat Cox, who stood in Pearse Wyse's former seat, following his retirement in Cork South Central, added a Dáil seat to the one he held in the European Parliament, where he went on to be a Commissioner. However a serious clash developed between Cox and O'Malley that was to lead to Cox's resignation from the party.

In 1997 they entered the election having lost three of their sitting deputies. Cox had left, Cullen had joined Fianna Fáil and Peadar Clohessy, who had represented Limerick East, had retired. The campaign began with a disastrous policy launch apart from which the party made the error of fielding far too many candidates. Mary Harney, who had proved herself to be a skilled legislator then made a number of uncharacteristic mistakes, for her next move all but sabotaged the party's carefully constructed campaign which was based on demonstrating the PDs independence from

Fianna Fail, thereby attracting support from Fine Gael voters. But without consulting the candidates or party workers, Harney suddenly announced that the PDs had agreed to give their second preference votes to Fianna Fail.

The result was an unmitigated disaster. Only four of their prospective candidates survived – Harney, O'Malley, Bobby Molloy and Liz O'Donnell – and Mc Dowell resigned from the party, angry at losing his seat due to an inept campaign. To many it seemed clear that Harney had become far too close to Fianna Fail and she had to face meetings of party activists who voiced their recriminations, but in fairness to her, it must be said that she accepted the criticism, without question.

During the next few years there was intense media speculation as to the PDs' future and at one stage their survival was in such doubt that a crisis meeting of the members was called. However the party was given a fresh lease of life after Mc Dowell accepted the position of Attorney General and in January 2002 he agreed to return to the party as President, while Tom Parlon, the leader of the Irish Farmers' Association, also unexpectedly agreed to join the party. Nevertheless the outlook appeared bleak and while the PDs and Fianna Fáil could both take credit for the continuation of the Celtic Tiger economy, this and Bertie Ahern's success at the peace process had resulted in a situation where the polls predicted that Fianna Fáil would romp home with an overall majority. The PDs had determined to fight the campaign as an independent party, despite the blandishments of Fianna Fáil. It was a high-risk strategy that could lose them a considerable number of second-preference votes from Fianna Fáil, but this was to prove the secret of their success.

Mc Dowell, against the judgement of some of the members of his party's National Executive, who feared that his plan might backfire to cause such anger in the ranks of Fianna Fáil as to make a further coalition with that party impossible, decided to mount a propaganda campaign aimed at persuading the electorate that Fianna Fáil could not be trusted to run the country on its own, thereby making coalition an election issue. A high risk strategy, this proved to be the turning point in the campaign and the fortunes of the PDs, creating the fear that Fianna Fail might be heading for a landslide victory and the print media coverage which followed also carried articles endorsing this message\ which was taken from door to door by PD canvassers as well as Mc Dowall and Harney in television interviews throughout the remainder of the campaign. When the voters went to the polls on 17 May this was the main issue, and the following morning it became clear that the party was well on target not only to retain its four seats but also to gain several more.

In the event they gained eight seats. Mc Dowell headed the poll and was to become the most respected though forthright, and therefore the most controversial, Minister for Justice since the foundation of the State. Fiona O'Malley, daughter of Des O'Malley, was returned for Dun Laoghaire and other leading PD candidates were returned with increased majorities. This pattern was repeated throughout the country, where Tom Parlon had a comfortable majority in Laois-Offaly and, to the surprise of many, May Sexton was elected for Longford-Roscommon and Noel Grealish for Galway West.

However with the honourable exception of Mc Dowell it would seem that, prior to the election campaign, the party had departed from its original agenda and the high ideals set by Des O'Malley. They failed to capitalise on the part they had played in bringing about the country's prosperity, being more interested in maintaining power than keeping a watchful eye on their partners.

When the votes were counted, it transpired that Fianna Fáil were two short of an overall majority and thus had the option of forming a government with friendly independents or re-entering a coalition with the PDs. The latter also had the alternative of going into opposition, where they would have the opportunity of making a reverse takeover for a weakened Fine Gael and positioning themselves to form the next government. Unfortunately they made the disastrous decision of accepting Bertie Ahern's offer to join him in forming an administration. This may have left them in power but they no longer had any real say in affairs.

They therefore became hopeless spectators while their Fianna Fáil partners introduced the very spendthrift, though populist, policies the PDs had been elected to oppose. This saw an unmanageable increase in the numbers and pay of those employed in the public service, particularly in the Health Service, despite the protests of Mary Harney who on being made Minister for Health had determined to streamline the service, once the HSE had been created, by retiring the redundant administrative staff from the old unwieldy health boards but was prevented from taking any such action by Ahern.

As Tánaiste she had little option but to agree to pay increases, that by far outstripped those available in the private sector without any commitment to productivity. Consequently those who had returned the PDs to ensure that their partners in government did not return to their past profligate policies, came to see them as irrelevant.

Similarly in 2003 they backed Mc Creevy's ill-thought decentralisation plans – yet another populist scheme they had been elected to oppose. This was not only extremely expensive but had nothing to do with planned regional development and undermined still further the efficiency of the public service by transferring government departments, rather than industries, to the regions. Yet it never appeared to occur to the Parliamentary Party, even when Ahern declared himself a socialist that he was planning to replace the PDs with the Labour Party at the next election.

It has often been said of the PDs that they punched above their weight. This was made possible because they were supported in cabinet by a number of Fianna Fáil colleagues who supported their views. Indeed had this not been so their position would have become untenable during the Reynolds era, as he was determined to return his party to an overall majority and did all he could to humiliate the PDs by denying them access to services and endeavouring to keep contact between the two parties to a minimum. Nevertheless O'Malley was able to push through a new Companies Act that was to make it possible, in a future administration, for Mary Harney to establish the Tribunals of Enquiry into the activities of certain high-profile politicians and businessmen, including C J Haughey.

Perceived by many as a niche party, inasmuch as the expansion of private enterprise formed a plank in the party's agenda, it was opposed to vested interests and was determined to root out the corruption caused by the link between politics and big business. Consequently it did not find favour with the section of the business community that benefited by its connection with Fianna Fáil, a good number of who did not pay taxes but relied on tax evasion schemes such as that operated by the Ansbacher Bank. The PDs therefore they had little support from the very wealthy who regarded them as a nuisance, particularly in regard to the revelations coming from the Tribunals.

The PDs were in a buoyant mood in 2007 following their successful national conference at White's Hotel in Wexford. A number of new candidates had been attracted to the party, including Colm O'Gorman, who had agreed to stand for the county. No sooner had the general election campaign begun than damaging and apparently incontrovertible allegations concerning Ahern's financial dealings appeared in the media, following his evidence to the Mahon Tribunal. So damaging were these charges that Michael Mc Dowell, now Minister for Justice, counselled that the party should pull out of government. But he was to find himself in a cleft stick because Ahern, due to his part in the peace process and his perceived part in bringing about the country's prosperity, was the most popular Taoiseach since the foundation of the State.

To bring down such a man when he was in he process of completing a deal with Ian Paisley that would see the Northern Assembly restored, as well as the entire peace process, would have seen the annihilation of the PDs. Therefore, very much against his will, Mc Dowell was persuaded by Harney to relent, stating the Fianna Fáil line that Ahern should be regarded as innocent until the Tribunal had completed its deliberations. This perceived flip-flop lost him his seat and the PDs, now divided, plummeted to an all-time low.

Only Harney and Noel Grealish succeeded in retaining their seats. Fianna Fáil formed a coalition with the Greens, who had taken six seats led by John Gormley, when Labour rejected their overtures, but Harney returned to her former post as

Minister for Health when Ahern formed a three-party coalition. Whether the PDs are now able to continue to survive became a matter of conjecture and a decision has now been taken to wind up the party.

Before they lost their way, following the 2002 General election, the PDs' policies had rescued Ireland from the destitution of the 1980s and laid the foundations for her subsequent prosperity, as well as achieving their aim of breaking the mould in Irish politics. But in recent years they parted a long way from the original agenda set by Des O'Malley and, with the honourable exception of Mc Dowell, they gave the appearance of being more anxious to retain power than to oppose measures that resulted in the government's misuse of public funds. McDowell was a loss not only to the PDs but also to the country. Never a populist, he believed in telling the people the facts, as they were, not necessarily what they wanted them to be. But as is conceded by his critics, it was his very honesty that brought him down.

CHAPTER 16

Haughey retains power by courtesy of Fine Gael

The 1987 general election was a closely fought and bitter contest and, when the votes were counted, so close was the outcome that Charles Haughey was forced to rely for support on two independent deputies. These were Neill Blaney, who had been expelled from the Fianna Fáil Party following the Arms Trial, and Tony Gregory, whom he had persuaded to vote for him during the 1982 election. But when the Dáil met and nominations were taken, Gregory abstained and Haughey only scraped home following the election of Sean Treacy, a former Labour TD as Ceann Comhairle, (Chair of the House) who had agreed to take this post when the Dail met.

Prior to this election some disquiet had been voiced among Fianna Fáil members, and it was an open secret that any nominee other than Haughey would be acceptable to them and possibly the PDs as well. But Haughey acted swiftly to crush any opposition to his leadership. Two days before the Dáil met, a statement was read out on his behalf by Sean Burke to the effect that no-one outside Fianna Fáil should have any illusion that they could influence Haughey's leadership. He would remain leader and Taoiseach and the only alternative would be a general election.

So keenly aware was Haughey of the danger to his position, that the day the Dáil met he called a meeting of his front bench and told them to prepare for an immediate general election. His plan was to get word round the House as to his supposed intentions in order to terrify his own members into silence, but he had overlooked the fact that he was in no position to call such an election. This was the prerogative of Garrett Fitzgerald, who until a government was formed was still acting Taoiseach. Not only had Fitzgerald no intention of calling such an immediate election, but even if he had been so minded the President would have had the right to veto the plan, as Fitzgerald no longer had an absolute majority.

Haughey had no intention of stepping down and immediately set about reviewing his options. He could call another election as he had threatened, but in view of the current result he dismissed this idea out of hand. It also seemed clear that he could not rely on any of the opposition parties for support, but just prior to the election he had had a meeting with Fitzgerald, who had agreed to deliver the support of Fine Gael provided that Haughey's administration adopt a policy of economic restraint.

He therefore announced a programme aimed at ending the economic crisis, which included a commitment to cutting public spending and the budget deficit.

This allayed the fears of the many who had been dismayed at the possibility of his election and who believed that under his leadership Fianna Fáil would revert to the policies that had been responsible for the economic crisis, in the first place. But they were still concerned that the result of the election could only produce instability, when quite the reverse was required.

The outcome of the election was a bitter blow to Fianna Fáil, which at the outset had had a clear lead in the opinion polls. Now their hopes of an overall majority, which would enable them to dispense with aid from Tony Gregory or anyone else had been shattered, and a palpable mood of despondency could be felt throughout the party from the grassroots up. For the fourth time in a row Haughey had failed to deliver unfettered power to them but he had the satisfaction of knowing that his bitter enemies the PDs, though they had done well, had failed in their bid to obtain sufficient seats to achieve a balance of power that would have threatened his position as party leader.

The PDs might have won 14 seats and 12 percent of the vote but they had made one cardinal error. Had they contested sufficient seats there is little doubt that they would have been in a position to unseat Haughey, for the groundswell of support for the new party had been obvious since the early days of the campaign. Moreover it is clear that they could have depended on the system of proportional representation to deliver them a substantial number of second preference votes from Fine Gael as well as Fianna Fáil. Still, many now had high hopes that the party would be included in the next government for it had the numbers to make up a strong and stable administration. Not only had the PDs established themselves as a force to be reckoned with, but they could take credit for forcing Haughey into making a substantial U-turn, as became clear when he announced his programme for government.

Many now looked to the PDs, whose policy of fiscal rectitude was not dissimilar from that contained in Haughey's announcement, which showed a marked contrast to that contained in his earlier policy. But, bitter enemies of Haughey and all that he stood for, they had been founded as a new and separate party, determined to end the Civil war differences that had been the root cause of the stagnation that had impoverished the country and subjected the body politic to a climate where corruption was rife. However both Fianna Fáil and Fine Gael were opposed to the PD policy of cutting taxation as a means of stimulating the economy and diffusing the unemployment crisis.

The question was whether the PDs would be prepared to enter a Haughey-led government. Some were opposed to any such arrangement, but when Haughey appeared to have undergone a Damascene conversion and added his own voice to the demand to control public spending, they came to the conclusion that the matter deserved serious consideration. By making it a precondition that they would enter government only as separate and equal partners they would have broken the mould in Irish politics, as it was a core value of Fianna Fáil that it should not entertain any coalition arrangement.

Such a condition would have enabled the PDs to put a stop to any attempt by Haughey to revert to his old ways and thereby enable them to stamp out corruption. However no amount of persuasion could convince Fianna Fáil to change its mind regarding the possibility of entering a coalition and Haughey announced his intention of forming a minority government. An astute politician, he felt safe in so doing for he envisaged that Fitzgerald's promise of support, made prior to the election, would translate itself into something similar to that announced some months later by Alan Dukes who, replaced Fitzgerald as leader of Fine Gael.

Following the election of the government, Dukes, now leader of the opposition, made the surprising announcement that his main priority was the destruction of the PDs. Both he and John Bruton accused them of stealing their policies, from which it became clear that Fine Gael feared that the new party would make inroads into their membership.

There had been some alarm when Ray Mac Sharry was made Minister for Finance, due to his now infamous speech made some time previously that he would replace Fine Gael "doom" with Fianna Fáil "boom". However his March 1987 budget introduced a programme of fiscal rectitude similar to that advocated by Fine Gael, but instead of recommending tax cuts to galvanise the economy, as suggested by the PDs, he announced drastic spending cuts. In fact when Ruari O'Hanlon, the Minister for Health, introduced the cuts that were applicable to his department he all but precipitated a general election.

Meanwhile Haughey's U-turn on the economy had been followed by an even more dramatic change in his policy towards Northern Ireland. Not only did he drop his objections to the Anglo-Irish Agreement, first adopted by the Fine Gael-Labour coalition and supported by the PDs, which he had pledged to tear up if elected, but he seemed anxious to redeem the reputation he had earned as an irreconcilable nationalist following the Arms Trial. Within months he was working the Agreement without any hesitation and stunned many in his own party by agreeing to operate the extradition arrangements, agreed by the previous government, with only minor modifications following one of the most atrocious outrages of the troubles – the Remembrance Day bombing in Enniskillen that killed 11 people and wounded 60 others.

Initially a critic of the severity of the health cuts, Dukes had been concerned at the narrow escape that the country had had from yet another general election. This was a risk that neither his own party nor Fianna Fáil could take and he was now satisfied that the government could be trusted both with the economy and the thorny question of Northern Ireland.

The PDs were feared by Fine Gael for purely party political reasons, and by Haughey for their clear intention to wipe out corruption in politics and business. Indeed their name will always be associated with the tribunals that they succeeded in having established by a future administration, to enquire into planning irregularities involving enormous profits gained through the rezoning of land, and the vast sums paid to politicians at government and local level.

Dukes was aware that if the election had been a disaster for Fianna Fáil, then his own party had not fared much better, when he announced what became known as the Tallaght Strategy – so called because he first divulged this plan at a meeting of the Tallaght Chamber of Commerce. This was an imaginative initiative by which he intended to restore Fine Gael's lost fortunes, while sidelining the PDs by presenting Fianna Fáil with an acceptable alternative to coalition.

Under this scheme Fine Gael would refrain from adversarial politics and back the government, so long as it remained committed to its new fiscal policy and conciliation towards Northern Ireland. A sound policy in itself, he envisaged that it would restore Fine Gael's lost fortunes, for they would be able to claim responsibility for the government's successes. By the next election he anticipated that he would have ended the danger of his own party being eroded by the PDs, whose demise he imagined would have occurred by then.

As a result of the Tallaght strategy the government was assured of an overwhelming majority in the House, while the PDs were neutered They could not vote against policies that they had initiated and consequently found themselves in the same camp as the Labour Party and the Workers' Party, whom they were able to back on matters extraneous to the economy, such as crime or social justice.

With the support of Fine Gael, Haughey set about his own rehabilitation. Indeed, had it not been for the aberration of the Arms Trial he might well have become Ireland's greatest ever statesman. But whatever ambition he might have had initially was annulled by the culture of his own personality and self-aggrandisement, which was to result in his becoming a byword for corruption. However his third term in office opened auspiciously. His new approach to the problem of Northern Ireland saw a thaw in Anglo-Irish relations that was illustrated by his meeting with Margaret Thatcher, an event that was widely welcomed in Ireland as well as in Britain.

His contribution to the arts world was immense. In a period that witnessed the emergence of a plethora of new authors, he presided over an Irish renaissance in the visual arts and music and, whatever his motives, he set about a programme of restoration of the once dull but imposing government buildings. An astute politician and an economist of note, he realised that a major cause of the country's instability stemmed from poor labour relations, which resulted in disputes being settled by strikes and periods of unrest, rather than by conciliation.

Haughey made it clear to all government departments, which invariably submitted annual claims and expected increases whether or not the exchequer could afford them, that they must expect a cutback in such expenditure. He opened direct talks with the Irish Congress of Trade Unions and those representing the employers, as well as the farming interests, in order to hammer out a programme of wage restraint, initially to cover the next three years.

In this he had the aid of Bertie Ahern, his Minister for Labour, who exhibited his negotiating skills for the first time. These talks resulted in the Programme for National Recovery, a master plan that was to guarantee industrial peace for the coming two decades. Not only did it peg public service pay increases to 2.5 percent for the coming three years, but it also paved the way for the establishment of the Labour Court to arbitrate between employers and unions in disputes regarding pay or conditions.

There can be no doubt that this national wage agreement was the foundation on which Ireland's economic recovery was built. With the country's new prosperity the government was able to concentrate on reducing the national debt, while it was possible to divert money to infrastructural development and other much needed projects rather than the previously insatiable demands of the labour market or the employers.

Meanwhile the PDs, in addition to being effectively neutralised, were confronted with a number of problems. The most serious resulted from the decision by the Minister for Health to close Barrington's Hospital in Limerick, an institution that was long past its sell-by date, and transfer its services to nearby St John's. This placed Des O'Malley in an awkward situation as Barrington's was in his constituency and the people were incensed by this decision.

Should he stand by his party's declaration against clientelism or should he support the demands of his constituents? Seeing the possible danger to his seat he chose the latter, even going to the extent of taking part in a protest march. This decision was an unmitigated disaster for his party, which emerged from the affair with its credibility irreparably damaged.

At their 1988 conference in Cork the PDs decided to update the 1937 Constitution and later in the year they issued a document that differed from that drawn up by de Valera, in that it abandoned the territorial claim to the North, contained in articles 2 and 3 of his Constitution, as well as the ban on divorce. But in endeavouring to emphasise the pluralist nature of their new Constitution they made the mistake of making no mention of God, leading to the accusation that the PDs were advocating a Godless state.

However in the same year they produced a plan for a radical overhaul of the tax system, based on a lower rate of taxation of 25 percent and an upper rate of 30 percent for personal tax, as well as a start in the reduction in corporation tax, in order to attract new industries and reduce the unacceptably high rate of unemployment. These reforms were dismissed as pie in the sky by the government, which was enjoying a near-record rating in the opinion polls thanks to the Tallaght strategy.

Haughey then saw the chance of consolidating his position and obtaining an overall majority for his party by calling a snap general election in June 1989. It was not long before he began to rue this decision for it soon came to light that, since his return to office some two years previously, he had restored the export credits in respect of the Goodman Group, Ireland's biggest exporters of meat. This scheme had been established to guarantee to exporters payments that were due from countries whose economic and political stability could be assured. It had been revoked for the Goodman Group by the Fine Gael-Labour administration, due to the unacceptable risk the company was taking in exporting £41.2 million tons of beef to Iraq, against the advice of the Minister for Industry and Commerce.

Not only had the government renewed this scheme with regard to a State that was regarded as a bad risk, but the figures for 1987/88 showed that the cover had increased to £78.5 million and in fact exceeded the amount of beef actually exported by £57 million. The Minister for Industry and Commerce therefore had no option but to withdraw the cover once more.

This was the second time a link between Haughey and Goodman had been established. Prior to this, within months of his return to office, he had announced the largest project in connection with the food industry in the history of the State. It involved the investment of £260 million in Goodman's operations, part of which was to be provided by the Industrial Development Authority, part from the European Union and the balance from a package of loans, under section 84 of the Finance Act.

This project had to be abandoned when it emerged that one of the Goodman Group of Companies, Food Industries, was in the process of making a takeover bid for the State-owned Irish Sugar Company. This bid was being examined by the Oireachtas Committee for State-sponsored Bodies, the chairman of which was none other than Liam Lawlor, who was also a director of Food Industries. Faced with this conflict of interests, Lawlor resigned and the £260 million scheme was dropped.

There now followed a dispute regarding a valuable gift, including jewellery that had been presented to Haughey by a member of the Saudi-Arabian royal family during a state visit to Ireland. Such expensive gifts presented to the Head of State are regarded as the property of the State, but Haughey had refused to part with them and rumours regarding his integrity now abounded.

These concerned his fund-raising activities and those of his closest friends. Under scrutiny were Padraig Flynn, who was said to have received a cheque for £50,000. According to the account given by Michael Collins, in his book, *Breaking the Mould,* this ended up in a foreign bank account in the joint names of Flynn and his wife, Dorothy; Ray Burke, who raised £60,000, part of which came from Century Radio at a time when he was minister for energy and communications. Rumours of these dealings spread like wildfire but they were small beer compared with the £150,000 that Haughey received from Ben Dunne, the supermarket tycoon, who was found to have financed him to the extent of £1.3 million between 1992 and 1997. These matters were only finally exposed following the setting up of the Flood, Mahon, Moriarty and Mc Cracken Tribunals set up to investigate wrong doing by politicians and businessmen, in particular those suspected of receiving of receiving bribes, in respect of the re-zoning of land for development purposes,

The 1989 election campaign began with the polls showing Fianna Fáil still holding a commanding lead, despite the many rumours surrounding Haughey and some of his senior ministers. Fine Gael's share of the vote was shown at 28 percent, but even given that the showing for Labour represented a substantial increase, it seemed clear that Fianna Fáil was set to gain an overall majority.

By contrast the opening of the contest proved most inauspicious for the PDs. Not only did it see them lose their deputy leader Michael Keating, but the previous March, before the declaration of the general election, Pat Cox had been selected as their candidate for Munster in the European Elections, Bobby Molloy had been selected for Connacht-Ulster and John Dardis for Leinster.

To add to their problems their poll showing had plummeted from 14 percent to five percent, in part due to the Tallaght strategy, which had resulted in many of the members of Fine Gael who had transferred their support to the PDs during the 1987 election, switching back to their original party. The PDs main support now came from former adherents in Fianna Fáil plus a number of floating voters.

In order to make any headway they needed a voting pact with another party and Fine Gael's policy was closer to theirs than any other. They therefore approached Alan Dukes, who at first dismissed the proposition out of hand. But having received reports from his constituency organisations of the return of former members who had defected to the PDs last time out, and having discussed the matter with his Parliamentary Party, he decided to negotiate a pact. He reasoned that another coalition with Labour would only be short-lived due to the re-emergence of the tensions that had resulted in the collapse of Dr Fitzgerald's administration. A voting pact with the PDs had at first sight seemed as unlikely, as was the possibility of seeing his own party back in government with any party other than Labour.

On the other hand if they could, as he expected, increase their share of first-preference votes, Fine Gael could afford to remain in opposition until the next election, while they set about rebuilding the party. By that time, Dukes anticipated, the party would have been considerably augmented by swallowing up the PDs. Meanwhile they could, if necessary, renew the Tallaght strategy to keep Fianna Fáil in power as long as it suited their purposes and ensure that they kept on the straight and narrow.

O'Malley now announced his party's policies, which, as well as restating their economic priorities, concentrated on a commitment to provide real improvements in the health service and social justice. This was designed to counteract the campaigns of Labour and the Workers' Party, both of which concentrated on health cuts and social issues. But while his opponents received considerable media coverage, his promise of honest government excited no-one because of the party's dismal performance in opposition, which was in part due to errors of judgement but mainly due to the fact that they had been incapacitated by the Tallaght strategy. As result the Labour Party's star was now in the ascendency according to the media coverage, which gave scant publicity to the PDs.

The main item on the agenda for the joint programme for government of the proposed Fine Gael-PD coalition included the PDs' tax-cutting policy and a concentration on Fine Gael's concern regarding the national debt. Privatisation was mentioned but there was little policy devoted to current issues and it did little to excite the attention of the electorate.

Polling took place on 15 June and Fianna Fail, far from getting an overall majority, received only 77 seats. The left-wing parties at the expense of the government and the main opposition parties made the main gains. While the election result may have been catastrophic for Fianna Fáil, it was an unmitigated disaster for the PDs, who lost eight seats, including some of their brightest stars. Among these losses were Anne Colley, who had topped the poll in Dublin South the last time out, as well as Geraldine Kennedy and Michael Mc Dowell.

When the Dáil met on 29 June the incredible happened. For the first time in the history of the State the Dáil failed to elect a Taoiseach, with Haughey, Dukes and the Labour leader, Dick Spring, all failing to receive sufficient support and neither party being prepared to call another election for fear of incurring the wrath of the electorate.

The Dáil adjourned for two hours to enable Haughey to consider his position. He made it clear that he was not prepared to resign, but in order to comply with legal niceties he agreed to forward a letter to President Hillery containing his resignation, as he announced to the Dáil when it resumed. Though he had failed to retain his position as Taoiseach he was still the head of a caretaker administration until such time as a new one was formed and, prior to the meeting of the Dáil, realising that his position might be precarious he had put out feelers to see if he could rely on the support of any other party or the Independents.

He had ruled out Labour and the Workers' Party as their policies were incompatible but had contacted Mary Harney, who in contrast to her leader, had suggested in a broadcast that her party should be prepared to support him in government. But this offer had to be withdrawn, following angry telephone calls to her party's central office, reminding her that the party's price was coalition and nothing less.

Nevertheless, no longer feeling confident that the main opposition party would be prepared to renew the Tallaght strategy, as he was aware that there had been considerable dissension within Fine Gael regarding the adoption of this policy in the first place, Haughey decided to take a calculated risk and opt for an arrangement, falling short of coalition, with the PDs. Though reduced in number, they had sufficient seats to make it possible for Fianna Fáil to form a government.

Haughey therefore decided on making a direct approach to Des O'Malley and offered him a package of concessions that included the chair of important Dáil Committees, the position of Leas Ceann Comhairle (Deputy Speaker of the House), three seats in the Senead and, although they had not the required number of seats to qualify, the position of group status. He also promised back-up staff but refused to budge on the possibility of a coalition.

Both men felt that sufficient progress had been made at this meeting to set up negotiating teams, with Albert Reynolds and Bertie Ahern for Fianna Fáil and Bobby Molloy and Pat Cox for the PDs. But while they appeared to agree on many issues, the talks seemed to be getting nowhere and collapsed on the thorny question of coalition. Haughey therefore decided to take the matter up himself.

There followed a stormy Cabinet meeting at which he introduced the subject of the dreaded C-word and suggested that the government reconsider its opposition to coalition. Reynolds met Haughey with angry interjections and the overwhelming majority of those present defeated the motion. Nevertheless he succeeded in getting agreement that he undertake the final negotiations with the PDs and meanwhile Bertie Ahern, who saw a future in coalition, was already working to secure such a deal but kept his views to himself during the Cabinet meeting.

So convinced was the Cabinet that coalition was now a non-runner that Padraig Flynn made a broadcast to reassure the Fianna Fáil faithful and the country as a whole that the matter would never be entertained. But meanwhile Haughey had asked O'Malley to meet him at a Dublin hotel. The PD leader had been informed of the Cabinet meeting and the decision that had been taken but he was also well aware, from previous experience, that Haughey was quite capable of defying it if it suited him.

When the two men met, O'Malley sounded the other out to discover, as he expected, that he was now prepared to discuss a coalition arrangement; but the problem was Haughey's Cabinet and the fact that he had found it impossible to sell the idea to them. O'Malley then played his trump card and suggested that he put them in their place by threatening to call a general election. For the first time since their meetings had begun the two men smiled and a meeting was set for the following day to formalise their agreement. O'Malley was joined by Molloy and Cox, but Haughey did not bother to invite his own negotiators.

Haughey's Cabinet colleagues, in particular Reynolds and Flynn, who had been making his broadcast while the meeting between Haughey and O'Malley was taking place, were indignant. But Haughey had the support of at least four members including Bertie Ahern, who had been a member of his negotiating team. When the prospect of a general election was put to them they had no alternative, however reluctantly, except to accept his decision. When the Dáil met on 6 July it was adjourned to enable Fianna Fáil and the PDs to prepare a programme for government.

This included the continuation of Fianna Fáil's national wage agreement, about which some scepticism had been expressed in the past, in particular by Michael Mc Dowell, as well as the PDs tax-cutting agenda and Northern Ireland policy. In addition their proposal for an Environmental Protection Agency was included, as were a host of other measures ranging from health to social welfare.

The only outstanding issue was the number of Cabinet Ministers that Fianna Fáil would be prepared to surrender to its coalition partners. Haughey endeavoured to limit this to one but the PDs were adamant that they would only be content with two and once this was conceded they agreed to vote for him as Taoiseach. Haughey was able to return to the Dáil on 12 July and, having been elected with the support of the PDs, was in a position to announce his new government, which included O'Malley as Minister for Industry and Commerce and Molloy as Minister for Energy.

In the 1989 election the PDs had snatched victory out of defeat by playing Haughey at his own game but their first term in office was to prove short-lived, for in doing so they had played into the hands of his enemies as well as their own. Reynolds' antagonism was not immediately apparent. As a businessman he shared the PDs' economic policy and when as Minister for Finance he announced his budget in 1990, a start was made in the tax-cutting agenda as set out in the programme for government. But the PDs soon realised what they were up against, for he had no difficulty in ensuring that he got all the credit in the ensuing media coverage.

Indeed such was the relationship that was to develop between Reynolds and the PDs following Haughey's defeat by him during the first Fianna Fáil-PD coalition, that before deciding to join Fianna Fáil in a coalition government the PDs might have done better to adopt something like the Tallaght strategy to keep Haughey in power until someone more to their way of thinking had mounted a challenge.

The period in office of the Fianna Fáil-PD coalition got off to a good start. In 1989 the Berlin Wall had come down and the following year it was Ireland's turn to have the presidency of the European Union, which saw Haughey at his best. He undoubtedly succeeded in securing a friend at court in Chancellor Kohl of West Germany, by giving his backing to the reunification of that country.

Despite their past differences, Haughey and O'Malley had a good working relationship. Mary Harney, who had received a junior ministry in the Department of the Environment, was to make a name for herself by introducing legislation making it obligatory to burn smokeless fuel in Dublin, thereby ending the smog with which the city had been cursed each winter. But by their insistence on coalition and good use of their position as partners, rather than mere supporters, the PDs had angered not only Albert Reynolds but also Padraig Flynn, formerly loyal lieutenants of Haughey's. Furthermore a number of backbenchers, who distained the PDs and regarded them as traitors, were now determined to overthrow Haughey, whom they blamed as the architect of the coalition arrangement.

Events were to play into their hands for it was not long before the potential for dissention between the coalition partners became apparent for O'Malley, in his new ministry, had access to papers relating to the export credit scheme as it related to the Goodman Group. They contained statements that conflicted with answers he had been given while an opposition deputy in the Dáil and he set up a departmental enquiry to discover the true facts.

Shortly afterwards it became clear that the Group was on the verge of bankruptcy and he discovered that much of the meat for which credit had been made available had originated not in Ireland but in Britain and Northern Ireland. Credits amounting to £40 million due to the Group were cancelled and, as it was deemed to be the beneficial owner of Classic Meats, that firm was closed down.

When the financial affairs of Goodman International came to light, a special Dáil session was convened. It was revealed that the Group owed £460 million to international banks and was owed £180 million respect of exports to Iraq. Had it been allowed to collapse, the effect on the farmers would have been devastating, so the government passed legislation to appoint an examiner to the Group, which would give it a breathing space to reschedule its debts.

Their handling of this matter illustrates just how good the working relationship that had been established between Haughey and O'Malley was, despite their past differences. This may well have been influenced by the fact that only a fortnight before the Dáil met, Haughey had been annoyed when Goodman had approached him with a request that he bale him out. But so great was the sum involved that not only was this impossible but was an embarrassment in view of Haughey's close business relationship with Goodman.

Nevertheless the PDs emphasised their independence from Fianna Fáil by refusing to vote for Sean Doherty, Fianna Fáil's nominee for the position of Cathaoirleach of the Senead. The honeymoon between O'Malley and Haughey, which proved to be short-lived, was to come to an abrupt end in 1990 during the presidential election campaign of that year. There were three candidates: Brian Lenihan, who was Tánaiste and Minister for Defence; Austin Currie from Northern Ireland for Fine Gael; and Mary Robinson for Labour. As coalition partners, although they had an open mind, the PDs felt honour bound to support Lenihan. For a while there was nothing unusual about the campaign, but when trouble arrived it came like a bolt from the blue.

Within days of the vote being taken Lenihan was accused of having contacted President Hillery in 1987, following the collapse of Dr Fitzgerald's government, and of having tried to prevent him from calling a general election. He had denied this accusation in a television interview, but he had also given an interview to a student, which had been tape-recorded, in which he had admitted making such an approach. When this was made public it caused a furore and Alan Dukes added fuel to the flames by tabling a no-confidence motion. If this had gone to a vote the PDs would have had no option but to withdraw from government and vote with the opposition if they were to retain their credibility.

Haughey, fearing the collapse of his government, approached Lenihan with a request that he resign. But as he showed no inclination to do so and it became clear that the PD ministers were clearing their offices pending their departure, Haughey took the unprecedented step of sacking a man who had been his Tainiste and Minister for Defence and who was now his party's presidential candidate.

This may have saved the day for him but the respite was only temporary for many in Fianna Fáil were angered at what they regarded as the intransigence of the PDs. Albert Reynolds and Padraig Flynn, who had been humiliated by Michael Mc Dowell during a telecast in which they were both panellists and he had attempted to besmirch Mary Robinson's good name, were all the more determined to get rid of Haughey and end what Reynolds contemptuously described as his party's temporary little arrangement with the PDs.

When the votes were counted Mary Robinson, who now had the unofficial support of the PDs, was returned as President although Lenihan gained a number of sympathy votes. Matters appeared to have returned to normal and O'Malley succeeded in passing a new Companies Act that closed a number of loopholes that had been the cause of past abuses.

Haughey, however, soon became involved in a number of controversies that exposed his close association with big business. The most outstanding of these involved the derelict site of the former Johnston, Mooney and O'Brien bakery at Ballsbridge, which had been purchased by Telecom Eireann, a state company, for £9.4 million. But when it emerged that Michael Smurfit, the Chairman of Telecom Eireann had an interest in the property company that had handled this transaction; questions were raised regarding the resale of the site. Following extensive media coverage of the matter both he and Seamus Parceir, who had been formerly the Chairman of the Revenue Commissioners, resigned from the board on Haughey's instructions.

Meanwhile Haughey's position had been further compromised by the evidence given in a court case taken by Greencore, in its dispute over the ownership of a Jersey-based company. This and the Telecom affair were followed by a controversy regarding Celtic Helicopters, a firm that Haughey's son Ciaran was a part owner, when it became known that his partner had approached Ben Dunne for finance as well as the sale of Blackrock College to a friend. This all resulted in Fine Gael's introduction of a no-confidence vote, but this could not be debated until the Dáil resumed after the summer recess.

At this stage, as the programme for government was due for review, Haughey's coalition partners were divided. Some felt that they should stay on, endeavouring to squeeze as many concessions as they could out of the government before it was brought down. In the end it was decided that no precipitant action should be taken until their proposed fiscal reforms were complete. Haughey was equally anxious to see a deal completed in order to re-establish his authority. However when the Dáil resumed Reynolds was adamant and indicated that, as Minister for Finance, he could not accept the budgetary implications involved in the proposed programme.

A final clash seemed inevitable but following the intervention of Bertie Ahern, whom Haughey had brought in as his fire-fighter, he was persuaded, among other concessions, to give a commitment to cut the basic rate of tax from 30 percent to 25 percent and set an upper rate of 44 percent. In addition the PRSI rate for employees was reduced from 7.75 percent to six percent. It was then that Haughey, relieved that a deal had been struck, described Ahern as "the most devious, the most cunning of them all".

Then the Goodman affair was resurrected following the broadcast of ITV's programme *World in Action* that alleged the connivance of the authorities in questionable practices in the operation of the Group's meat plants. Haughey's obfuscation when the matter was brought up in the Dáil was sufficient to bring the coalition to the brink of collapse, but the situation was diffused when he agreed to set up an enquiry into the beef industry.

When the Beef Tribunal began its hearings at Dublin Castle the sleaze factor predominated, as the inconsistencies between the evidence and that previously given in the Dáil by Haughey, was illustrated by witness after witness. This resulted in yet another vote of no confidence and Reynolds and Flynn were forced to leave the Cabinet on November 7, having voted with the opposition. The PDs, who were well aware that they had an ulterior motive, namely to break up the coalition, decided to stay clear of the affair having expressed their concern.

A Cabinet reshuffle took place in 1991 during which Bertie Ahern, who had been chief whip and also remained Fianna Fáil's national treasurer until the following year, during which time he remained co-signatory of the party leader's bank account and admitted that he had signed blank cheques for Haughey, was appointed Minister for Finance. His coalition partners and the opposition parties were stunned when Dr Jim Mc Daid was appointed Minister for Defence, a man whom they accused of having provided an alibi for an IRA man facing extradition. This provoked considerable outrage and resulted in a crisis between the coalition partners.

Once again it looked as if the government's days were numbered but it was saved when Mc Daid offered to withdraw his nomination. However, this spelt the end of his political career. Fianna Fáil members were incensed when it became clear that the PDs had forced the issue. At the end of 1991 Ray Burke published the Phone-tapping Bill, which was regarded as a personal affront by Sean Doherty, who had been Minister for Justice and had been disgraced in 1982 when this affair came to light. Doherty therefore agreed to appear on an RTE television programme, produced by Shay Healy, in which he justified his actions in tapping the telephones of two journalists, Geraldine Kennedy and Bruce Arnold, inasmuch as a decision had been taken in Cabinet to put an end to leaks to the press. He stated that Haughey was fully aware that Doherty was following this Cabinet decision.

O'Malley and a number of ministers who had served in Cabinet reacted with amazement. They were aware that the matter had never been discussed in Cabinet and it was clear that Haughey himself must have given the order, without any consultation with his ministers. His coalition partners decided that there could be no further prevarication and were not prepared to find themselves faced with further embarrassing compromises, so Haughey had to go if they were to justify their existence. However once Haughey had resigned they realised that life under Reynolds would be anything but easy.

CHAPTER 17

Albert Reynolds

Albert Reynolds assumed the reins of power for two short periods, the first lasting a year and the second being replaced by a rainbow coalition, but both his administrations collapsed due to differences with different coalition partners, mostly of his own making. Nevertheless under his watch Anglo-Irish relations took a leap forward due to his friendship with John Major, the British Prime Minister. The Northern Ireland peace process also progressed when he succeeded in bringing about the first of a number of meetings between the SDLP leader John Hume and Sinn Fein President Gerry Adams.

This was a brave move, for the policies of the two men were poles apart. Hume was a man of peace while Adams was waging a war of attrition in order to bring about the reunification of Ireland. But Reynolds' motives in bringing about this meeting were widely misinterpreted in the North as an attempt to establish a pan-nationalist front; in the South, and many feared that he was getting too close to Sinn Fein.

It is more than probable that he was aware, through his contacts with John Major, that secret talks were already taking place between Sinn Fein and the British government and it is clear that both leaders appreciated that this seemingly insurmountable conflict could only be resolved by talks with the combatants. As it transpired, the Hume-Adams talks proved to be essential building blocks in the peace process and were to result in the first IRA ceasefire, in August 1994. Reynolds can also take credit for capitalising on the goodwill established by his predecessor, during his presidency of the European Union, by succeeding in negotiating the first of a number of grants, involving the transfer of funds from Europe, to modernise Ireland's creaking infrastructure.

But when he replaced Haughey in 1992 he determined on a policy of non-cooperation with his partners in government, despite the fact that he owed his position as Taoiseach to them. This seemed inexplicable to the PDs, particularly as he had appointed Charlie Mac Creevy, a man who could well have acted as a catalyst between them, as his Minister of Social Welfare. Mac Creevy, as well as Reynolds, shared the pro-enterprise agenda adopted by O'Malley.

From the outset Reynolds found himself involved in controversies outside his control, due not so much to policy but to faulty administration. He had hardly established himself in office when he found himself embroiled in a situation resulting from a decision by his Attorney General, Harry Whelehan, to forbid a 14-year-old rape victim from travelling to England for an abortion.

Known as the X-case, this and matters relating to it were to bedevil and occupy almost his entire first term of office. Members on all sides of the Dáil viewed the handling of this matter with distaste and there was considerable sympathy throughout the country for the predicament of this child. Many in political circles felt that the complexities and circumstances of the case were such that the Attorney General should have turned a blind eye. It added to the strains between the coalition partners, as the PDs maintained that not only was compassion lacking, in the manner with which this case had been dealt, but questioned why she had been denied information about abortion let alone forbidden to travel.

Matters came to a head during the debate on the referendum to ratify the Maastricht Treaty. It had the backing of Fianna Fáil, Fine Gael and the PDs, but was opposed by Labour and the left-wing parties. What should have been a normal political decision was jeopardised when the Pro-Life Movement, which opposed abortion, endangered assent to the Treaty by branding it pro-abortion, and while the artificial termination of a pregnancy was legal in Europe, the same was not true in Ireland. Reynolds, however, saved the day by having a protocol inserted into the treaty recognising Ireland's constitutional position regarding abortion, and with the help of Fine Gael the Treaty received the assent of the people when the vote was taken.

This solution only added to the agitation occasioned by the X-case and Reynolds therefore decided to put a triptych of resolutions to a referendum to change the Constitution concerning the issues of the right to travel, the right to information about abortion, and a proposal to make abortion illegal except in cases where the life of the mother was in danger. This latter proposal became known as the substantive issue, as the first two issues were not particularly controversial.

While the PDs agreed that it was necessary to change the Constitution, they were fundamentally opposed to Reynolds approach to the wording of the substantive issue as it was at variance with that of the Supreme Court, which had subsequently allowed the child to travel in view of the girl's threat of suicide, which was deemed to be a threat to her life.

Reynolds then approached the Attorney General, who advised that this ruling had been given in a specific instance and that there was nothing, in law to prevent the Taoiseach from proceeding with his proposed amendment to the Constitution. The PDs decided to hold their fire for the success of Reynolds' policy had seen the poll rating for his party soar to 50 percent compared with that of their junior partners, which had stuck at around six percent. This was possibly due to the fact that they had been denied the ability to participate in government by Reynolds who, when Minister for Finance, had been able to take the credit for the economic reforms initiated by them.

The PDs were also well aware that they could not withdraw from government, as in the event of a general election being precipitated by them on this issue they could face annihilation. Fianna Fáil could count on the support not only of the Roman Catholic Church but also that of the powerful pro-life lobby. The PDs would simply be playing into the hands of Reynolds, who had long sought a means of jettisoning his partners.

This antagonism came to a head, in June, when O'Malley gave his evidence to the Beef Tribunal. Reynolds had been Minister for Industry and Commerce in 1987/88, when the export credit scheme had been misused by the Goodman Group, and he was determined to get his revenge on O'Malley and anyone else whose evidence had implicated him.

In his evidence O'Malley described Reynolds's actions during this period as "wrong, reckless and foolish". Reynolds, whose evidence was marked by a hesitation in answering direct questions, replied by accusing him of being "irresponsible and dishonest" – a charge he refused to withdraw despite the advice of his counsel.

As a result of his mishandling of the X-case and the public's disbelief in the evidence Reynolds had given to the Beef Tribunal, the fortunes of Fianna Fáil and the PDs had been reversed, with the former plummeting and the latter appearing to be staging a recovery, The PDs therefore decided to withdraw from the coalition while the going was good, but they delayed doing so until Sean Dargan, O'Malley's department head, had given his evidence. They did not announce their decision until the night before the Dáil was due to debate a motion of no confidence in the government, and their ministers resigned the following day in order to enable them to vote with the opposition.

The subsequent general election was called for 25 November and the timing could not have been better for the PDs. The first opinion poll showing a massive drop of 20 percent in the Taoiseach's share of the vote, for the electorate blamed him for the breakdown of the coalition. Fianna Fáil's slide in the opinion polls was further accentuated at the beginning of the campaign when Reynolds, unable to rebut O'Malley's assertion that he was responsible for the collapse of the government, referred to his remarks as "crap – total crap", in an interview with RTE's Charlie Bird. He worsened the situation by repeating the comment to the editor of *The Sunday Tribune*. So great was the backlash that he was forced into a humiliating climb-down. Labour, whose leader Dick Spring made the most of the difference between the coalition partners, made the greatest gains.

When the count took place, the turnout for Fianna Fáil proved to be the lowest since 1927. Fianna Fáil and Fine Gael both lost 10 seats while the Labour Party returned a record 33 seats. The PDs also did well, gaining back the seats they had lost at the last election, including those of Michael Mc Dowell. Liz O'Donnell and Helen Keogh replaced Anne Colley and Geraldine Kennedy, who had resigned following their defeat in 1989. Pat Cox, now the PDs' European representative for Munster, replaced Pearse Wyse, who had resigned, in Cork South Central.

Once again the Dáil failed to elect a Taoiseach and talks took place, between Fine Gael, Labour and the PDs with a view to forming a rainbow coalition, but they broke down due to irreconcilable policy differences between the Labour Party and the PDs. However the principle of coalition had now been established and Reynolds had no option but to enter into a partnership with Labour if he wished to remain in office.

The Fianna Fáil-Labour coalition assumed office on 12 January 1993 and the following month Bertie Ahern, the Minister for Finance, introduced a budget that appeared to indicate a return to the old Fianna Fáil policy of tax and spend. This was a deliberate snub to the PDs, for it aimed to reverse many of the changes introduced by them during the past three years.

In the very first meeting of the 29th Dáil, O'Malley complained of a matter that had occurred in December of the previous year during the Beef Tribunal. He said that there had been an exchange outside the Tribunal between his counsel and a State's counsel, Gerry Danaher, who had boasted that the State had access to private papers concerning O'Malley's evidence. They related to his rebuttal of an accusation that he had received a bribe from Tara Mines, which he maintained had been leaked to Fianna Fáil sources by Reynolds, who was a close confidant of Danaher. According to Michael Collins, in his book *Breaking the Mould* what began as a storm in a teacup was to have unexpectedly serious political implications. According to Collins, Danaher, who was a member of Reynolds 'kitchen cabinet' made these remarks to Des O'Malley's Counsel, in the Shelbourne Bar, just before Christmas; making the information public knowledge. Consequently he was investigated by the Bar Council but the nature of these enquiries would never have been made public but for the fact that the story was published by the *Sunday Tribune*.

However, this matter sparked off unfounded rumours that resulted in O'Malley's decision to give up the leadership of the PDs, in case any damage should be done to the party, and seek the nomination for the European Parliament, held by Pat Cox, who had now become a member of the Dáil, lest the constant publicity should prove an embarrassment to his party. But this decision was to lead to a split within its ranks.

O'Malley's decision itself was not unreasonable, due to the party's stand against the dual mandate that allowed Dáil deputies to retain their seats in the assembly while holding a similar position in a local authority or the European Parliament. In addition Cox was now his party's shadow Minister for Finance and O'Malley wished to enable a leadership contest between Cox and Mary Harney.

Cox would not agree, as legislation had not yet been passed to do away with the dual mandate. This led to considerable bad blood between the two men and Cox announced that he would step down from his Dáil seat to concentrate on European affairs. Salt was added to the wound when O'Malley confirmed his intention of putting his name forward for the Munster seat in the forthcoming European elections. Cox then resigned from the PDs but succeeded in retaining his seat in Europe as an independent. Harney replaced O'Malley unopposed and was able to capitalise on the fact that she was the first woman to be elected leader of a political party since the foundation of the State.

The PDs had not yet got over the trauma of the upheaval that had taken place within the party when an event occurred that was to see the beginning of the end of the Fianna Fáil-Labour coalition. The Dáil had been recalled at the end of August to discuss the report of the Tribunal investigating the beef industry. This was to lead to angry exchanges between Reynolds, who considered himself to have been vindicated, and Dick Spring, who took a line closer to that of John Bruton, the Fine Gael leader and Mary Harney, the PD leader. This resulted in the government coming under increasing pressure.

Trouble between Reynolds and his new coalition partners reached breaking point in November 1994, when following an incident that has never been satisfactorily explained Harry Whelehan, the Attorney General, failed to act on an extradition warrant issued by the RUC in respect of Brendan Smyth, a priest from Belfast, who was being sought to answer charges of child abuse.

Spring demanded the dismissal of the AG but Reynolds, unwilling to see an old friend humiliated, removed him by promoting him to the position of President of the High Court. This was too much for Spring, who now had the support of the entire opposition, and he announced the withdrawal of his Parliamentary Party from the coalition with Fianna Fáil.

The collapse of his government put Reynolds in a quandary. He was well aware that he had burnt his boats with Labour and such was the antagonism of the entire opposition that he was unlikely to get another partner. He feared that his own party would be crushed in the event of a general election, but he envisaged that if the opposition succeeded in cobbling together a rainbow coalition its divisions would be such as to render it impotent. They and not he would therefore be forced to call an election and Fianna Fáil could take the opportunity to rebuild its forces.

Bertie Ahern now replaced Reynolds as leader of Fianna Fáil, but despite his best efforts he was unable to forge a new coalition with Labour and, following negotiations, a Rainbow Coalition came into being involving Fine Gael, Labour and Democratic

Left. This was a new party that included Prionsias da Rossa and Pat Rabbitte, who had broken away from the Workers' Party, as well as independents, but had no PD representatives due to the implacable opposition of Labour.

Led by Fine Gael's John Bruton, who became Taoiseach, the new government defied Reynolds' predictions by bonding well. Fianna Fáil and the PDs also acted together so well in opposition that Harney came to the conclusion that the future of her party lay in coalition with Fianna Fáil. This led to the gradual realignment of the parties, following a number of opinion polls and persuasion by the media. However when Bruton introduced the Divorce Referendum he emphasised that he too was committed to a liberal agenda and both Labour and the PDs backed his call for a 'Yes' vote.

The Rainbow Coalition also had its successes, with perhaps its greatest being in the economic sphere when it persuaded the European Union to allow Ireland to reduce its rate of Corporation Tax to 12.5 percent. This had long-term positive repercussions for the country by making it attractive to companies seeking to establish themselves there and take advantage of Ireland's membership of the EU. This setting provided the basis for the boom years.

During this period the Mc Cracken Tribunal began its hearings into evidence relating to the affairs of Haughey and Michael Lowrey, a Fine Gael minister, both of whom were alleged to have received substantial payments from supermarket tycoon Ben Dunne. But a disagreement developed between Bruton, who wished to defer the forthcoming general election until after the 1997 summer recess, when the Tribunal was due to present a report, and Dick Spring, who favoured an immediate election. It was subsequently agreed it would take place on 6 June and the Dáil was dissolved on 25 May.

CHAPTER 18

The PDs return to coalition under Bertie Ahern

When Bertie Ahern addressed his party's Ard Fheis (annual general meeting) shortly before the general election was called, he made great play of his determination to clean up Fianna Fáil and rid the organisation of the sleaze factor that had dogged it, ever since the Haughey era. No doubt this was meant for public consumption as much as for his immediate audience, but it might well have been directed in particular at the PDs for there is little doubt that a new relationship existed between the two parties with the departure of Reynolds. However he refrained from making any reference to a potential coalition.

During the course of the rainbow administration, when the realignment of the parties had taken place, a decision had been made by the partners in the coalition to campaign as one, with an agreed programme for government. Successive opinion polls and media pressure also suggested that Fianna Fáil and the PDs should fight the election as an alternative coalition. As the two parties shared many of the same policy objectives this seemed on the cards but no decision had yet been made, yet when the campaign began the PDs, as before, adopted an independent strategy.

At the outset both parties had a healthy lead in the opinion polls. Nevertheless Ahern, who had been a protégé of Haughey's, had a number of questions to answer for it would seem that he had learned much from his former boss. Judging by his toleration of corruption among his chosen associates he would appear to have emulated Haughey except that his own his financial dealings, however questionable, do not appear to have been motivated by self-aggrandisement.

However questions regarding these dealings had been raised in the Dáil some years earlier. In addition a tax assessment in respect of £2 million that had been received by Haughey in 1994 from Ben Dunne, had been reduced to nil by the Appeals Commissioner, Ronan Kelly, who was Ahern's brother-in-law. This matter was raised in the Dail. However due to the stonewalling of Brian Mc Creevy and the refusal of the Ceann Comhairle to allow the debate to continue after it had lasted 45 minutes, the matter remained unresolved.

With the approach of the general election the opposition had held their fire, fearing an adverse reaction from the electorate, such was Ahern's popularity, but during the campaign itself the country was awash with rumours of financial wrongdoing by his close associates, leading Geraldine Kennedy of the *Irish Times* to question him.

He had dodged the issue, intimating that if her questions related to a certain individual he was well aware of the matter and could assure her that there was no truth in the speculation. That individual was Ray Burke, whom he intended to appoint as his Minister for Foreign Affairs if elected, despite allegations of planning corruption that had been published in the media prior to and during the election campaign. Like Ahern, Burke had been a member of Haughey's old guard and ever since the 1970s his name had been the subject of considerable speculation regarding alleged links with builders and planning irregularities, and he had also been the subject of a Garda enquiry.

Their putative coalition partners also had a satisfactory poll rating, but following their successes in 1992 the PDs had become over-confident and contested 30 seats. This confidence might have been justified had it not been for the ensuing catalogue of errors. As well as the fact that eyebrows had been raised when Harney had announced her intention to introduce water charges, the party manifesto was a disaster in that it contained a highly controversial plan to have single mothers remain at home with their parents rather than set up their own one-parent homes.

Harney, who had started the campaign with the highest opinion poll rating of any of the party leaders, was accused of setting the clock back to the bad old days of stigmatising the illegitimate. The media portrayed the party as an uncaring, right-wing group, an impression given further weight when Harney announced a policy that would see the numbers employed in the public service reduced by 25,000 over the next four years.

This played straight into the hands of her opponents and the trade unions were particularly incensed. In the middle of the campaign, instead of keeping her options open until it came to forming a government, and without consulting party members in advance, she decided to make a vote transfer pact with Fianna Fáil. This announcement came like a bolt from the blue to party candidates and activists, who had been canvassing successfully to maximise the party's vote from both Fine Gael and Fianna Fáil supporters but who were now faced with the collapse of their campaigns.

Following her statement it became clear that Ahern and Harney, who had been close friends for the past 20 years, had envisaged the return of a Fianna Fáil-PD coalition, for whatever else divided them they were united by their tax cutting agenda. This became a major issue in that the Rainbow Coalition parties opposed it, their preferred option being a widening of the tax bands and an improvement in the various allowances.

In an attempt to undo the damage done by his putative coalition partner, Ahern caused a joint Fianna Fáil-PD statement to be issued promising specific tax cuts that would be of considerable benefit to the overburdened PAYE sector, as well as pay increases for public service workers. Among other fringe benefits there would also be a 15 percent shareholding given to staff in Telecom Eireann, should that company become privatised.

This statement had been carefully planned to catch the attention of the media and receive the maximum publicity before polling day. It had the desired effect with both the *Irish Times* and the *Irish Independent* urging voters to vote for the Fianna Fáil-PD coalition. But it was too late as Fianna Fáil failed to regain any of the seats they had lost in 1992 and the result for the PDs was a disaster. They had started the campaign with the polls giving them a rating of 11 percent but they lost six seats, including that of Michael Mc Dowell, the brain behind much of their more radical policies, who lost his seat for the second time and who was so infuriated at the errors that had dogged their campaign that he resigned from the party. However Harney, O'Malley, Molloy and Liz O'Donnell succeeded in retaining their seats.

The Labour Party's results were equally disastrous for they plunged from a high of 33 seats to a mere 17. This was no doubt due to the fact that they had lost the confidence of the electorate, for contrary to pledges given during the 1992 election, they had entered into a coalition with Fianna Fáil.

With only 77 of their candidates returned, Fianna Fáil were once again unable to form a government, even with four from the PDs. Likewise the Rainbow Coalition, with 54 Fine Gael seats plus Labour's 17 and Democratic Left's 4, had fewer seats, even if they were able to attract two from the newly elected Greens as well as one each from the Socialist and Sinn Fein members.

However there were six independents, among them Mildred Fox, Harry Blaney and Jackie Healy-Rae, all of whom were close to Fianna Fáil and could be persuaded to vote for Bertie Ahern as Taoiseach. This would give the Fianna Fáil-PD coalition a majority of just one vote, sufficient to make Ahern Taoiseach and they could begin to form a government.

As the two parties had already agreed a programme for government, the only question now remaining was what ministry would be available to Mary Harney, as with her depleted party Ahern would no longer be in a position to justify giving the PDS more than one out of the 15 members making up the Cabinet. Harney felt that she would be too isolated on her own and fortunately there was a precedent for dealing with this situation, which had resulted from a similar predicament when allocating ministries in the Rainbow Coalition, when John Bruton had agreed with Prionsias da Rossa that Democratic Left be allowed to nominate Pat Rabbitte to accompany him at the Cabinet table as a junior Minister.

Consequently, as well as being Tánaiste, Harney became Minister for Enterprise and Employment while Bobby Molloy was given special status as junior Minister in charge of Housing and Urban Renewal, enabling him to attend Cabinet meetings. Liz O'Donnell was given a position with responsibility for overseas development in the Ministry for Foreign Affairs. At a meeting called by the members Mary Harney accepted that she had made disastrous mistakes during the campaign and also went out of her way to placate those members of the public service whom she had angered.

It would seem that Pat Rabbitte was incorrect in his assumption that a coalition made up of 81 out of the 166 seats in the Dáil, which depended on the support of three independents, was incapable of survival. However not only did its fortunes improve but it was still intact in 2007.

The Teflon Taoiseach as he became known, Ahern is perhaps the greatest enigma in the Irish political sphere to have appeared since the foundation of the State. A statesman of world renown, he was a brilliant negotiator and shrewd strategist who transformed Anglo Irish relations to such an extent that he was invited to address the joint Houses of Parliament at Westminster. His place in history is assured as the leader whose patient persuasion and tireless work brought peace to Ireland. Yet it would seem, like those who preceded him, that he was by no means incorruptible.

First elected as Taoiseach on 26 July 1997, he headed the third Fianna Fáil-Progressive Democrat coalition that was guaranteed to last by virtue of the fact that its first and second terms in office coincided with the beginning and continuation of the boom known as the Celtic Tiger. As the social partnership established by Haughey, which had led to industrial peace, was continued together with the PDs' low-tax regime, the old age of unemployment and emigration gradually disappeared to make way for a new era of prosperity and immigration.

Ahern's consensus-style politics, which was in marked contrast to that adopted by Reynolds, was aided by his appointment of Charlie Mc Creevy as Minister for Finance, whose analysis of the economic problems facing the country was similar to that of the PDs. In that capacity he acted as a valuable intermediary when difficulties arose between the two partners in government. Things seemed to favour the new regime, for within three weeks of its appointment the IRA declared its second ceasefire, which paved the way for talks leading to the Good Friday Agreement the following year.

However his first few months in office were overshadowed by a controversy regarding some of his appointees to Cabinet, in particular Ray Burke as his Minister for Foreign Affairs. Following reports in the media that a certain James Gogarty had given Burke a substantial payment to facilitate a planning application on behalf of JMSE, his employers, Ahern sent his brother, who was Chief Whip, to London to meet the company's CEO prior to the first session of the Dáil. Ahern also spoke to Michael Bailey, a builder who was said to have been present when money had exchanged hands and who was later found guilty of corruption by the Mahon Tribunal, in connection with this matter. Yet for some unexplained reason he had failed to inform his brother that he had made this direct contact, nor the result of it.

Nevertheless Ahern had gone ahead with Burke's appointment and stated in the Dáil, in response to enquiries, that he had made extensive enquiries. But despite his assurances, the veracity of these rumours was to be confirmed by James Gogarty in evidence given to the Flood Tribunal in January 2000. To the surprise of many, Burke received the backing of Harney.

In fact Harney was in a quandary for while she knew that her judgement would questioned by her own supporters, she was equally conscious that to bring the government down now would revive memories of the Lenihan affair, which had led to considerable criticism of her party's influence. Furthermore an election at this stage would fly in the face of her party's good fortune in getting into office and might well see them wiped out. For the same reason she was to find herself unable to take any action when confronted with Ahern's evasion when questions were raised regarding payments to Haughey and his amnesia relating to blank cheques that he had signed and given to him.

However during the summer recess Burke was forced to admit that he had received £30,000 from Gogarty. The government then came under pressure to set up the Moriarty Tribunal to further investigate the Mc Cracken Report into Haughey's affairs and those of Michael Lowrey. During the ensuing debate when the Dáil resumed, having given a spirited defence of his actions Burke found himself with no option but to admit that he had received this money. The following month he resigned from both his ministry and his seat. Later both the Flood and Mahon Tribunals found him guilty of a number of counts of corruption

This resulted in a by-election that deprived the government of its slim majority. It then transpired that Burke was under investigation by the Flood Tribunal in respect of two further payments of £30,000, allegedly received by him during the 1989 election. One in his capacity as Minister for Energy and Communications, from Century Radio in connection with its application for a licence from the Irish Radio and Television Commission.

It was also revealed by Vincent Browne, in his *Magill Magazine*, that during the same election Tom Gilmartin, a property developer, had given Padraig Flynn, the Minister for the Environment, a cheque for £50,000 intended for Fianna Fáil. It had, however, ended up in an account controlled by Flynn and his wife Dorothy. Gilmartin subsequently confirmed making a payment to Flynn in his evidence to the Flood Tribunal. This ended Flynn's ambition to become a European Commissioner, a post that was filled by David Byrne, a former Attorney General.

During the debate on the Mc Cracken Report, Ahern demonstrated a remarkable degree of equivocation in dealing with questions concerning his own part in matters relating to the payment to Haughey of £1 million, which he had received in respect of a State grant as the party leader's allowance, to enable him to run his party. There had been rumours, which now amounted to allegations, that for the better part of two decades, instead of being used for the purpose for which it was intended, the money had been used to finance his expensive lifestyle.

But Ahern told the House that he had discussed the matter with the person who had charge of the account, without disclosing that that person was himself, and was satisfied that it had been used for bona fide political purposes. Fortunately he was believed, for within three weeks of his assumption of office the IRA had declared its second ceasefire and events were beginning to take place in Northern Ireland that were to shape not only the government's and the country's destiny, but would require all Ahern's dedication throughout his first two terms in office.

As the spotlight shifted to Northern Ireland and more of the Taoiseach's time was taken up with the subsequent negotiations, Charlie Mc Creevy prepared his first budget, which was crucial to the advancement of the Celtic Tiger phenomenon by introducing the first cut in corporation tax, aimed at the 12.5 percent negotiated with the EU by the Rainbow Coalition. The budget also included two percent cuts, in both the standard and top rates of income tax and increases in the rates of old-age and social-welfare pensions. However to the surprise of many the rate of capital gains tax was halved from 40 percent to 20 percent.

This and future budgets can be explained by looking into the political backgrounds of Mc Creevy, who had decided to remain Fianna Fail, and Harney, both of whom shared the same economic outlook and had been partners in the early days of the foundation of the Progressive Democrats. They now held the two key economic ministries, so this and future budgets reflected PD policy. However in his second budget, anxious to dispel the criticism that had been levelled at him, Mc Creevy concentrated on concessions to the lower paid and exempted the first 120 of income from tax. This also had the effect of encouraging those still on social welfare to enter the workforce and paved the way for the acceptance by the trade unions of a new wage agreement.

Subsequent budgets saw the introduction of the individualisation of the tax code, a highly controversial move that abolished the treatment that until then had been afforded to married couples where only one spouse worked. This gave substantial benefits to families where both spouses were employed. Together with Harney's Employment Action Plan, these introductions proved highly contentious as they appeared to be designed to benefit the better off.

Nevertheless this went largely unnoticed by the trade unions, as this was a time of unprecedented development and progress made possible by the Celtic Tiger, which was to see Ireland transformed from a sleepy, inward-looking rural hinterland into one of the most vibrant economies in Western Europe. Mary Harney, as Minister for Enterprise and Employment, oversaw a vast plan to put the country back to work in the new industries that had been attracted to the Ireland, not only by its low tax regime but in order to take advantage of its membership of the European Union.

This was to see much of the work formerly carried out in California's silicon valley being transferred to Ireland. The country gradually became the main base for the manufacture and export of the hardware and software needed to service the new technological age. Other industries followed, as did giant multinationals, and such was the demand for skilled labour that the country became a magnet for immigrants.

CHAPTER 19

The Peace Process

Following the completion of Mc Creevy's first budget, Ahern lost no time in grasping an opportunity to establish himself as a statesman, ensuring his rehabilitation at home by becoming a main player in the talks now taking place at the Clonard Monastery in County Louth. These were hosted by Fr Reid, a priest from the monastery, and attended by representatives of the British and Irish governments, the SDLP's John Hume, and Gerry Adams and Martin Mc Guinness of Sinn Fein. A formula for peace was being hammered out to end the long-running civil war in the North that had cost over 3,000 lives and wrecked thousands of families, in addition to causing damage to property amounting to millions of pounds and threatening to spread to the South as well as mainland Britain.

The peace process had initially been made possible by Garrett Fitzgerald's conclusion of the Anglo-Irish Agreement, but in order to appreciate the extent of the hurdle that had to be overcome it is necessary to restate the problem. It had its origins in the unpopular and ill-timed 1916 Rising, which might have been long forgotten but for the War of Independence and the introduction by the British of the Black and Tans – hardened unemployed war veterans whose actions alienated the entire population, thereby rendering country ungovernable.

However the anger that had been aroused, not only in Northern Ireland but throughout the UK, by the Rising, which had not only taken place when Britain was at war with Germany but whose leaders had invoked Britain's enemies, had made the completion of the passage of the Home Rule Bill impossible. Consequently the Treaty of 1921 was a compromise by Lloyd George who sought to minimise the possibility of sectarian conflict, caused by the perception among Unionists, fostered by Sir Edward Carson among others, that Home rule by a predominantly Catholic Ireland would be threat to their Protestant faith. Thus two confessional states were created, the Free State and the North-East of Ulster, which remained in the UK.

This was opposed by those who were demanding control of the whole island of Ireland and was the cause of the Civil War, which lasted until 1926 when De Valera formed his constitutional republican party, Fianna Fáil. This then saw a split when the militant wing broke away to form a new Sinn Fein and IRA, which continued to mount sporadic attacks on the border between the two States. But in order to keep the peace a blind eye was turned to these activities by future governments.

When De Valera enacted his 1937 Constitution he had no option, in order to prevent a further split, other than to include a claim, as expressed by articles 2 and 3, to the territory of Northern Ireland. This claim was to remain a core principle of the party he had founded. However not only did it become an insuperable barrier to a resolution of the impasse between the Northern and Southern States, but it was also to provide the IRA with a *raison d'être* for the continuation of their campaign.

It was not until 1965 that the first tenuous steps were taken to bring about an accommodation between the two States, when Sean Lemass met Captain Terence O'Neill with a view to finding a means of resolving the resultant hostility. This led to the latter's downfall, and such was the ensuing violence against Catholics that the non-sectarian civil rights movement was formed to protect them. Made up largely of nationalist social democrats, they held marches that were broken up by militant Unionists and in 1969 the British government sent troops to the North to protect Catholics and restore order.

This year also saw a split in Sinn Fein and the emergence of the militant Provisional IRA movement, which was itching to go on the offensive. Haughey, who was well aware of the British Labour Party's support for the civil rights movement and seeing it as a threat to his entrenched position, engaged in a cynical plot to send arms to the IRA to bring them into conflict with the British army. The Irish authorities foiled this but the damage had been done, for the subsequent trial of Haughey and three of his ministers saw a split in the Fianna Fáil Party. This revealed that ambivalence to violence was still very much alive in the South, which gave the impression to the IRA that they could count on not inconsiderable support.

May 1973 saw a general election in the South and Fianna Fáil was replaced by a Fine Gael-Labour coalition led by Liam Cosgrave, who almost immediately made contact with his British counterpart, Edward Heath. Meetings followed with Brian Faulkner, the Northern Prime Minister, which culminated in the Sunningdale Agreement and the establishment of the first Power Sharing Executive to replace direct rule from Westminster, which had been imposed to replace the old, discredited Stormont regime. This arrangement was brought down in 1974 by Unionist agitation and the Ulster Workers' Strike, supported by paramilitaries on both sides of the political divide.

This led to the collapse of the accord, direct rule returned and with it the bloody insurrection that lasted in varying degrees of intensity until 1997. This period also saw the Nassau Street bombings in Dublin. In 1977 Jack Lynch's Fianna Fáil government was returned but he made the error of inviting Haughey back in an effort to restore unity to his party. Haughey was to become Taoiseach three times before his resignation in 1992, when Albert Reynolds replaced him.

Reynolds gave the peace process a fresh lease of life by establishing the Hume-Adams talks as well as opening negotiations with John Major, the British Prime Minister, who made secret contacts with the IRA. This earned him ill-informed criticism after the event by those who failed to appreciate that conflict resolution involves talking to your enemies rather than simply listening to your friends. The Unionists, who saw it as an attempt to form a pan-Nationalist front, rejected Reynolds initiative. Nevertheless the Rainbow Coalition under John Bruton advanced the talks until the arrival on the scene of Bertie Ahern.

Ahern had no illusions as to the hurdles that would have to be overcome, not only between North and South but in particular among his own supporters. This was a period that saw his negotiating skills at their best, for in order to reach an agreement it would be necessary for the South to give up articles 2 and 3 of its Constitution, which laid claim to the territory of Northern Ireland. This was no easy task as this claim, which could only be altered by a referendum, was regarded as sacrosanct by many members of Ahern's party, as evidenced by their reaction to the arms trial and the Anglo-Irish Agreement.

Not only did Ahern succeed in persuading his Parliamentary Party of the necessity for change but he also toured the entire country to ensure that the grassroots members understood the reasons why it was essential. His success was reflected in the ensuing referendum to change the Constitution, which was passed by 90 percent of the electorate.

He then prepared for negotiations with all the political parties in the North, aiming at a consensus on the way forward. But he realised that if agreement were to be reached, seemingly irreconcilable conditions would have to be met and in order to make any progress he would need to understand the mindset of all the protagonists. His first contacts with David Trimble and Gerry Adams showed that, whilst both men wanted peace, they were to a large extent the prisoners of their own organisations. They would have great difficulty in convincing their rank and file members that the solution to the problem lay not in terrorism, nor in reliance on the forces of law and order, but in peaceful dialogue.

Though both Trimble and Adams bore a responsibility for the violence that had broken out following the collapse of the Sunningdale Agreement, Adams, who had become the leader of Sinn Fein, made it clear from the outset that if he was to bring his supporters with him that he would have no option but to remain not only active but be seen to take a prominent part in its activities. Similarly it seems logical that Trimble may have had to turn a blind eye to the activities of some of his more extreme supporters.

Ahern had earned a reputation for dealing with seemingly intractable situations, as illustrated during his period as Minister for Labour and during the negotiations that had brought about the entry of the Progressive Democrats into a coalition with Fianna Fáil, despite the opposition of the majority of his party. But negotiating between two warring factions was a very different matter and he realised that if he was to succeed he would have to involve himself in painstaking, lengthy, and somewhat frustrating negotiations.

His patience paid off and the ensuing talks had the support of US President Bill Clinton as well as Tony Blair, who had succeeded John Major. They were to pave the way for the Good Friday Agreement, signed in Easter week 1998, which was to see the restoration of a Power Sharing Executive at Stormont. Unlike its predecessor it had the enthusiastic support of the Official Unionist Party and was not subjected to attacks by Ian Paisley's Democratic Unionist Party, whose members accepted ministries in the new government even though they had initially opposed the accord.

As 2001 approached Ahern not only had the triumph of the Belfast Agreement under his belt but his government could also claim credit for the economic miracle produced by the Celtic Tiger. He decided to call a snap election and Mc Creevy was instructed to prepare the customary pre-election giveaway budget. Plans had to be temporarily shelved by an outbreak of foot and mouth disease, which inhibited canvassing in the rural areas, but the outbreak was short lived and the election was called on the 25 April to be held on 17 May 2002.

Fianna Fáil was in an extremely strong position as demonstrated by the polls. Not only had the economy outperformed all others in the Western world, due to the Celtic Tiger and the Mc Creevy-Harney, axis but a growth rate of 10 percent had been achieved, unemployment had fallen to four percent, tax rates had been reduced and the debt/GDP ratio stood at around 30 percent.

By contrast the PDs had never been given credit for the upsurge in the economy that would never have taken place had Fianna Fáil been left to govern on their own. Nevertheless their support of Burke and their failure to oppose such measures as the benchmarking of pay awards to public service workers – a spectacular illustration of profligacy and a thinly veiled ploy to buy votes that had just been announced by their Fianna Fáil partners – had convinced the electorate that their influence was to all intents and purposes non-existent.

To make matters worse, the PDs appeared to have become accident-prone. In 1997 old files containing details of sensitive financial matters relating to donations received by the party from prominent businessmen, including one for £12000 from the Smurfit Group, were discovered in a skip outside their head office instead of having been shredded. Such a payment, as distinct from one made to elicit a favour was not unusual, for companies often make donations to political parties, in particular new organisations whose policies they approve. But this caused the PDs no little embarrassment for it sparked off rumours that demoralisation had set in and that the PDs were in the process of disintegration.

Such was the erosion of support for the party that in October 1998, when a by-election took place in Cork South Central, the scene of victories in three successive elections, it only succeeded in polling 971 votes. So serious was this crisis that a special meeting was held in November to consider the party's future.

In May 1999 Michael Mc Dowell was approached by John Bruton and invited to rejoin Fine Gael. A meeting was set up between them, but on hearing of it Harney decided to make Mc Dowell an offer he could not refuse by inviting him to become Attorney General, a post that had become vacant on David Byrne's departure for Europe. Harney had been endeavouring to lure him back ever since his departure from the party following his defeat in 1997, which he had blamed on her mismanagement of that year's election campaign.

Since then relations between them had been strained and her efforts had been without success, although she had managed to persuade him to chair a meeting on company law that resulted in the establishment of the office of Director of Corporate Enforcement. He had also agreed to head a committee to look into the workings of the Central Bank and the financial services industry on her behalf.

As she anticipated, he jumped at the chance of becoming Attorney General but she had not yet succeeded in mending fences with him, and it soon became clear to her that he preferred to remain in this important non-governmental position rather than become involved in the political scene. However in the run-up to the 2002 general election she approached him once more, and following lengthy negotiations an agreement was reached between them whereby he would rejoin the PDs on condition that he was made President of the party.

His decision to return and run as a candidate in his former constituency of Dublin South East gave a much-needed boost to the PDs, whose morale was at a low ebb. Des O'Malley and Bobby Molloy had both announced their intention of retiring, leaving them with no more than two sitting deputies – Harney and Liz O'Donnell. With the party's poll rating standing at no more than three percent, many wondered if the media's oft repeated prediction of its demise was about to be fulfilled. But when Mc Dowell's re-emergence was followed by Molloy's announcement that he would stand for a further term and the unexpected decision of John Parlon, leader of the Irish Farmers' Association, to join the PDs and stand as a candidate, the corner appeared to have been turned.

With renewed confidence they set themselves a target of eight seats, because whatever the outcome of the election they saw themselves as pivotal to the formation of a government and therefore set out to return sufficient candidates to place the party in a strong negotiating position. With this aim they decided to target those constituencies where they could maximise their vote. Nevertheless they chose to fight the campaign as an independent party because, although it might result in their losing Fianna Fáil second preference votes, it would make them attractive to a wider section of the electorate, which had withdrawn its support from the party the last time out, following its disastrous pre-election voting pact with Fianna Fail.

Only a fortnight before the dissolution of the Dáil, however, their carefully laid plans were almost brought to nought when one of their most outstanding candidates, Bobby Molloy, who found himself caught up in a controversy not of his making and felt obliged to resign his seat. This blow was reflected in the national opinion polls, which showed a further drop in the party's rating to two percent. Michael Mc Dowell, one of their key candidates, was also trailing disastrously, with his showing being no better Sinn Fein's.

It now seemed that an overall majority for Fianna Fáil was not only possible but probable. It was then that Michael Mc Dowell came up with a brilliant strategy to turn their strength to the PDs and his own advantage. The idea was to play on the electorate's latent distrust of Fianna Fáil, which had existed ever since the Haughey era, and Mc Dowell thought up an imaginative scheme to convince voters that Fianna Fáil could not be trusted if left to their own devices.

It was at this critical stage in the election campaign that, having climbed to the top of a lamp-post, he had himself photographed as he was about to hang a poster bearing the simple message "One-party government? NO WAY!" This appeared prominently on the front page of the national dailies the following morning. The effect was electric and was to have a decisive effect on the result of the election, for Mc Dowell had succeeded in re-igniting the misgivings about Fianna Fáil that were still very much alive among voters, and such was the reaction on the doorsteps that by polling day it had become clear that his message was a major issue.

When the counts were held, Harney and Liz O'Donnell had been comfortably re-elected, to be joined by Tim O'Malley in Limerick East, Fiona O 'Malley for Dun Laoghaire and Tom Parlon with a sound majority in Laois-Offaly. Noel Grealish was returned against all the odds for Galway West, as was May Sexton in Longford-Westmeath, and Michael Mc Dowell, the architect of the PDs' resurgence, had the satisfaction of topping the poll in Dublin South East.

Not only had the PDs reached their target of eight seats but also they had denied Fianna Fáil, who had returned 81 of their candidates, an absolute majority. Only the question of the composition of the next administration remained, for both the parties making up the outgoing government had two options.

Mary Harney had insisted throughout the campaign that the PDs would not go into any Fianna Fáil administration if they had an overall majority. They had not achieved one but they had, nevertheless, increased their representation sufficiently to make it possible for them to rule with the help of friendly independents. In these circumstances it should have been clear to her that should her party to go into government with them it would have no leverage.

She had already experienced sufficient humiliation at the hands of Ahern, particularly in the early days of the previous administration when, although her party had power, it was so weak electorally that she feared a wipe-out should she bring his government down. This was despite the Burke affair, the early revelations of the Taoiseach's financial impropriety and that of his cronies, and the Sheedy affair. This last case which revolved round representations made by Ahern to secure the early release of a young man convicted of causing death by dangerous driving, the ramifications of which had resulted in the enforced resignation of a Supreme Court as well as a High Court Judge. Harney had been concerned and requested Ahern to make a statement in the Dáil, which he agreed to do. Later however, when he publicly denied that he had given her any such undertaking, a row had developed between them and it seemed that the coalition would collapse. Nevertheless she relented and it survived.

It was now clear that Fianna Fáil was about to become involved in some of the most irresponsible spending, totally at odds with PD policy, as had been indicated by its announcement of the benchmarking of public service pay, which would have to be paid for by the enormous revenue received by the State from the property boom. However this could not last for ever and was therefore unsustainable.

If the PDs entered into a coalition with Fianna Fáil they would have power, but though they might be able to push through some much needed legislation as long as they had the approval of their senior partner in government, the ultimate sanction of withdrawal in the event of a serious disagreement on policy would have been taken away from them.

Alternatively they could go into opposition with Fine Gael, which had emerged from the election deeply demoralised, having lost 20 seats. They were desperately searching for a leader and as their economic policies were not dissimilar from the PDs', it would not be impossible to engineer a reverse takeover. It was perhaps a risk, but one well worth taking for if successful it could well see the PDs as the main opposition party at the next election.

It was at this stage that Ahern, realising that he no longer had anything to fear from the PDs should they join him in coalition, put it to Harney that he would prefer to have them with him to form a stable government, as required by the electorate, rather than rely on the independents for support.

For some unaccountable reason Harney failed to see through this ploy, despite her previous experience, and made the disastrous decision to go back into office. It was a move that could only result in the annihilation of the PDs, who would be seen as irrelevant next time out.

Ireland had previously relied to a large extent on agriculture and tourism to provide a living for its people, but now found itself at the centre of an industrial revolution. Despite the efforts of the Industrial Development Authority, however, Ireland had few native industries until the arrival of Lemass, who established Aer Lingus and was responsible for the mini boom in the construction industry that was to become the driving force behind Ireland's economic miracle.

CHAPTER 20

The Coalition's Second Term in Office

On Ahern's return to office in the spring of 2002, Fianna Fáil was in a strong position. While their junior partner's performance in the election warranted their being given extra seats at the Cabinet table, they could afford to dispense with their services and fall back on the independents for support if necessary. Nevertheless they preferred a coalition arrangement with the PDs. Not only did it give the appearance of a stable government, but also the PDs were policy driven and would bring forward useful proposals that Fianna Fáil could implement and claim as their own. Meanwhile, even if they chose to oppose measures introduced by them, they had no leverage.

Harney therefore remained as Minister for Trade and Enterprise and Michael Mc Dowell was made Minister for Justice – a particularly challenging portfolio and both Tom Parlon and Tim O'Malley were appointed to junior ministries. However despite its strong showing it was not long before the new government became involved in a controversy regarding Mc Creevy's proposed cuts to control public spending, for both he and Ahern had maintained during the general election campaign that no such cutbacks were envisaged by them, despite the projected downturn in the economy.

Within weeks of the election, however, a leaked report from the Department of Finance confirmed that a number of such cuts were being prepared even at the height of the election campaign. This was confirmed by a leaked memo and resulted in a furore, public anger being directed both at the government and the PDs in particular, who were known to support such a move.

Such a disclosure was to have serious repercussions both for Mc Creevy and the junior partners in the coalition, who maintained that it would be better to introduce corrective measures now to secure the stability of the economy in the long term. This was a view that most of the electorate would have been prepared to accept, as the reason the government had been returned in such strength was that the people believed that the economy would be safer with them were it to hit troubled waters. But Mc Creevy's plans had not only angered Fianna Fáil backbenchers but Ahern himself, who determined to rid himself of both Mc Creevy and his supporters in the PDs, who he feared would wreck his populist policies.

As Minister for Trade and Enterprise, Harney was able to continue expanding the jobs market, despite the proposed corrective measures. She was also responsible for reducing the exorbitant cost of insurance premiums by introducing the Personal

Insurance Assessment Board as a means of counteracting the compensation culture that had seen insurance companies having to pay excessive damages as well as heavy legal costs in response to bogus insurance claims. Indeed such was the extent of this fraud that many chose to settle such claims out of court rather than face the cost of a trial.

Michael Mc Dowell was faced with the problem of reforming the Garda Siochana, as a result of the Mc Brearty scandal. This had involved a Donegal publican who was arrested as a murder suspect following a hit and run accident in which a cattle dealer, Ritchie Barron, from Raphoe, was killed. No charges were brought when it transpired that the evidence of the Gardai was too flawed to warrant a prosecution. As a result, in March 2002 the Morris Tribunal had been set up to investigate this matter as well as a number of complaints that had been brought against the Gardai in Donegal.

In 2004 this Tribunal published a report into caches of explosives said to have been found in this county. It was a damning indictment of a number of officers who were alleged to have planted false evidence of IRA activity, and without any foundation had charged people with involvement in subversive activity in order to obtain promotion. Mc Dowell's reaction was swift and he produced reforming legislation in a number of key areas. His Garda Siochana Bill, the first to be enacted since 1922, established local policing divisions and provided for an independent ombudsman as well as a Garda Inspectorate.

Meanwhile, within months of the signing of the Belfast Agreement, such problems had arisen that it seemed that the original high hopes would never be realised. While the Assembly remained intact, it had been prorogued on three occasions due to espionage campaigns carried out by the IRA and counter-surveillance operations taken by the authorities in retaliation.

This saw a downturn in relations between the two communities and the outbreak of sporadic acts of violence, not only by the IRA but also by the UVF and UDA paramilitaries who had remained active, despite being condemned equally by the Official Unionists and Paisley's DUP. Intensive negotiations had been continued by the two governments but it would seem that concessions made to one side were simply blocked by new demands from the other. Nevertheless it seemed that an agreement was at last in sight on the question of decommissioning the IRA's arsenal of weapons.

One of Sinn Fein's demands had been the release of the IRA killers of Garda Jerry Mc Cabe, who had been murdered during a raid on a post office in Adare, County Limerick, during a period when there was supposed to be on ceasefire. Because of this his release had been specifically excluded under the terms of the Belfast Agreement. Ahern, however, had agreed that this provision be set aside. This caused an uproar in the South and Mc Dowell, as Minister for Justice, was determined to ensure that he would only agree to consider such an arrangement on receiving a cast-iron guarantee that the IRA would not only disarm but would give up all criminality.

However while this matter had caused intense anger in the South, it was controversial because many on both sides of the border believed that the conditions for the release of prisoners should be the same in both jurisdictions. But following further prevarication by the IRA with regard to the decommissioning issue, the talks were suspended.

Elections to the Northern Assembly, held in November 2003, had seen Trimble's Official Unionists ousted by Ian Paisley's hard-line Democratic Unionist Party, while the SDLP lost out to Sinn Fein. David Trimble's loss of power was attributed to defections within his own ranks, due to his perceived vacillation in his dealings with Sinn Fein. However his defeat might well have been averted had it not been for Ahern's dalliance with Sinn Fein and his pressure on Tony Blair to give in to them every time there seemed a likelihood of a breakdown in the delicate talks that had been taking place since the Assembly was first prorogued. It would seem that this had hampered Trimble's scope for decision-making.

Similar perceptions to those that had affected Trimble's vote were also reflected in support for Ahern, as was demonstrated during the Local and European elections held in 2004. The Fianna Fáil vote in both contests dropped by 30 percent while Sinn Fein did well. Of the 32 seats gained by them, 24 were at the expense of Fianna Fáil, while their Mary Lou O'Donnell captured a seat in the European Parliament. Ahern, having seen what had happened to the SDLP at Sinn Fein's hands, now saw the party as a threat and withdrew his support from them in time to adjust to a new set of circumstances. But he refused to accept that his own indulgence of Sinn Fein over the years had, like Trimble's defeat, been responsible for his own party's poor showing.

With Paisley's DUP now the dominant political force in the North, it seemed that Ahern was faced with having to go back to the drawing board when he remembered the advice given by David Irvine in the run-up to the Good Friday Agreement. A leading member of the UVF, Irvine he had met a number of members of Sinn Fein while serving a term of imprisonment in the Maze prison., and had come to realise that many like himself, though convicted of crimes of violence, believed that only a political solution could solve the impasse between the two communities. But this could only be achieved if the extremists on both sides could be brought to talks.

Despite the less than auspicious circumstances, the British and Irish Governments both concentrated on getting Paisley and all the parties, including Sinn Fein, to the negotiating table to find a means not only of restoring the Assembly but also of completing the work of the Belfast Agreement. It was a marathon task, but it was Ahern's vision and understanding of Paisley, whose name had become synonymous with intransigence, that won the day. In future discussions with him Ahern realised that though they came from diametrically opposite viewpoints and backgrounds, they had one thing in common – and it was the factor that had motivated Paisley to form the DUP.

Ahern did not have to look far back in history to discover a parallel. Like Wolfe Tone, who had founded the United Irishmen in opposition to the oppression of the established Church, Paisley was a nonconformist and an egalitarian, who though a staunch Unionist did not take kindly to the Official Unionist Party. It was made up of the landlord and upper classes, which had used the sectarian divide to prevent their workers from uniting, thereby ensuring that they had an abundant and compliant workforce.

The Protestant worker, even if he had work, was little better off than his Catholic neighbour as his ability to obtain employment was conditional on his religious affiliation. Sectarianism had therefore become deeply ingrained. Consequently Paisley, the head of the Free Presbyterian Church, which treated all its members as equal, had considerable support among the ordinary Protestant people.

When they met, Ahern was intrigued by Paisley's interest in the workings of the Southern State, he was also clearly impressed by the way with which the Irish Government had dealt with the thorny question of Church-State relations. During their future discussions they discovered that they had more in common, politically, than either would have imagined.

Their talks had begun almost immediately after Paisley's installation as First Minister of the Northern Ireland Assembly, and though they may have been protracted and frustrating, due to foot dragging by Sinn Fein, they gave Ahern and Paisley the opportunity to get to know each other. The first six months of 2004 had been taken up with intensive discussions in an endeavour to get Sinn Fein to agree a deal that would allow for the restoration of the Assembly as well as the completion of unresolved issues. But the summer saw a breakthrough when it seemed that Mc Dowell's hard line on the issue of criminality had paid off.

When the two Northern parties met in September 2004 at Leeds Castle, Kent, such progress appeared to have been made that the way now seemed open for a final settlement, despite the continuing controversy over the release of the Mc Cabe killers. It had really only been delayed by the IRA's failure to give firm assurances on the questions of decommissioning and criminality, which were being demanded equally by Paisley and the Irish Government.

Meanwhile the autumn also saw Ahern grappling with problems at home. He was now determined on a showdown with Mc Creevy, who was insistent that the country was heading for a downturn and maintained that spending cuts were necessary in order to correct the position and sustain the progress that had already been made.

But seeing that he was getting nowhere and that his leader was intent on forcing his resignation, he accepted the inevitable and agreed to take up a vacant position as a European Commissioner.

This saw a Cabinet reshuffle and Brian Cowan, who had held office in the Ministry for Agriculture as well as Health, a portfolio he had described as "Angola", became Minister for Finance. Mary Harney replaced Micheal Martin, Minister for Health, whose department had been unable to get to grips with the problems facing it despite being the government's biggest spender. She offered to take on this portfolio to the surprise of many, as it was a poisoned chalice that had defied the best efforts of a succession of ministers, ever since the time of the Inter-Party Government,.

Ahern was well satisfied with these changes for he was aware that Cowan's loyalty to whoever was leader of Fianna Fáil would inhibit him from interfering with any of his more populist spending plans, while any mistakes made by Harney could be blamed on the PDs, whom he intended to replace with Labour the next time out.

However, if there had been concerns about the continued growth of the economy during the general election, this was about the most inopportune moment to lose a Minister for Finance who was determined to bring spending under control. It was now clear that the boom, which had been driven by the construction industry and consumer demand, could not be sustained forever and that a slowdown was on the cards. While the Celtic Tiger had brought great prosperity to Ireland, dark forces were at work for corruption was growing like weeds alongside sound economic developments.

This year saw a further example of Ahern's negotiating skills, when as President of the European Union he succeeded in getting the member States to agree to the changes required to secure Ireland's assent to the Lisbon Treaty, which would provide for the accession of 10 new members. This had proved to be a controversial piece of legislation that was required to be ratified by each State in the EU and, in Ireland, endorsement by a referendum.

This had required a rerun due to the fact that the Irish electorate following a low turnout, possibly due to an injudicious remark by Mary Harney, had rejected it. During the initial campaign to secure its adoption she had stated "Geographically we are closer to Berlin than Boston, but spiritually we are a lot closer to Boston." This inadvertently added weight to the Eurosceptics' campaign.

Meanwhile Mc Dowell feared that the possibility of a breakthrough in the North was yet another delaying tactic to wring further concessions from the British and Irish Governments. But following weeks of discussions he appeared to accept that Sinn Fein had accepted his terms. Therefore Ahern and Blair, expecting to conclude an agreement, travelled to Belfast on 8 December only to discover that though an outline text of an accord had been prepared by Sinn Fein, no mention had been made of the issue of criminality, despite the fact that the form of words used would have to be endorsed by the Irish Minister for Justice.

The DUP now entered their own deal-breaker – a demand that there be photographic evidence of the destruction of the IRA's weaponry. Sinn Fein refused to agree to this, the talks broke down and Ahern withdrew his offer to free the killers of Garda Mc Cabe.

Then on 20 December, following Sinn Fein's rejection of the demand to give up their criminal activities, there was a massive raid on the Northern Bank in Belfast and it appeared that all was lost. Described as the biggest currency heist in history, there would seem little doubt that it was the work of the Provisional IRA, as was confirmed by Hugh Orde, Chef Commissioner of the Police Service of Northern Ireland.

Ahern had come a long way towards coming to an understanding with Paisley, only to see his hopes dashed by the Northern Bank raid. But following the discovery of some of the proceeds in Cork, as well as an international money-laundering network, he redoubled his efforts to restart negotiations. This resulted in unprecedented pressure from the Irish government on Sinn Fein to live up to their obligations under the Belfast agreement.

However this was overshadowed by a disagreement between the Northern parties as to how or who should verify the decommissioning of the IRA's weaponry. This involved a matter of principle but was of so little import that it was dismissed by many as irrelevant. It is nonetheless possible that both parties wished to delay a final settlement in the hope of bringing their dissidents on board.

It was now plain to Sinn Fein that they could no longer rely on Ahern for support, and the public reaction to the expressed views of Michael Mc Dowell served to convince them that they could make no further progress if they continued to prevaricate. Thus on 5 July 2005, seven years after signing the Belfast Agreement, an order was given for the IRA to dump all its arms. Plans were made for agreed witnesses to oversee their destruction, in accordance with the instructions given by John de Chastelaine's decommissioning body, which had been set up some time previously in anticipation of this event. Sinn Fein also gave an undertaking to pursue their aims only by peaceful and democratic means.

Not only had the way been prepared for a permanent peace but also it became clear, when Paisley visited Dublin in 2007 that a strong rapport had developed between him and Ahern. It was an amazing development in view of the mutual antagonism that had been evident on the first occasion that Paisley had paid a visit to Ireland's capital city

CHAPTER 21

Ahern resigns

Ahern was now undoubtedly the most popular leader since the foundation of the State, though like others before him, it would seem that he was by no means incorruptible. Under his watch Ireland had developed from being an insular backwater into one of the most prosperous multi-cultural States in Europe, due to the necessity to import labour to service its ever-growing industries. But in common with many of the leaders in the developed world, although Ahern's government negotiated a number of wage agreements it failed to control costs and prices, all of which had been high even before the boom started in 2000. The consequence of the Celtic Tiger was that Ireland was to become one of the most expensive states in Europe.

By the beginning of 2005 the Celtic Tiger had reached its zenith but the economy, which was both labour intensive and consumer driven, was overheating. Warnings to this effect not only from economists but also from the IMF were ignored. The problem, although to a greater or lesser extent reflected throughout the Western industrialised world, threatened to be more of a potential risk to Ireland than to its neighbours, as a result of the extent of the influx of American capital that supported the new industries, apart from the fact that the banks, there, were off-loading potential risks to European institutions, and especially due to Ireland's dependence on the construction industry the biggest single employer.

In Ireland the problem had been exacerbated by corruption, as illustrated by the rezoning scandals exposed by the various tribunals of enquiry set up to examine them. They revealed the vast sums of money paid to politicians, many of them household names, to secure the change of use of agricultural and other lands so as to make them available for construction.

Other than land speculation, this was the principle factor in inflating the cost of building sites, thereby making housing unaffordable for many, particularly first-time buyers and those on low incomes. Property developers found themselves forced to borrow huge sums from banks or other financial institutions to enable them to complete their projects.

Consequently as the cost of housing rose, intending purchasers had no option but to take out larger and larger mortgages and it became the practice to offer inappropriate loans, often amounting to 100 percent, to those who could least afford them. Dishonest mortgage brokers were prepared to falsify the details of their clients' incomes in order to make them eligible for such credit.

As a result, so great was the demand for finance that the banks were forced to borrow from each other, leading to a dangerous situation that could threaten their liquidity in the event of a downturn in the economy. Yet the government took no action, no doubt due to the fact that the construction industry was the exchequer's most lucrative source of revenue.

Already the economists were predicting a soft landing for the economy, but neither Brian Cowan, the new Minister for Finance, nor the Taoiseach took any action to control the situation. Rather, the politicians fed the country 'lies, damned lies and statistics' that bore no relation to reality. In fact the country was suffering from hyperinflation, as evidenced by the cost of property and consumer goods.

It was now clear that a downturn in the economy was inevitable; the only question was when and the extent of its severity. However it was possible to conceal the truth from the electorate, as an OECD report published in February 2005 showed that not only had Ireland succeeded in maintaining its level of employment, but illustrated that Irish workers were paying the third lowest rate of taxes in the industrialised world while enjoying a standard of living unheard of by their forefathers.

At this time came the first inkling of crisis of a very different kind that was to dog Ahern until his resignation, soon after his return to office for a third term. Indeed there is no doubt that he would have been subjected to questioning by the Mc Cracken Tribunal early during his first administration, regarding his collusion with Haughey, but he had been spared an interrogation then as the whole of that period had been taken up with ensuring that the Peace Process did not collapse.

However during the hiatus caused by the proroguing of the Assembly, the Mahon Tribunal, which was looking into the question of bribes paid by property developers to corrupt politicians, demanded that Ahern make himself available for interview. But as he was then engaged in talks with Paisley he had once again been enabled to evade being questioned.

Already his first term had seen the exposure by the tribunals of a number of scandals involving ministers and top politicians, many of whom he had been forced to sack, but as these proceedings were held in public they received extensive coverage in both the print media and on radio and television. Such was the extent of the problem that the tribunals are still dealing with matters that occurred as far back as the late 1980s. The concept of the tribunals was in itself excellent, but apart from exposing corruption and those responsible for it they have achieved little other than enriching lawyers, many of whom became millionaires from fees obtained from the State and clients who engaged them as defence counsel. Naturally it suited them to drag out cases as long as possible in order to obtain the maximum profit.

This misuse of the tribunals could have been prevented had a cap been put on the fees paid to those in the legal profession engaged in these enquiries. Worse still, no doubt vested interests among the political establishment ensured that the tribunals did not have the power of prosecution. The best they could do was to ensure that corrupt politicians and businessmen were exposed, and while some of them lost their positions of influence and power as a result, criminal action did not follow. The evidence obtained by a tribunal was not admissible in a court of law and if such a prosecution were to be undertaken, the serious fraud division of the Gardai would have to start gathering the evidence all over again.

Because the vast majority of those brought before the tribunals happened to be Fianna Fáil politicians and their supporters, it does not mean that only that party was involved in corrupt practices, as evidenced by the exposure of Michael Lowrey's dealing with Ben Dunne, who was stated to have paid him IRL 395,000 for an extension to his house in Tipperary, during the hearings of the Mc Cracken Tribunal. Nor does it mean that all those concerned were senior politicians. In fact the vast majority were councillors elected to serve in local government, as well as civil servants, who received bribes from large property developers to ensure that they voted to ensure the rezoning of land from agricultural to industrial use. Nevertheless the tribunals proved useful in uncovering other frauds, such as the Ansbacher tax-evasion scheme.

So great was the degree of corruption during the Ahern era that even the courts were not immune, as evidenced by the Sheedy affair during his first term in office. This was not an isolated case and there was considerable comment in the media concerning the lenience of sentences handed down by the courts to certain individuals. Indeed when members of the judiciary themselves came before the courts, the sentences handed out to them would have been laughable were it not for the fact that they can be said to have been in contempt of the very justice they were supposed to be upholding.

As the date of the 2007 general election drew near, the Mahon Tribunal's inquiry into Ahern's personal finances had intensified, although so far he had succeeded in evading giving evidence due to his heavy commitment to the peace process. The original case brought by the Tribunal against Ahern had resulted from evidence given by Tom Gilmartin that he had been informed by a property developer involved in the Quarryvale development that Owen O'Callaghan, who was involved in the same project, had paid Ahern £80,000, £50,000 of which he had received in 1989. Ahern had denied this, as did O'Callaghan, but the paper trail unearthed in the search for the truth regarding Ahern's financial dealings revealed an astounding state of affairs that led the Tribunal to begin a private investigation into them.

Its enquiries led to the discovery that lodgements totalling several times his declared income had been made to accounts controlled by him between 1989 and

1995. The Tribunal wrote to him in 2004, asking him to explain the source of these lodgements but his replies were evasive, incomplete and slow in coming. In 2005 he failed to fulfil a November deadline to provide the Tribunal with explanations.

As a result in March 2006 he was warned that if he did not supply the required information he would be summonsed to a public meeting. In April he told the Tribunal, in response to allegations made against him, that he had accumulated more than £50,000 in cash savings in the period up to 1993 and had also received two large dig-outs from friends in 1993 and 1994, in respect of the expenses involved in his separation agreement with his wife. He also said that he had received an amount in sterling from friends in Manchester in 1994.

The Tribunal continued its pursue its private enquiries to discover that Ahern's new partner, Celia Larkin, had also made a considerable lodgement in December 1994 which, according to her evidence, was in connection with a house he was planning to rent from Thomas Wall, a Manchester businessman. But when it was discovered that Wall had made a will leaving the house to Ahern, they suspected that Wall was in fact merely acting as his nominee.

As they dug deeper these transactions became so convoluted that they decided to call Ahern to give evidence, but the hearing had to be deferred when Ahern called a general election for September 2007. However the enquiries of the Tribunal had become public knowledge in September 2006, when the *Irish Times* disclosed that the Tribunal had been told that Ahern had received payments, including cash, from a number of individuals.

In order to try and stamp out the controversy resulting from the revelations of the evidence he had given to the Mahon Tribunal, Ahern gave an interview to Bryan Dobson of RTE and also answered questions raised by the opposition in the Dáil. But as the contradictions between his statements to Dobson, the Dáil and the Tribunal became ever more manifest, they were to have a dramatic result on the election campaign, which in the absence of a Fine Gael pact with Labour saw the distinct possibility of Ahern's bringing about his plans to replace his present junior partner in government.

Fianna Fáil could undoubtedly have swept all before them had it not been for the conflicting accounts given by Ahern in connection with his business affairs. It was an issue that was to dominate the election, despite his outstanding diplomatic successes, and many looked back to the irregularities in which he had been involved during the Haughey era.

Meanwhile as the 2007 general election got under way it would appear that a split was developing between the coalition partners and there was talk of the PDs pulling out of government. This came to a head when Michael Mc Dowell, now the party's candidate for Dublin South East, made an announcement to that effect. But such was the popularity of Ahern, who had much to his credit, that pressure was put on him, by Mary Harney and others to reverse his position and he had had no option but to withdraw his stance and adopt a legalistic approach. In effect he gave his backing to the contention of Fianna Fáil that the Mahon Tribunal should not judge Ahern until the final outcome of the deliberations into the matter.

His apparent flip-flop was to prove disastrous not only for his own campaign but for that of the PDs, for Fianna Fáil had no difficulty in exacting their revenge. Not only were their candidates instructed not to give their second preference votes to their former partners in government, but in Mc Dowell's own constituency their canvassers called from door to door to assure his known supporters that his vote was so strong that he was guaranteed a surplus and that their candidate, rather than he, should be given a first preference vote. Consequently many of the PD candidates, who had confidently expected to retain or gain a seat, lost out; Mc Dowell was defeated by John Gormley of the Green Party.

Following the count Mc Dowell decided to bow out of politics. Though controversial, he had unquestionably been the best Minister for Justice since the foundation of the state, as evidenced by the testimony of many who were bitterly opposed to some of his decisions while in office. Not only was he noted for his honesty but he was prepared to take on vested interests including, if necessary, the Law Society. His defeat was cynically engineered but also those whose dishonesty he had spent his political career endeavouring to counteract and there can be no doubt that Irish politics will be the poorer without him.

The election saw Fianna Fáil lose seats to Fine Gael under their new leader Enda Kenny, as well as to Labour, whose leader Pat Rabbitte, having consulted his party colleagues, made it clear that they would not be prepared to enter a coalition arrangement with Fianna Fáil. As expected the result saw the virtual wipe out of the PDs, with only two of their number, Mary Harney and Noel Grealish, being returned for Dublin South West and Galway West. The independents had remained static. Ahern was therefore left with no option but to form a coalition of three parties, having persuaded the six Greens, under John Gormley, and the two remaining PDs to join him in forming an administration.

However his own tenure in office proved to be short lived, for following the Christmas recess he once again found himself under examination by the Mahon Tribunal and, according to the *Irish Times*, by March he had been questioned about lodgements and transactions made during the period 1984 to 1997, amounting to 866,830 in today's money. He stated in reply to enquiries that £70,000 sterling of this sum represented money that he had withdrawn and deposited back into his account, but he was unable to produce any evidence to prove this contention.

These transactions concerned large sums of cash and other lodgements involving some nine accounts, to which he had access, opened at various branches of the Anglo Irish Bank and the Irish Permanent Building Society. One of these accounts was in the name of the Cumann (branch) of Fianna Fáil to which he belonged, but the address given for it was that of Ahern's office and there was no record of any transaction passing through it since the introduction of legislation governing the banking of donations to political parties.

One of the most controversial of these deposits was an account opened at the Irish Permanent Building Society Drumcondra Branch by Tim Collins, who was not even a member of Fianna Fáil. In reply to questions, both Ahern and Collins insisted that the name B/T on the account referred to the Building Trust and not to the Bertie/Tim account, as suggested by the Tribunal, yet there appeared to be no evidence of the existence of such a trust.

The deeper the Tribunal delved into Ahern's affairs the greater the contradictions became, not only in his evidence, which was not supported by documentary evidence from the banks, but in his replies to questions in the Dáil, which became increasingly unbelievable. The die was finally cast when his former constituency secretary, Grainne Caruth, gave evidence regarding lodgements she had made to his account on his behalf. Ahern insisted, when questioned by the Tribunal, that these referred simply to his salary, but this flew in the face of the documentary evidence produced by the bank and Caruth tearfully admitted that the lodgements must have been made in sterling.

On 2 April Ahern made a statement from the steps of government buildings that he would submit his resignation to the President on 6 May following his proposed trip to America. This valedictory statement, which was full of self-praise, made no apology for his past actions and neither did he make any attempt to explain them. He simply stated that his decision to bring forward the date of his proposed retirement from office had been solely influenced by the need to ensure that the work of his ministerial colleagues was not distracted by the publicity given to the Tribunal.

Indeed the government could ill afford any such diversion, for Ahern left much unfinished business that needed the urgent attention of his successor, Brian Cowan, including the preparation of the electorate for a referendum to endorse the Lisbon Treaty. However during the hiatus between the resignation of his predecessor and his installation in office this matter was neglected by the government, allowing the opponents of the Treaty valuable time to ensure its rejection At the same time ominous signs of a severe downturn in the economy were appearing on the horizon, but both the Taoiseach and his Minister for Finance spent their time playing down the possibility of any such an eventuality.

Epilogue

If the reports emanating from RTE and the media, in general are confirmed in the final report of the Mahon Tribunal, it seems likely that Ahern, despite his undoubted diplomatic triumphs as distinct from his political actions, will be judged to have been one of the most corrupt Taoiseach in the history of the State. However the administration of his successor, Brian Cowan, who gives the impression of being completely unable or unwilling to confront the problems facing it, must surely be the most incompetent government yet to have achieved office in Ireland.

At a time when he should have been concentrating his efforts on informing the people of the reasons why they needed to give a resounding endorsement to the ratification of the Lisbon Treaty, he spent his time in his constituency, celebrating his elevation to the rank of Taoiseach. This hiatus allowed Declan Ganley and his Libertas Movement to steal a march on the government by distributing leaflets to every household in the State, giving cogent and well-documented reasons why the electorate should oppose the treaty.

The treaty was contained in a long and convoluted document that was never properly explained by the government despite media pressure to do so, and regardless of opinion polls during the campaign that indicated a "No" vote. Both the Taoiseach and Brian Mc Creevy, Ireland's representative at the European Parliament, admitted that they had not read it, and what literature the government distributed was evasive and gave the impression that something was being hidden from the electorate. Consequently, when the referendum was held on 12 June, the "Yes" camp was overwhelmingly defeated.

Meanwhile it had become clear that the economic situation was such that the prospect of a serious recession could not be discounted. But Brian Lenihan, junior, who had become Minister for Finance, on Cowan's elevation to the office of Taoiseach, continued to play down this eventuality until some of the worst predictions of the economists began to make themselves evident. But instead of taking action to take control of events he appears to have be swept along by them. He gave the appearance of not knowing his own mind; such were the number of volte-faces that followed his original decisions.

Lenihan began his career in this ministry by announcing that he was bringing forward his budget due to the deteriorating financial situation, while appearing to be in a state of denial as to the extent of the problem when announcing his proposals. He blamed everything on the international financial crisis, when in fact many of the reasons why Ireland appears to have suffered disproportionately from the recession were home grown, beginning with the refusal by Cowan to heed the warnings of the IMF some four years previously, that the boom would not go on for ever and it was time to consider putting money aside to prepare for a downturn.

Instead he allowed the housing market to grow unchecked. It was inevitable that the bubble would burst and when it did the price of property crashed, leaving many people with rapidly deteriorating negative equity that aggravated the problems already being experienced by the banks, which had originated with excessive or inappropriate lending.

In fact the country was now suffering from a hangover that resulted from the excesses of the Celtic Tiger and the corrupt business practices that accompanied it, in addition to the high costs that resulted from increasing demands by labour and the employers, which saw Ireland priced out of the market. Manufacturers are moving their bases to Eastern Europe and even China in order to remain competitive, resulting in the beginning of a return to mass unemployment.

In June 2008 Lenihan issued his first budget, but instead of concentrating his taxation proposals on those who had done well out of the Celtic Tiger and who could well afford to contribute to solving the economic crisis, he chose to deal a devastating blow to the most vulnerable in Irish society. Included in his proposals was a plan to abolish the free medical card scheme for those over 65 years of age; cutbacks were to be made in the education system, which was already underfunded; and the disability allowance paid to those aged 18, who were unable to find work, was to be abolished.

This led to angry protests when some 5,000 angry pensioners, as well as many thousands of students and their teachers, took to the streets and demonstrations were held outside Dáil Eireann. So great was the disenchantment with the budget, which also included a one percent levy on all incomes, including those earning the minimum wage, that it had to be abandoned and redrafted. Future projections also proved to be so wide of the mark that no sooner were they made than they had to be increased by several billions.

If indecision had marked the government's handling of its budget, this was nothing compared with its dealings with the banks. At first the people were assured that these institutions were perfectly sound, as was the economy, which was better able to withstand a downturn than most. The first admission that all was not well came on 20 September 2008 when the government undertook to guarantee depositors.

This decision, although it had its critics, was perfectly sound in itself, in that banks' ability to lend depends on a multiple of the amount they have on deposit. This is checked daily and if they are unable to comply with this provision they are said to have a liquidity problem, which they solve in normal times by borrowing from other banks, on a fixed-term basis. However in a recession this source of finance may be unavailable to them.

The government announced in October that it had no plans to recapitalise the banks but that private investors would be welcome, yet in December it was decided to recapitalise the three main Irish banks, to the extent of 7.5 billion, by taking preference shares in each. This decision should only have been taken having first obtained a fully independent audit of all the banks' current assets and undeclared liabilities, but no such declaration was forthcoming. Despite this, and although it was known to every dog in the street that the banks had not only been mismanaged but that obscene payments had been made to their directors and executive members of staff, the question of nationalisation was not even considered.

Anglo Irish Bank, Ireland's third largest, had acquired its position by lending enormous sums to the building industry, both in Ireland and the UK, as well as to land and property speculators. Consequently it was particularly vulnerable to the stagnation that followed the collapse in property prices. 1.5 billion was to be used to recapitalise this institution despite the fact that the price of its shares had fallen from a high of 17 to 28 cents by September. But when in December Sean Fitzpatrick resigned as the bank's chairman, having admitted that he had hidden loans by the bank to himself, totalling 87 million, by transferring them to another bank before the audit on eight separate occasions a can of worms was opened that revealed the indescribable misuse to which funds entrusted to the bank by its shareholders had been put.

This was followed by the resignation of the bank's CEO, David Drumm, and a number of other directors, and it appeared that the Bank Regulator, Patrick Neary, had turned a blind eye to these operations, which Fitzpatrick described as inappropriate.

Anywhere but in Ireland these gentlemen would have faced criminal proceedings. However it now appears that a number of shareholders have banded together to take a civil action against not only Anglo Irish but also its auditors Ernst and Young and the Irish Nationwide Building Society. Meanwhile the price of Anglo Irish shares plunged to 20 cents and at long last the government announced its decision to nationalise the bank, but without full disclosure of its liabilities this move would involve the taxpayer issuing a blank cheque to meet them.

On 23 January 2009 an urgent and long-delayed meeting was scheduled to be held between the government and the social partners, including the employers and the trade unions, to discuss pay cuts. But when the meeting took place neither the Taoiseach nor the Minister for Finance bothered to turn up and the meeting was described as a farce.

No normal government other than a dictatorship could have survived such negligence. It happened in Ireland because it relies on adversarial politics and the party system is so rigid that it cannot be challenged. No one dares defy the party whip by voting for the opposition unless they are prepared to resign or be expelled from the group to which they belong. This negates the very meaning of democracy, which is best exemplified in the Swiss Constitution. This provides for all deputies to have a free vote in the National Assembly, thereby not only ensuring that they participate in running the country but also that the Central Government, which may consist of a number of parties, is elected by the entire Assembly.

Consequently ministers are appointed on their suitability for the job, irrespective of their party affiliation. Furthermore the freedom of action of deputies is guaranteed by clauses that forbid the coercion of any member by the party to which they belong, to vote for a given proposition and provide for a popular referendum not only to initiate laws, other than those passed by the Central Government, but to remove a government that is deemed to be corrupt or incompetent. Such a system provides for constructive debate rather than the circus that so often passes for such not only in Ireland but elsewhere.

Ireland may be living through the worst recession since 1929 but this is no time for despair. Rather it could be a time for hope, for not only did the country undergo an industrial revolution during the Celtic Tiger years, but such is the innovative nature of the Irish that it could well become a leader in the development of a green technology that would see an end to the world's dependence on oil. Meanwhile unemployment need not be the end of the road for many but could result in a new breed of entrepreneurs; many others have developed skills to enable them to become self-employed.

Ireland could set about modernising its political system, which is at present designed so that it is virtually impossible to depose a corrupt or incompetent government that has lost the confidence not only of the opposition but also of a significant proportion of the electorate. Currently the only time a government can be removed is at a general election unless, in the case of a coalition or minority administration, it loses the support of its partner or independents that are keeping it in office.

Index